THE SIX MILLION: FACT OR FICTION?

Peter Winter

Revised, Updated and Expanded Fifth Edition
July 2015

The Revisionist Press

All material copyright
© 2015 The Revisionist Press

Revised, Updated and Expanded edition

http://peterwinterwriting.blogspot.com

ISBN 978-1499174922

Dedicated to Karl. S.

TABLE OF CONTENTS

Introduction..1

CHAPTER 1: NAZIS AND ZIONISTS BEFORE THE WAR......................................1

Section 1: Nazi Anti-Semitism and Jewish Emigration from Greater Germany 1933–1940
Section 2: Zionist and Nazi Collaboration on the 1935 Nuremberg Laws
Section 3: "A Nazi Travels to Palestine"—How the SS Supported the Zionist Colonization of Palestine
Section 4: Nazi Financial Assistance to Zionism: the "Haavara" Transfer Agreement
Section 5: The Jewish Declaration of War against Germany and the Organized Boycott of German Goods
Section 6: The Truth about Kristallnacht
Section 7: The Creation of the Concentration Camps
Section 8: Zionists Offered to Fight for the Nazis against the British

CHAPTER 2: THE NUMBER OF JEWS UNDER NAZI CONTROL............................9

Section 9: There Were 4.5 Million Jews under Nazi Control
Section 10: 4.3 Million Postwar "Holocaust Claims" against German Government
Section 11: Yad Vashem's "Victim List" Compiled on Hearsay
Section 12: Dieter Wisliceny and Wilhelm Höttl—The Spurious Origin of the "Six Million" Number
Section 13: Jewish Holocaust Scholar Raul Hilberg Reduces Total Death Toll to 2.8 Million—but Media Still use the "Six Million Dead" Figure
Section 14: Auschwitz "Death Toll" Officially Reduced by 2.5 Million—but Media Still use the "Six Million Dead" Figure
Section 15: The Shrinking Number of Dead at Auschwitz: From 9 Million to 73,000
Section 16: The Korherr Report

CHAPTER 3: COMMONLY USED LIES AND DISTORTIONS..................................15

Section 17: The Outrageous Lies and Distortions of the "Kurt Gerstein Statement"
Section 18: Jewish Scholars and Yad Vashem Forced to Deny "Soap," "Lampshades" Horror Stories
Section 19: What Was Really Said at the Wannsee Conference
Section 20: What the "Final Solution" Actually Meant: Deportation to the East
Section 21: Hitler's 1939 Reichstag "Threat to the Jews" Speech
Section 22: What Hitler Said about the "Extermination" Rumors
Section 23: Himmler's 1943 Posen Speech and the Meaning of "Ausrotten"
Section 24: Himmler's Personal Correspondence Never Mentions "Extermination" Claims
Section 25: The Bad Arolsen "International Tracing Service" Archives Provides No Evidence of any Mass Murder Program

CHAPTER 4: THE NUREMBERG WAR CRIMES TRIALS................................19

Section 26: The Legally-Flawed Nuremberg "War Crimes Trials" Did Not "Prove" the Holocaust
Section 27: The Katyn Massacre—How the Soviets Tortured Nazis to "Obtain Confessions"
Section 28: Official "Holocaust" Journal Admits Soviet Torture used to Obtain Nazi "Confessions"

CHAPTER 5: THE EINSATZGRUPPEN—MYTH AND REALITY..22

Section 29: Anti-Partisan Warfare—The Real Purpose of the Einsatzgruppen ("Task Forces")
Section 30: Benjamin Ferencz, Jewish Chief Prosecutor at the Einsatzgruppen Trials, Admits to Using Forced Confessions and Death Threats
Section 31: The Einsatzgruppen Ereignismeldungen ("Event Reports")
Section 32: The Babi Yar Massacre in Kiev: Wartime Aerial Photography Exposes the Lie
Section 33: The "Confession"—and Retraction—of Einsatzgruppen Commander Otto Ohlendorf
Section 34: The Wildly Varying Numbers of Einsatzgruppen "Victims"
Section 35: The Oswald Pohl "Confessions"—Textbook Example of the Nuremberg Miscarriage of Justice
Section 36: The Perjured Testimony of Erich von dem Bach-Zelewski

CHAPTER 6: THE ADOLF EICHMANN TRIAL....30

Section 37: Eichmann Only Admitted Deporting Jews, Never Murdering Them
Section 38: Eichmann's Doctored "Memoirs"

TABLE OF CONTENTS (Continued)

CHAPTER 7: THE JOHN DEMJANJUK TRIALS..31

Section 39: John Demjanjuk—Acquitted in Israel!
Section 40: "Survivor" Testimony Identifies Demjanjuk—But Israeli Supreme Court Dismisses them as Liars
Section 41: German Court Ignores Israeli Decision

CHAPTER 8: THE PSYCHOLOGY OF CONFESSIONS..................34

Section 42: Why Would Anyone "Confess?"
Section 43: The Suchomel "Confession" in Claude Lanzmann's "Shoah" Movie

CHAPTER 9: "DEATH CAMPS" VERSUS "LABOR CAMPS"........................37

Section 44: The Distribution of the Concentration Camps

CHAPTER 10: AUSCHWITZ-BIRKENAU................38

Section 45: Auschwitz Founded as a POW Camp for Polish Soldiers in 1940
Section 46: Auschwitz "Gas Chamber" Shown to Tourists Is Officially Admitted to be Fake
Section 47: Auschwitz Museum Finally Admits that "Gas Chamber" Was Built After the War
Section 48: Auschwitz II: Architect's Plans Show No "Gas Chambers"
Section 49: Real Showers in Auschwitz and the "Gas through the Shower-head" Legend
Section 50: Steam Disinfection Stations for Prisoner Clothing as Part of the Anti-Typhus Measures
Section 51: Delousing Chambers for Clothing Used Zyklon-B in All Camps
Section 52: The Real Auschwitz Gas Chambers—The "Kanada I" Delousing Chambers Which Used Zyklon-B
Section 53: Photographs of Auschwitz's Kanada I and Its Clothing Delousing Installation Gas Chamber in Action
Section 54: Forensic Investigation of "Gas Chamber" Ruins Reveals No Evidence of Gassings
Section 55: The Rudolf Report Confirms the Lack of Forensic Evidence
Section 56: The Auschwitz "Gas Chambers" Change Location
Section 57: Auschwitz's Real Purpose: A Massive Labor Camp
Section 58: Photographs of Auschwitz Inmates Belie Mass Gassing Allegations
Section 59: The Rudolf Höss Memoirs
Section 60: The Auschwitz Swimming Pool
Section 61: The Frankfurt Auschwitz Trial of 1963

CHAPTER 11: THE AKTION REINHARD CAMPS................................53

Section 62: Details Unknown for Decades
Section 63: The Höfle Telegram
Section 64: Problems with "Gassing by Diesel"
Section 65: The Purpose of the Reinhard Camps

CHAPTER 12: CHELMNO AND "GAS VANS".......55

Section 66: Chelmno—"Operational" for Eighteen Months
Section 67: Yad Vashem's Gas Van That Wasn't
Section 68: Walter Rauff and the "Gas Van" Story
Section 69: Forensic Digs Contradict "Official History" by Finding "Crematoria" in Chelmno
Section 70: The Chelmno Trials

CHAPTER 13: BELZEC 57

Section 71: The Belzec Camp—Given Little Prominence Because of Unbelievable Allegations
Section 72: Belzec's Incredible Execution Methods: Electrocution and Drowning in Excrement
Section 73: The Belzec Trial
Section 74: Forensic Digs at Belzec Contradict "Official" History and Fail to Find "Gas Chambers"

CHAPTER 14: SOBIBÓR..........................59

Section 75: Sobibór—A Temporary Camp Which Only Existed for 15 Months
Section 76: Chlorine and Electricity: "Survivors" Claim Bizarre Execution Methods in Sobibór
Section 77: Yitzhak Arad's Contradictory Official History of Sobibór
Section 78: Official Documents Show Sobibór's True Function
Section 79: The Sobibór Trials
Section 80: Archaeological Digs Fail To Find Sobibór "Gas Chamber"
Section 81: 2014 Archaeological Dig Contradicts Earlier "Gas Chamber" Claims

CHAPTER 15: TREBLINKA.......................63

Section 82: Treblinka— Another Temporary Camp Which Only Existed for 15 Months
Section 83: Treblinka I and II—Labor Camp and Transit Area
Section 84: The Famous "Black Book of Polish Jewry" Claims Execution by "Steam" in Treblinka

TABLE OF CONTENTS (Continued)

Section 85: "Survivors" Claim Execution by "Vacuum Chambers"
Section 86: First 1999 Forensic Examination of Treblinka Site Reveals No Mass Graves
Section 87: US National Archive Aerial Photography of Treblinka Shows No Sign of "Extermination Camp"
Section 88: The 2010 Second Forensic Analysis of Treblinka Reveals No "Mass Graves"
Section 89: The 2013 Third Forensic Analysis of Treblinka and the "Star of David Gas Chamber Tiles" Hoax
Section 90: The "Evidence" of "Treblinka Guard" Paval Leleko
Section 91: The Franz Stangl Trial and His "Memoirs"

CHAPTER 16: MAJDANEK..70

Section 92: Majdanek, Lublin—Originally Built as POW Camp for Soviet Army Prisoners
Section 93: First Majdanek Soviet Show Trial, November 1944
Section 94: Number of Madjanek "Victims" Varies Wildly from 1.7 Million to 79,000
Section 95: "Gas Chamber" Added to Postwar Rebuilt Madjanek Crematorium Building
Section 96: The Impossibility of the Majdanek "Gas Chambers"
Section 97: Majdanek's Real Showers for "Gassing Victims"
Section 98: Majdanek's "Gas Bottles" on Display are Carbon Dioxide, Not Carbon Monoxide
Section 99: The Anomalies of Majdanek's Second and Third "Gas Chambers"
Section 100: The Plain Glass Window in Majdanek's Fourth "Gas Chamber"
Section 101: The Operation "Harvest Festival" Hoax
Section 102: The Mußfeldt "Confession"
Section 103: The Second Madjanek Trial of 1975

CHAPTER 17: DACHAU..81

Section 104: Dachau and Its Mysterious "Gas Chamber"
Section 105: The Real Dachau Gas Chambers—Delousing Cubicles
Section 106: Dachau Casualty Figures Officially "Reduced" from 238,000 to 20,000

CHAPTER 18: SACHSENHAUSEN............................85

Section 107: Sachsenhausen: Gas Chamber Built in November 1945, Knocked Down in 1952

CHAPTER 19: BERGEN-BELSEN..............................87

Section 108: Typhus Deaths—Origin of Horror Images in Bergen-Belsen—No Gas Chambers

CHAPTER 20: "EYEWITNESS" ACCOUNTS.........88

Section 109: Simon Wiesenthal's Faked "Holocaust Memoirs"
Section 110: The Diary of Anne Frank—Father Admits "Transcribing" to "Explain" Ball Point Pen Use
Section 111: Rudolf Vrba's "I Cannot Forgive"
Section 112: Olga Lengyel's "Five Chimneys"
Section 113: Kitty Hart's "Return to Auschwitz"
Section 114: Martin Gray's "For Those I Loved"
Section 115: Jean Francis Steiner's "Treblinka"
Section 116: Miklos Nyiszli's "Auschwitz: A Doctor's Eyewitness Account"
Section 117: Filip Müller's "Eyewitness Auschwitz: Three Years in the Gas Chambers"
Section 118: Truthful Survivor Books Not Given Prominence
Section 119: Paul Rassinier—The Holocaust Victim Who Argued Against the "Gas Chambers"
Section 120: Martin Gilbert's "Auschwitz and the Allies"

CHAPTER 21: OUTLANDISH HOLOCAUST CLAIMS..96

Section 121: Bears and Eagles in Cages Eating Jews; Jewish "Soap Burial" in Atlanta, USA; Sausages Made out of Jews; Mummified Thumbs as Light Switches; "Pedal-driven Brain-bashing Machines"—And More, All in Nuremberg Court as "Evidence."

CHAPTER 22: CONCLUSION....................................99

Section 122: The "Holocaust"—What Actually Happened
Section 123: Why Was the Holocaust Story Invented?

APPENDIX 1: ALOIS BRUNNER AND THE "I WOULD DO IT ALL AGAIN" LIE..........................101
APPENDIX 2: DECEIT, LIES AND SWINDLES: THE PSYCHOLOGY BEHIND "HOLOCAUST SURVIVOR TESTIMONIES"..................................103
APPENDIX 3: THE ONGOING "SURVIVOR" FINANCIAL SWINDLES..105
APPENDIX 4: THE OSKAR GROENING "I SAW THE GAS CHAMBERS" STORY............................106
APPENDIX 5: AUSCHWITZ—PHOTOS SHOW REALITY VERSUS THE CLAIMS........................113
Index..116

Introduction

The story of the "Six Million" has, for many people, become an article of faith. Some will therefore find it surprising to be confronted with the reality that the entire story is at the very best, a poor concoction of lies, and at the worst, an utterly evil conspiracy designed to besmirch the German people.

Constant repetition in the media, combined with endless Hollywood films, character assassination of any historical researcher who has dared to investigate the topic, and finally legislation outlawing revisionism (only for the Second World War) has created the impression amongst the general public that the so-called Holocaust cannot be questioned.

The truth has, however, nothing to fear from open inquiry, and only those who have something to hide seek to outlaw books.

It is therefore, highly ironical, that those who seek to outlaw historical revisionism, do so in the name of "democracy"—and fail to see that their very desire to censor historical research and differing opinions are the very opposite of democracy!

The reader is, without further delay, invited to read further, critically evaluate, and form their own conclusion on whether the Six Million is fact or fiction.

The Author

CHAPTER 1: NAZIS AND ZIONISTS BEFORE THE WAR

Section 1: Nazi Anti-Semitism and Jewish Emigration from Greater Germany 1933–1940

The first thing that any rational person notices about media coverage of the Third Reich, Hitler, or the "Six Million" story, is that although there is always plenty of coverage of Nazi Anti-Semitism, there is hardly any attempt to explain why Hitler was able to come to power on such a strongly anti-Jewish political platform.

If this topic is addressed at all, it is quite often claimed that the Nazis were "jealous" of Jewish money, intellect or achievements, or any variation on that topic. The reality is, like the entire Six Million narrative, very different to the postwar propaganda.

The real reasons for Nazi anti-Semitism were far deeper:
- Jews were identified as a racially-alien group engaged in political, social and moral subversion. Politically, the Nazis pointed to the undisputed facts that the founder of Communism, Karl Marx, had been a Jew; that a majority of the Communists who had seized power in the "Russian Revolution" of 1918 had been Jews (for example Leon Trotsky, whose real name was Bronstein); that the majority of post First World War Communist leaders in Germany had been Jews (Rosa Luxemburg and Karl Liebknecht); that much of the mass media in Germany was owned by Jews; that Jews were largely responsible for "modern art,"; that those convicted of war-profiteering and financial swindles of the 1920s were Jews (the Sklarek scandal, which also involved the Social Democratic Party, being the most famous case), etc.

- The Nazis also associated Jews with extremist capitalist exploitation, which was linked to a much older—and European-wide—objection to Jewish financial dealings. Objections to Jewish money lending practices were as old as the Jewish community in Europe, and were even specifically mentioned in the English *Magna Carta*. They were also the primary reason why Jews were expelled from every single European nation during the Middle Ages.

In summary then, the Nazis sought to expel Jews from all aspects of Germany political cultural and social life, and it was to this end that their anti-Semitic policies were aimed.

To this end, by order of Reich Marshal Hermann Göring, a "Reich Central Office for Jewish Emigration" was set up, whose official tasks were listed as follows:
a) to make all necessary arrangements for the preparation for an increased emigration of the Jews,
b) to direct the flow of emigration,
c) to speed the procedure of emigration in each individual case." (*Wannsee Protocol*, January 20, 1942.)

According to official figures, there were approximately 523,000 Jews in Germany as of January 1933, prior to the

Figure 21. Waiting at the Palestine Office, Berlin, for permits to enter Erez Israel, 1939. Courtesy Yad Vashem, Jerusalem.

Contrary to postwar propaganda, the Nazi government actively encouraged Jewish emigration. This illustration is from the Encyclopeadia Judaica *(1971), Vol. 7, col. 494, and shows Jews waiting at the Palestine Office, Berlin, for permits to enter Palestine ("Eretz Israel") in 1939.*

The Six Million

Nazis coming to power. At the time of the annexation of Austria in 1938, there were approximately 181,882 Jews in that country.

The Nazi efforts to encourage Jews to leave this combined "Greater Germany" were largely successful. By September 1939, approximately 282,000 Jews had left Germany and 117,000 had left Austria. Of these, some 95,000 emigrated to the United States, 60,000 to Palestine, 40,000 to Great Britain, and about 75,000 to Central and South America, with the largest numbers entering Argentina, Brazil, Chile, and Bolivia. More than 18,000 Jews went to Shanghai, in Japanese-occupied China, creating a long-lasting Jewish settlement there.

By 1940, official figures showed that 131,800 Jews remained in Germany, and 43,700 in Austria—a total of 175,500. (*Wannsee Protocol*, January 20, 1942.) This was a significant decline from the pre-war total of 704,882.

Section 2: Zionist and Nazi Collaboration on the 1935 Nuremberg Laws

It is one of the great ironies of history that the Zionists and National Socialist government policy with regard to Jews coincided to a very large degree. In fact, National Socialist and Zionist policy coincided prior to the war, and cooperation carried on at least until 1943, as will be shown below.

The reason for the Zionist-Nazi cooperation was simple: the Nazis wanted the Jews to leave Germany, and the Zionists wanted the Jews to come to Palestine to help create the Zionist state.

The 1935 Nuremberg Laws, for example, which are now dismissed as "Nazi anti-Semitic laws," were in fact drawn up with the active assistance and support of the German Council of Jews.

What makes this fact even more astounding is that the definition of who is a Jew, as created by Israel's Law of Return, as amended in 1970, is based on the definition as contained in the Nuremberg Laws (Jewish Virtual Library, *The Law of Return: An Introduction,* 2014, The American-Israeli Enterprise).

Thus it is no surprise that soon after the Nazis came to power, the Zionist Federation of Germany submitted a document to Hitler's office which offered its support in "solving the Jewish question" (Memo of June 21, 1933, as reproduced in *The Third Reich and the Palestine Question,* Francis R. Nicosia, Austin: University of Texas, 1985, p. 42). The document continued:

> "Zionism believes that the rebirth of the national life of a people, which is now occurring in Germany through the emphasis on its Christian and national character, must also come about in the Jewish national group. Our acknowledgment of Jewish nationality provides for a clear and sincere relationship to the German people and its national and racial realities. Precisely because we do not wish to falsify these fundamentals, because we, too, are against mixed marriage and are for maintaining the purity of the Jewish group and reject any trespasses in the cultural domain, we—having been brought up in the German language and German culture—can show an interest in the works and values of German culture with admiration and internal sympathy" (*ibid.*).

When the Nuremberg Laws were first adopted by the Nazi Party at its congress of 1935, they were specifically welcomed by the Zionist-supporting Jewish German newspaper, the *Jüdische Rundschau,* which published an editorial which read:

> "Germany ... is meeting the demands of the World Zionist Congress when it declares the Jews now living in Germany to be a national minority. Once the Jews have been stamped a national minority it is again possible to establish normal relations between the German nation and Jewry.
>
> "The new laws give the Jewish minority in Germany its own cultural life, its own national life. In future it

The Jüdische Rundschau, *Sept. 17, 1935, the official Zionist newspaper in Germany, which welcomed and supported the Nuremberg Laws. This support for the legal definition of who is a Jew—as created by Nazis and Jews working together—is still referenced to the present-day in Israel's "Law of Return" which regulates Jewish immigration into that state.*

will be able to shape its own schools, its own theater, and its own sports associations. In short, it can create its own future in all aspects of national life.

"Germany has given the Jewish minority the opportunity to live for itself, and is offering state protection for this separate life of the Jewish minority: Jewry's process of growth into a nation will thereby be encouraged and a contribution will be made to the establishment of more tolerable relations between the two nations" (*Jüdische Rundschau,* Sept. 17, 1935).

The head of the Zionist State Organization, the Jewish Cultural League, and former head of the Berlin Jewish Community, Georg Kareski, declared in an interview with the Nazi newspaper *Der Angriff* that:

"For many years I have regarded a complete separation of the cultural affairs of the two peoples [Jews and Germans] as a pre-condition for living together without conflict . . . I have long supported such a separation, provided it is founded on respect for the alien nationality. The Nuremberg Laws . . . seem to me, apart from their legal provisions, to conform entirely with this desire for a separate life based on mutual respect . . . This interruption of the process of dissolution in many Jewish communities, which had been promoted through mixed marriages, is therefore, from a Jewish point of view, entirely welcome" (*Der Angriff,* Dec. 23, 1935).

Section 3: "A Nazi Travels to Palestine"—How the SS Supported the Zionist Colonization of Palestine

The SS—supposedly the epitome of evil, if postwar propaganda is to be taken at face value—was particularly enthusiastic in its support for Zionism. A June 1934 internal SS position paper urged active and wide-ranging support for Zionism by the government and the Party as the best way to encourage emigration of Germany's Jews to Palestine.

The Zionist-SS co-operation became public when SS officer Leopold von Mildenstein and Zionist Federation official Kurt Tuchler, toured Palestine together for six months in order to assess the progress of the Jewish colonization efforts.

Von Mildenstein wrote a series of twelve illustrated articles for the important Nazi paper, published by Joseph

Ein Nazi Fahrt Nach Palastina—"*A Nazi Travels to Palestine.*" *A selection of articles from the Joseph Goebbels-edited newspaper,* Der Angriff, *as penned by SS officer Leopold von Mildenstein.*

The medallion ordered struck by the Joseph Goebbels-edited newspaper, Der Angriff, *to mark the Zionist-Nazi cooperation with regard to Palestine. The medallion contained the title of the article which appeared in his newspaper, "A Nazi Travels to Palestine," encircling a Star of David.*

Goebbels, *Der Angriff,* in late 1934 under the heading *A Nazi Travels to Palestine.* The articles expressed great admiration for the pioneering spirit and achievements of the Jewish settlers.

"A Jewish homeland in Palestine," von Mildenstein wrote, "pointed the way to curing a centuries-long wound on the body of the world: the Jewish question."

Der Angriff issued a special medal, with a Swastika on one side and a Star of David on the other, to commemorate the joint SS-Zionist visit. A few months after the articles appeared, von Mildenstein was promoted to head the Jewish affairs department of the SS security service in order to support Zionist migration.

The official SS newspaper, *Das Schwarze Korps,* proclaimed its support for Zionism in a May 1935 front-page editorial: "The time may not be too far off when Palestine will again be able to receive its sons who have been lost to it for more than a thousand years. Our good wishes, together with official goodwill, go with them."

Section 4: Nazi Financial Assistance to Zionism: the "Haavara" Transfer Agreement

The centerpiece of Nazi-Zionist cooperation was something called the "Transfer Agreement," a pact that enabled tens of thousands of German Jews to migrate to Palestine with their wealth.

The Agreement, also known as the Haavara (Hebrew for "transfer"), was concluded in August 1933 following talks between German officials and Chaim Arlosoroff, Political Secretary of the Jewish Agency, the Palestine center of the World Zionist Organization.

Through this arrangement, each Jew bound for Palestine deposited money in a special account in Germany. The money was used to purchase German-made agricultural tools, building materials, pumps, fertilizer, and so forth, which were exported to Palestine and sold there by the

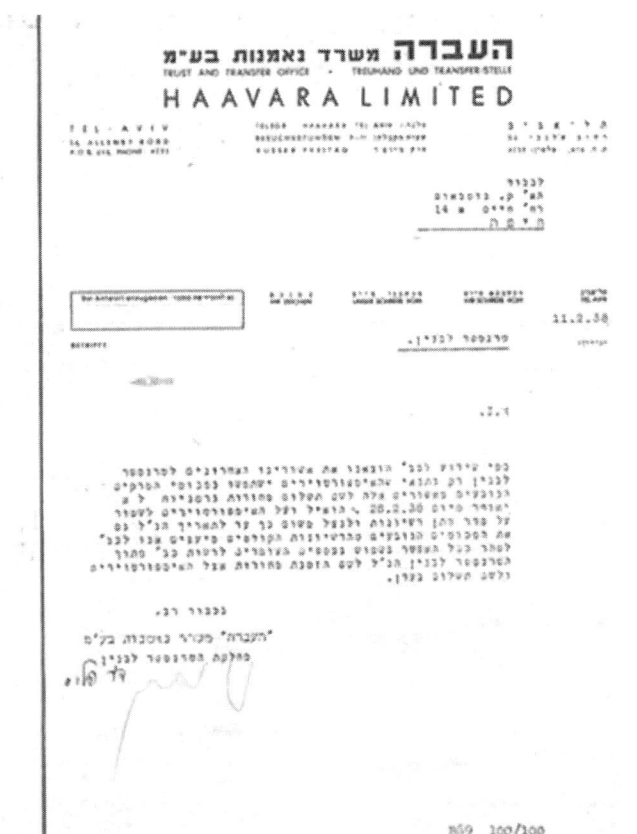

A Nazi-Zionist Haavara certificate issued in Hebrew and in English.

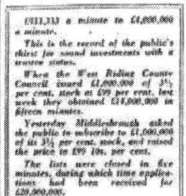

As early as March 24, 1933, World Jewry had declared war on Germany. Despite the Nazis' best efforts to cooperate with the Zionists, who also sought the removal of Jews from Germany, the German government regarded the Jewish population as subversives and justified their physical expulsion by pointing to announcements such as this one.

Jewish-owned Haavara company in Tel-Aviv. Money from the sales was given to the Jewish emigrant upon his arrival in Palestine in an amount corresponding to his deposit in Germany. German goods poured into Palestine through the Haavara, which was supplemented a short time later with a barter agreement by which Palestine oranges were exchanged for German timber, automobiles, agricultural machinery, and other goods.

The Agreement thus served the Zionist aim of bringing Jewish settlers and development capital to Palestine, while simultaneously serving the German goal of freeing the country of an unwanted alien group.

Hitler personally reviewed the policy in July and September 1937, and again in January 1938, and each time decided to maintain the Haavara arrangement. The goal of removing Jews from Germany, he concluded, justified the drawbacks, which included alienating the Arab world.

The Reich Economics Ministry helped to organize another transfer company, the International Trade and Investment Agency, or Intria, through which Jews in foreign countries could help German Jews immigrate to Palestine. Almost $900,000 was eventually channeled through the Intria to German Jews in Palestine.

Other European countries eager to encourage Jewish emigration concluded agreements with the Zionists modeled after the Haavara.

In 1937 Poland authorized the Halifin (Hebrew for "exchange") transfer company. By late summer 1939, Czechoslovakia, Romania, Hungary, and Italy had signed similar arrangements. The outbreak of war in September 1939, however, prevented large-scale implementation of these agreements.

Section 5: The Jewish Declaration of War against Germany and the Organized Boycott of German Goods

Zionist cooperation with the National Socialist German government was however marked by extreme schizophrenia. While some Jews actively sought out German assistance in building Palestine, others viewed the Nazis as mortal enemies. On September 5, 1939, Chaim Weizmann declared war against Germany on behalf of the world's Jews, stating: "the Jews stand by Great Britain and will fight on the side of the democracies... The Jewish Agency is ready to enter into immediate arrangements for utilizing Jewish manpower, technical ability, resources etc."(*Jewish Chronicle,* September 8, 1939).

This announcement was repeated in banner headlines in many newspapers of the time. World Jewry therefore

Left: A mass rally of Jews in New York City, 1933, calling for a boycott of Germany. Right: The organized Jewish boycott is announced in London, 1933, using the same headline as in the Daily Express.

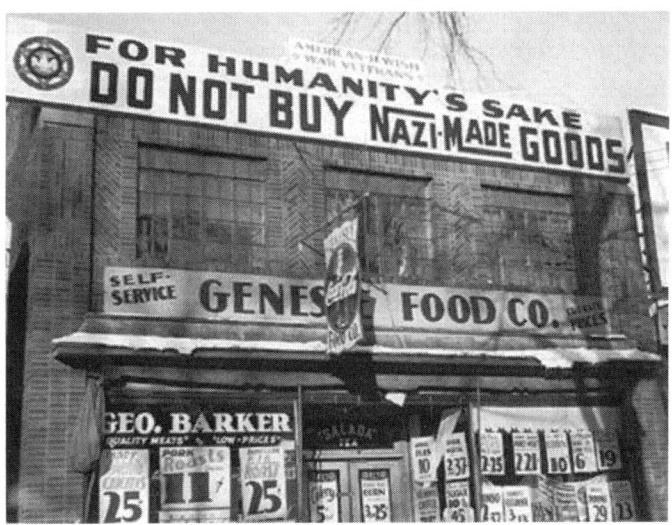

Advertising by the American Jewish War Veterans calling for a boycott of Germany, 1933. The boycott started in March 1933 in both Europe and the US and continued until the entry of the US into the war.

The Nazi boycott of Jewish businesses in Germany, was, unlike the Jewish boycott of Germany, a one-day affair held on April 1, 1933. Images such as these are always presented without the explanation that the Nazi boycott was only a reaction to the international Jewish measures implemented elsewhere in the world.

declared itself to be a belligerent party in the Second World War, and there was therefore ample basis under international law for the Germans to intern the Jewish population as a hostile force. In response to these campaigns, the National Socialist government organized its own boycott of Jewish businesses within Germany. These images are most often shown without it being explained that they were reactions to the Jewish-initiated boycott outlined above.

Section 6: The Truth about Kristallnacht

One of the most commonly referred to events in pre-war Germany was the wholesale attacks by crowds of Germans on Jewish shops during the night of November 9–10, 1938.

Large numbers of shop windows were smashed out, with the broken glass then giving rise to the "crystal" name.

The events of Crystal Night are important because they provide a valuable lesson in how postwar propaganda presents events in Nazi Germany—and how important information is deliberately left out to provide as incomplete a picture as possible.

The attacks on Jewish businesses was not "pre-planned" as the postwar allegations claim, but were a spontaneous outburst of anger which followed two high profile murders—by Jews—of important German figures outside the country.

The first murder occurred on February 4, 1936, when the Jew David Frankfurter shot dead Wilhelm Gustloff, the

Left: The NSDAP leader in Switzerland, Wilhelm Gustloff, murdered by the Jew David Frankfurter, right.

Left: The German diplomat in Paris, Ernst vom Rath, murdered by the Jew Herschel Grynszpan, right.

German leader of the Nazi Party in Switzerland. Gustloff's murder was greeted with outrage in Germany, and his funeral was attended by tens of thousands of mourners, including Hitler, Goebbels, Göring, Himmler, and German foreign minister Joachim von Ribbentrop. Gustloff was proclaimed a Nazi *Blutzeuge* (martyr) and had a large ship named after him.

German public outrage over the Gustloff murder had barely subsided when the Jew Herschel Grynszpan murdered the German diplomat Ernst vom Rath inside the German embassy in Paris on November 7, 1938.

When news of the second murder reached Germany, angry crowds turned out in the streets all over Germany and attacked Jewish shops and synagogues.

The vehemence of the reaction took Germany's leadership by surprise, and the attacks only stopped after Goebbels issued a public order for the violence to stop, as was reported in the *New York Times* of November 11, 1938. That newspaper also reported that the attacks were "revenge" for the Vom Rath murder.

Postwar coverage of Kristallnacht almost always omits to provide the two most important facts around this unfortunate incident: namely that:

– The attacks were spontaneous responses to a series of murders committed by Jews on prominent Germans; and

– That the "pogrom" was stopped after the Nazi leadership, taken by surprise over its violence, ordered it halted.

This technique of "omitting" all the facts and instead presenting only one aspect—in this case the events of the night of November 9–10, 1938 in isolation so as to create an "impression" rather than the full story—is the model used by all postwar propaganda around the Six Million story, as will be seen below.

Section 7: The Creation of the Concentration Camps

The concentration camp system lies at the core of the Six Million story, and, just like Kristallnacht, has also been subjected to an ongoing series of "impressions" rather than the full facts since 1945. Firstly, as is well-known amongst historians, the first concentration camps were not German, but British, and date from the Second Anglo-Boer War of 1899–1902.

Disease—typhus in particular—was a great killer in these British camps, and photographs of dying internees display the characteristic thinness and weakness which post-World War II propaganda has most commonly—and falsely—associated with "gassings" in German camps.

Secondly, the legal basis for the creation of the concentration camp system in Germany was not, as is often claimed, Nazi in origin, but based upon the Weimar Constitution, which preceded Hitler's coming to power. Article 48 of the Weimar Constitution specifically allowed for emergency measures to be taken to suspend civil liberties, a fact which was used to set up the legal framework for the concentration camp system

Thirdly, the camps were not set up to "imprison all Jews," as postwar propaganda has claimed. The camps were first and foremost prisons for political dissidents, then

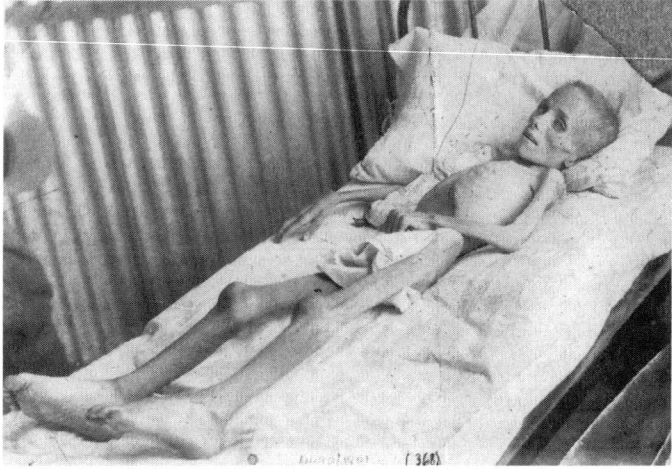

Lizzie Van Zyl (1894 –May 9, 1901), a child inmate who died from typhus in the British-built Bloemfontein, South Africa, concentration camp during the Second Anglo-Boer War of 1899–1902. The thin body—caused by dehydration which follows massive diarrhea—was also seen in the German concentration camps. While pictures of thin bodies are most often presented as evidence of "gassing," they are in fact the product of typhus.

specially-created labor camps, then prisoner of war camps (Auschwitz, dealt with below, was for example originally a POW camp for Polish soldiers), and then finally, transit camps meant to facilitate the deportation of Jews to the Far East.

It is important to note—because, once again, the erroneous belief has been created that only Jews were interred—that the concentration camps in Germany were primarily built to house political prisoners prior to the outbreak of the war.

At every camp, where Jews and other nationalities were detained, there were large industrial plants and factories supplying material for the German war-effort–the Buna rubber factory at Bergen-Belsen, for example, Buna and I. G. Farben Industrie at Auschwitz and the electrical firm of Siemens at Ravensbrück.

The old entrance to the Siemens factory at Ravensbruck, photographed in 2011.

In many cases, special concentration camp money notes were issued as payment for labor, enabling prisoners to buy extra rations from camp shops.

The Thereisenstadt settlement—which was certainly not a concentration camp, even though the Holocaust storytellers claim that it was—had specially issued bank notes which can still be found today in the hands of specialist collectors.

Nazi-issued banknotes for use in the Thereisenstadt settlement—called a "Ghetto" by the proponents of the extermination legend. Why would Nazis print up special banknotes for Jews if their intention was actually just to kill them all?

Section 8: Zionists Offered to Fight for the Nazis against the British

Yet another fact which is pertinent to the Six Million story is the reality that late in the course of the war, the leading Zionists in Palestine offered to take up arms against the British in order to facilitate a German victory.

The background to this astonishing—and suppressed— reality lies with the Jewish settlers in Palestine who found the British colonial administration unwilling to accede to the Zionist demand to turn the region into an exclusively Jewish homeland. The British were, of course, well aware of what the potential consequences would be for the existing Arab Palestinian population, and also the aftereffects such a development would have on the rest of the Arab world.

As a result, the Zionists in Palestine launched a terrorist war against the British and Palestinians, with the aim of driving both of these groups out. Many massacres of Palestinians took place (the most famous of which was at Deir Yassin, where hundreds of Arabs were killed by armed Zionist terrorists) and British soldiers were also regularly murdered and attacked.

The leading Zionist terrorist organization was called Lehi, although it is better known as the "Stern Gang," after its leader Yair Stern. Lehi assassinated Lord Moyne, British Minister Resident in the Middle East and took part in many other incidents, including the Deir Yassin massacre which was carried out in cooperation with another Zionist faction called the Igrun.

In December 1940, Lehi contacted Germany with a proposal to aid German conquest in the Middle East in return for recognition of a Jewish state open to unlimited immigration (Colin Shindler, *The Land Beyond Promise: Israel, Likud and the Zionist Dream,* 1995, I.B. Tauris. p. 22).

Late in 1940, Lehi representative Naftali Lubenchik went to Beirut to meet German official Werner Otto von Hentig (who also was involved with the Haavara or Transfer Agreement, which had been transferring German Jews and their funds to Palestine since 1933).

On the assumption that the destruction of Britain was the Germans' top objective, the Zionists offered cooperation in the following terms: Lehi would support sabotage and espionage operations in the Middle East and in eastern Europe anywhere where they had cells.

Germany would recognize an independent Jewish state in Palestine, and all Jews leaving their homes in Europe, by their own will or because of government injunctions, could enter Palestine with no restriction of numbers. Stern also proposed to recruit some 40,000 Jews from occupied Europe to invade Palestine with German support to oust the British.

On January 11, 1941, Vice Admiral Ralf von der Marwitz, the German Naval attaché in Turkey, filed a report (the "Ankara document") conveying an offer by Lehi to "actively take part in the war on Germany's side" in return for German support for "the establishment of the historic Jewish state on a national and totalitarian basis, bound by a treaty with the German Reich."

By then, however, pressing demands of the war had eclipsed German government time, and nothing came of this particular offer.

It is however important to note that one of the leaders of Lehi was Yitzhak Shamir, who later became prime minister of Israel. Lehi therefore represented an important and leading element in Zionist thought, and the concept of a Nazi-Zionist alliance in the middle of World War II makes a mockery of the later "extermination" claims.

CHAPTER 2: THE NUMBER OF JEWS UNDER NAZI CONTROL

Section 9: There Were 4.5 Million Jews under Nazi Control

If there was one group which would have been interested in establishing exactly how many Jews were under German control, it would have been the Nazis themselves.

In this regard, the official German records offer an astonishing insight. The Nazis estimated that the maximum number of Jews under their control at the Reich's height was no more than 4.5 million, and they would have had no particular reason to lie or exaggerate.

Figures produced by the German government and submitted to the famous Wannsee Conference in January 1942, listed the following numbers of Jews in territories under Nazi control:

Germany, (131,800);
Austria (43,700);
Eastern territories (420,000);
General Government (2,284,000);

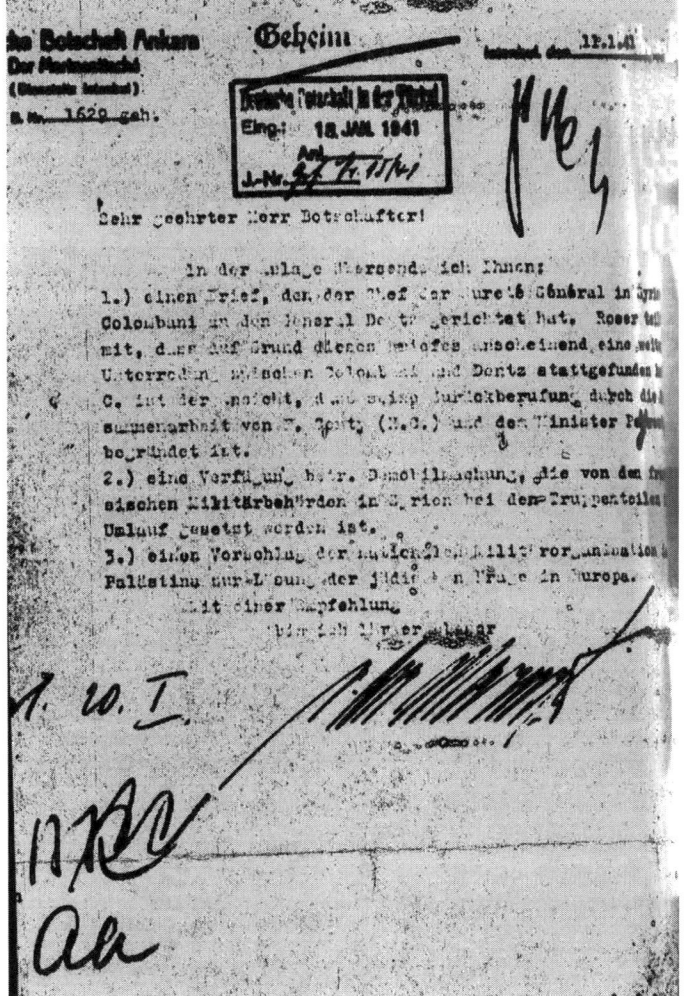

The 1941 covering letter from the German embassy in Ankara, Turkey, to the German foreign office, reporting on the offer by the Zionist Stern Gang to join the war on Germany's side in return for Nazi support for the creation of a Jewish state in Palestine. The relevant section translates as: "3.) a proposal of the National Military Organization in Palestine regarding the solution of the Jewish question in Europe."

Bialystok (400,000);
Protectorate Bohemia and Moravia (74,200);
Estonia (0);
Latvia (3,500);
Lithuania (34,000);
Belgium (43,000);
Denmark (5,600);
France /occupied territory (165,000)/ unoccupied territory (700,000);
Greece (69,600);
Netherlands (160,800);
Norway (1,300).

This gives a total of 4,536,500 Jews under German control.

The Wannsee Conference listed a further number of countries with significant Jewish populations which were not under Nazi control. They were named as follows:
Bulgaria (48,000);
England (330,000);
Finland (2,300);
Ireland (4,000);
Italy including Sardinia (58,000);
Albania (200);
Croatia (40,000);
Portugal (3,000);
Romania including Bessarabia (342,000);
Sweden (8,000);
Switzerland (18,000);
Serbia (10,000);
Slovakia (88,000);
Spain (6,000);
Turkey (European portion) (55,500);
Hungary (742,800);
USSR (5,000,000, including as subdivisions the Ukraine (2,994,684) and Byelorussia (446,484).)

This gives a total of 6,755,800 Jews in Europe not under direct German control.

It is incorrect to assume that the Jews in countries allied to the Germans were handed over to the Nazis.

The most famous example of this is Bulgaria, whose entire Jewish population was protected by that country's government, as recounted in Jewish historian Martin Gilbert's Book *The Holocaust* (Holt, Rinehart & Winston, 1985).

The Yad Vashem, Israel's official Holocaust memorial institute, claims that Denmark only lost 60 Jews dead, that Finland lost 7 Jews dead, that Italy lost 7,600 Jews (out of the total of 58,000, by Nazi estimates).

Section 10: 4.3 Million Postwar "Holocaust Claims" against German Government

The figure of 4,536,500 Jews under German control is important when it is considered that, until the end of 1987,

Page 6 from the minutes of the Wannsee Conference, detailing how many Jews were in all of Europe (11 million), and how many were under German control (4.5 million). Section "A" is the list under German control, and section "B" is not under German control.

some 4,384,138 individual claims for compensation had been made by Holocaust survivors against the postwar German government. According to the German Federal Ministry of Finance, "During the period from 1 October 1953 to 31 December 1987, 4,384,138 applications for compensation were submitted pursuant to the Additional Federal Compensation Act of 18 September 1953 (Federal Law Gazette I p. 1387), the Federal Compensation Act of 29 June 1956 (Federal Law Gazette I p. 559) and the Final Federal Compensation Act of 14 September 1965 (Federal Law Gazette I p. 1315). (West German Federal Indemnification Law-BEG "Wiedergutmachung." German Finance Ministry, *Leistungen der öffentlichen Hand auf dem Gebiet der Wiedergutmachung Stand: 31. Dezember 2009, Bundesministerium der Finanzen, Referat V B 4*).

This means, by the Nazis' own reckoning, that of the estimated 4.5 million Jews directly under their control in 1942, at least 4.3 million had claimed compensation from the German government for persecution by 1987.

These figures by themselves speak volumes about the true number of Jewish casualties during the war.

Section 11: Yad Vashem's "Victim List" Compiled on Hearsay

Yad Vashem, Israel's official memorial to the "Jewish victims of the Holocaust" claimed in 2014 to have a database of at least five million names of Jews who allegedly died during World War II. This list, even though it falls short of the "Six Million" (or even the "nine million") has been compiled purely on hearsay.

Yad Vashem's "Holocaust victims" database list is compiled online, and anyone, from anywhere, can submit a name by simply filling in an online form.

This "submission" is then automatically added to the "official death list," a process which has resulted in almost all names appearing twice, and some as many as five times. Any submission is automatically accepted as "fact" without any further investigation.

The Yad Vashem "list of Holocaust Victims" is comprised of utterly vague and unverifiable entries such as this one. Anyone, from anywhere, can make an entry and it is automatically added to the list of "victims."

Above is a typical Yad Vashem "Victims' list" entry, made by someone claiming to be a nephew of a Berlin Jew. Note the complete lack of detail in this "report"—the "nephew" claims his uncle was arrested in 1941 in Berlin, and has no idea of the circumstances of his death, or any other details at all. The vast majority of entries in Yad Vashem's register are of this nature.

Clearly, a list of names compiled under these conditions is open to the most outrageous fraud, and is no way reliable.

Despite this, Yad Vashem and the media regularly tout this "list of victims" as "proof" of the Holocaust.

Section 12: Dieter Wisliceny and Wilhelm Höttl—The Spurious Origin of the "Six Million" Number

The first mention of the figure of "six million Jews killed" was contained in a statement made by Wilhelm Höttl, a former employee of the Reichssicherheitshauptamt (RSHA) or Reich Main Security Office.

In 1944 Höttl became the acting head of Intelligence and Counter Espionage in Central and South-East Europe. Höttl never had any dealings with the concentration camp system, and therefore possessed no first-hand knowledge of any of the numbers involved.

Nonetheless, a written statement he made after the war while in detention after the war during the Nuremberg War Crimes Trials, claimed that SS-Obersturmbannführer (lieutenant colonel) Adolf Eichmann had informed him in Budapest that "Approximately 4 million Jews had been killed in the various concentration camps, while an additional 2 million met death in other ways, the major part of which were shot by operational squads of the Security Police during the campaign against Russia" (*Nuremberg Trial Proceedings Volume 3,* Friday, December 14, 1945, Morning Session).

For his part, at his trial (see below), Eichmann denied saying any such thing, and was quoted not long after the war as saying that Höttl should be killed for making up this claim.

Höttl never actually gave evidence at Nuremberg, despite the importance of his allegation, a fact which was seized upon by Dr. Kurt Kauffman, defense attorney for RSHA Chief Ernst Kaltenbrunner.

In the afternoon session of the court proceedings following the morning reading of Höttl's statement, Dr. Kauffman asked the court for Höttl's "evidence" to be struck off, saying:

> "I request that the evidence of Dr. Höttl, which was read into the record this morning be stricken out again for the following two reasons. . . As can be seen from the affidavit, Dr. Höttl was interrogated on the 26th of November hardly 3 weeks ago. Moreover I gather that Dr. Höttl is kept in custody here in Nuremberg. No delay would therefore be involved if this witness were called to the stand. This man held a significant position in the SS and for that reason I have already applied in writing that he be called as a

witness. I am convinced that there is a large amount of important evidence which he can reveal to the Court. Dr. Höttl's deposition is infinitely important. The death of millions of people is involved here. His affidavit is based largely on inferences, on hearsay; I believe that the facts are very different, and I would not like to apply later, after weeks or months, for the witness to be brought into Court" (*Nuremberg Trial Proceedings Volume 3,* Friday, 14 December 1945, Afternoon Session).

This perfectly reasonable request to cross-question Höttl was denied by the court, just one of many aberrations of justice which took place at those trials, of which more examples are given below.

Needless to say, Dr. Kauffmann's objections are never recounted when the Höttl statement is recounted as "evidence" for the Six Million story.

The only other "source" for the Six Million figure is supposedly the "confession" from a low-ranking Gestapo figure, Dieter Wisliceny.

Leader of the Gestapo in Bratislava, Wisliceny, like Höttl, never actually had anything to do with the camps themselves, and provided his "evidence" purely on hearsay.

The relevant part of Wisliceny's "confession" reads as follows: "Eichmann personally always talked about at least million Jews. Sometimes he even mentioned 5 million. According to my own estimate I should say that at least 4 million must have been destined for the so-called final solution. How many of those actually survived, I am not in a position to say" ("Twenty-Sixth Day, Thursday, 1/3/1946, Part 30", in *Trial of the Major War Criminals before the International Military Tribunal Volume IV.* Proceedings: 12/17/1945-1/8/1946. Nuremberg: IMT, 1947. p. 355.).

When Adolf Eichmann was put on trial (see below) he called Wisliceny's comments "theater," and said that he never had any figures of "exterminated" Jews.

Needless to say, Wisliceny was never able to produce any evidence to back up his claims, but this did not stop his "confession" from being accepted as the literal truth, contrary to all normal laws of evidence and procedure.

Soon after making this "confession," Wisliceny was extradited to Communist-controlled Czechoslovakia, where he was hanged in 1948.

Why would both Höttl and Wisliceny have made such outrageous statements, based purely on hearsay without any other evidence? The answer to this question was provided by US Senator Joe McCarthy, who was officially sent to Nuremberg by the US Senate as an observer. Senator McCarthy was shocked at the abuses which he saw, and made a complete speech in the US Senate on the matter (*Congressional Record—Senate No. 134,* July 26, 1949, pp. 10397ff.).

In this speech, Senator McCarthy revealed that the Allied prosecutors had a standing order (Order SOP No. 4) which promised that any accused who offered to give State's evidence to incriminate others would be set free.

This had the effect of encouraging witnesses to agree to make any statement at all—as long as they could possibly be released or found not guilty.

But that was not all. Senator McCarthy went on to reveal the manner in which confessions were extorted from accused persons, or statements were taken from reluctant witnesses subjected to automatic arrest both in the prisons for those awaiting trial.

The "interrogations," he revealed, left clearly visible marks: the methods used were: skin burns; destruction of the bed of the (finger-, i.e., toe-)nails with burning matches; torn-out fingernails; knocked-in teeth; broken jaws; crushed testicles; wounds of all kinds due to beatings with clubs; brass knuckles and kicks; being locked up naked in cold, damp and dark rooms for several days; imprisonment in hot rooms with nothing to drink; mock trials; mock convictions; mock executions; bogus clergymen, and many more (*Congressional Record—Senate No. 134,* July 26, 1949, pp. 10397ff.).

Senator McCarthy was never forgiven for daring to speak out against the abuses at Nuremberg, and they were a major reason for his later demonization by the mass media.

Section 13: Jewish Holocaust Scholar Raul Hilberg Reduces Total Death Toll to 2.8 Million—but Media Still use the "Six Million Dead" Figure

Raul Hilberg (died 2007) was an Austrian-born Jew, considered to be the world's preeminent scholar of the Holocaust, famous for his three-volume, 1,273-page *The Destruction of the European Jews.*

According to Hilberg, as quoted in an article written by himself in the 1998 Microsoft *Encarta Encyclopedia* under the heading Holocaust, the six camps, their means of killing, and their total number of victims was as follows:

- Chelmno had gas vans, and its death toll was 150,000;
- Belzec had carbon monoxide gas chambers in which 600,000 Jews were killed;
- Sobibór's gas chambers accounted for 250,000 dead;
- Treblinka's for 700,000 to 800,000;

At Majdanek, some 50,000 were gassed or shot; and in Auschwitz, the Jewish dead totaled more than 1 million (Raul Hilberg, *Holocaust,* Microsoft "Encarta" 98 Encyclopedia. 1993-1997 Microsoft Corporation).

This only accounts for 2.8 million dead.

If Hilberg's figures are correct, then the number of six million dead drops, by this foremost Jewish "expert," by more than half. Hilberg offers no explanation for the fact that the Nuremberg trials (both Höttl and Höss) claimed figures twice as large (or in Auschwitz's case, four times as large).

More disturbingly, no attempt is ever made to correct the still quoted figure of six million which is so popular with the media to this day, and which has been repeated so often that it has become an article of faith.

Hilberg, who spent 36 years studying the Holocaust and the subsequent Nuremberg trials, has often changed his estimates. In 1985, he told a Canadian court that five million Jews were killed during the war, substantially higher than his 1998 estimate of 2.8 million ("Scientific evidence of Holocaust missing," *The Sault Star*, Sault Ste. Marie, Ontario, January 18, 1985).

Section 14: Auschwitz "Death Toll" Officially Reduced by 2.5 Million—but the "Six Million" Figure Remains!

In July 1989, the Auschwitz Museum dramatically announced that the "actual" number of deaths in the camp were nowhere near the four million initially claimed, and that the real figure was a "million." (Auschwitz Deaths Reduced to a Million," Daily Telegraph, July 17, 1990; "Poland Reduces Auschwitz Death Toll Estimate to 1 Million," *The Washington Times,* July 17, 1990.)

Significantly, the "new" figures were endorsed by the head of research at Israel's Yad Vashem, Dr. Shmuel Krakowsky, who added the following revealing comment:

> "The four million figure was let slip by Captain Rudolf Höss, the death camp's Nazi commander. Some have bought it, but it was exaggerated." (Auschwitz Deaths Reduced to a Million," *Daily Telegraph,* July 17, 1990.)

Of course, Dr. Shmuel did not try to address why Höss had "let slip" the four million figure, obviously not wanting to draw attention to the torture used by the Soviets to extract that confession.

An important by-product of this dramatic reduction in the number of deaths at Auschwitz should have been that the "Six Million" total figure also be reduced by three million. The "Holocaust" scholars and media should therefore be talking about the "Three Million," not the "Six Million"—but this logic has never been applied.

Section 15: The Shrinking Number of Dead at Auschwitz: From 9 Million to 73,000

The best example of how the figures for the number of Jews killed varies can be seen from a review of the available official "Holocaust" source books.

Left—This was the plaque on display at Auschwitz until 1989. Note the "4 million" victims. Right—The plaque on display at Auschwitz after 1990, showing the sudden reduction in the number of deaths to 1.5 million. This 2.5 million shrinkage in the number of dead Jews was widely reported in the media, but no attempt was made to reduce the "Six Million" figure accordingly. The Holocaust storytellers and the media have continued to claim that six million or even more Jews were killed in World War II, despite unilaterally deducting millions at a time from the total figure.

– The "confession" of former Auschwitz commander Rudolf Höss, said that between 5,000,000 to 5,500,000 Jews had been killed in Auschwitz. (Discussed below.)

– A Soviet document submitted at the Nuremberg War Crimes trial on May 6, 1945, and reported in the *New York Times* on April 18, 1945, said that 4,000,000 Jews had been killed in Auschwitz.

– The *New York Times* and the *Washington Post* slashed the figure to 1,500,000 Jews killed in Auschwitz in 1990, citing "new findings" by the Auschwitz Museum officials.

– The 1991 edition of Filip Müller's book, *Three Years in an Auschwitz Gas Chamber,* claimed that 3,500,000 Jews had been killed at Auschwitz.

– During the Adolf Eichmann trial in Jerusalem in 1961, star prosecution witness Rudolf Vrba, who claimed to have escaped from Auschwitz in April 1944, claimed that 2,500,000 Jews had been killed at Auschwitz.

Leading Jewish Holocaust "expert" and Professor of Holocaust Studies at the Avraham Harman Institute of Contemporary Jewry at the Hebrew University of Jerusalem, Yehuda Bauer, however dismissed Vrba as "embittered, furious, and not credible."

– The 1989 version of *A History of the Holocaust,* by Bauer, claimed that the number of Jews killed at Auschwitz was "lower than 1,600,000." Bauer cited this new figure on September 22, 1989 in the *Jerusalem Post,* in which he wrote "The larger figures have been dismissed for years, except that it hasn't reached the public yet."

– In 1995, the "official" number of Auschwitz deaths was put at 1,500,000 and announced by Polish President Lech Walesa as determined by the historians at the Auschwitz museum. This number was inscribed on the monument at the Auschwitz camp at that time, thereby "replacing" the earlier 4,000,000 figure that had been formally repudiated (and withdrawn from the monument) five years earlier in 1990.

On July 17, 1990, the *Washington Times* reprinted a brief article from the London *Daily Telegraph* citing the "new" figure of 1,500,000 that had been determined by the authorities at the Auschwitz museum. This new figure was reported two years later in a UPI report published in the *New York Post* on March 26, 1992.

– In 1985, Raul Hilberg in his book, *The Destruction of the European Jews,* claimed that 1,250,000 people had been killed at Auschwitz. According to Hilberg, of those dead, some 1,000,000 were Jews.

– Yisrael Gutman and Michael Berenbaum (later of the US. Holocaust Memorial Museum) in their 1984 book, *Anatomy of the Auschwitz Death Camp,* claimed that 1,500,000 Jews had been killed at Auschwitz.

This estimate was later also cited by Walter Reich, former director of the US Holocaust Memorial Museum, writing in the *Washington Post* on September 8, 1998.

– Jean-Claude Pressac, writing in his 1989 book *Auschwitz: Technique and Operation of the Gas Chambers,* claimed that 1,000,000 Jews had been killed at Auschwitz.

– Gerald Reitlinger in his 1953 book, *The Final Solution,* claimed that between 800,000 and 900,000 Jews had been killed at Auschwitz. This figure is notable, considering the fact that it reduces the Auschwitz death total from the 4,000,000 figure that was widely in vogue in 1953.

– Jean-Claude Pressac revised his earlier estimate of the number of people killed at Auschwitz from one million down to "775,000 to 800,000" in his 1993 book, *The Crematoria of Auschwitz: The Mass Murder's Machinery.* He added that of this number, some 630,000 were Jews.

– The *New York Times* reported on December 3, 1990 that the total number of deaths in Auschwitz was "nearly 70,000." This was based on the wartime German concentration camp records that had been captured by the Soviets and just released.

According to this figure, of those dead, 38,031 were Jews. These records state that the total of all persons who died in the entire German prison camp system from 1935 to 1945 were 403,713. This figure is worth repeating: a total of 403,713 persons of all races and religions was officially recorded to have died (of all causes: typhus, old age, measles, and execution) in the entire prison camp system over a ten year period.

This figure is made more plausible when compared to the number of "survivors" of Jews under German control (see sections 9 and 10 above). According to those figures, there were 4,536,500 Jews under German control, and some 4,384,138 individual claims for compensation were made against the German government after the war—indicating that the difference between these two figures (152,362) had not survived. Allowing for possible errors in population estimates and other variable factors, it is therefore very possible that the true death rate in the camp system from 1935 to 1945 was somewhere between this lower figure—152,362—and the higher number—403,713. It is worthwhile, however, repeating once again that these figures would include deaths from all causes, and all ethnic groups, not only Jews.

Section 16: The Korherr Report

Another favorite standby of the Holocaust storytellers is the famous "Korherr Report" which, it is claimed, was a report drawn up by the chief inspector of the statistical bureau of the SS, Dr Richard Korherr "on the progress of the Holocaust" up until December 1942. A supplemental report covered the first quarter of 1943.

A reading of the full Korherr Report reveals however that there is no mention of gas chambers or extermination.

Significantly, the report specified how many Jews had been detained in all concentration camps over the ten year period from 1933 to 1943 as being 73,417; while only 9,127 Jews were in the camps in December 1942.

The report calculated that, from 1937 to December 1942, the number of Jews in Europe had fallen by 4 million.

Korherr ascribed this fall to "emigration, partially due to the excess mortality of the Jews in Central and Western Europe, partially due to the evacuations especially in the more strongly populated Eastern Territories, which are here counted as ongoing."

After the war, Korherr denied all knowledge of the Holocaust, saying that he had "only heard about exterminations after the collapse in 1945" (Ernst Klee, *Personenlexikon zum Dritten Reich,* Aktualisierte Ausgabe Frankfurt/M 2005, S. 331).

In a letter he sent to the German magazine *Der Spiegel* in July 1977, Korherr also protested against the misinterpretation given to the words "special treatment," writing "I must protest against the word 'died' in this context. It was the very word 'Sonderbehandlung' ['special treatment'] that led me to call the RSHA by phone and ask what this word meant. I was given the answer that these were Jews who were settled in the Lublin district" (*Der Spiegel*, Nr. 31, 25. Juli 1977, S. 12).

There is thus nothing in the Korherr Report which could substantiate the "Holocaust" legend.

On the contrary, the revelation that there were only 9,127 Jews in all the concentration camps as of December 1942 (including the camps in Poland) serves as a devastating indictment against the Holocaust myth.

CHAPTER 3: COMMONLY USED LIES AND DISTORTIONS

Section 17: The Outrageous Lies and Distortions of the "Kurt Gerstein Statement"

One of the most commonly quoted sources for the "mass gassings" claim is a series of statements made after the war by Kurt Gerstein, a former SS Officer. His statements, now known as "The Gerstein Statement" contain what he claimed were to be eyewitness accounts of mass gassings at camps in Poland.

The Holocaust storytellers always omit to explain that there are several different versions of Gerstein's "statement"—so that should be "Gerstein statements" in the plural.

The reason why they try and obscure the fact that there are a number of different Gerstein statements is because they all differ so radically.

The Holocaust storytellers also omit to say that Gerstein conveniently "committed suicide" as soon as he had completed his "revised" affidavits—and so never testified

Kurt Gerstein—Despite the most fantastic and patently false claims in his "confession," his statement is still offered as "proof" even though a casual reading shows that they cannot be true.

in court, nor was ever cross-questioned on his fantastic claims.

A selection of some of the more incredible claims in the Gerstein Statements include:

– Gerstein's first statement said the Nazis had gassed 40 million people—and did not specify that they were Jews. His second statement reduced this figure to 20 million.

– He claimed to have seen, while on a visit to the Treblinka, 8 gas chambers and "whole mountains of clothes and underwear about 35–40 meters high."

If it is borne in mind that the average height of a house story is 2.66 meters, then an idea is gained of exactly how high 40 meters is—in other words, he claimed that there were heaps of clothes as high as 15-storey buildings. The sheer physical impossibility of such a mountain of clothes proves the statement to be false.

– He claimed to have been present at a gassing near the Polish town of Belzec in August of 1942, describing the "gas chamber" as follows: "The people are stepping on each other's feet, 700–800 persons to 25 square meters, 45 cubic meters." This translates to between 28 and 32 persons were crammed into each cubic meter, something which is nearly physically impossible.

This physical impossibility was acknowledged quite early on by the Holocaust storytellers, and the author Leon Poliakov in particular, who in his 1951 work *Breviary of Hate,* contained a version of the Gerstein Statement which changed the area of the gas chambers to 93 square meters, thus cutting down Gerstein's figures to a much more believable 7.5–8.6 persons per square meter.

– Gerstein claimed that the "gas chambers" he saw generated poison gas through the use of diesel engines. The corpses, he said, of the victims were blue afterward from the gas—but in fact carbon monoxide poisoning turns bodies cherry-red, not blue.

There are many other obvious errors and fabrications in the Gerstein statements (including, for example, a claim that Hitler visited Lublin in August 1943—which definitely never happened), but, in spite of these issues which clearly indicate that the "Gerstein Statements" are either completely fabricated or the work of an insane liar, they were used by almost all the "Holocaust experts" in their accounts of the camps.

Acclaimed "expert" Raul Hilberg quoted Gerstein as a major witness no less than six times in his *The Destruction of the European Jews,* and in 1955, the German government mandated that their schools teach the Gerstein "confessions" to all schoolchildren.

One version of the Gerstein Statements was submitted as evidence to the International Military Tribunal (the main Nuremberg War Crimes Trial) and accepted into evidence—even though the "author" was long since dead and could not testify in person.

Section 18: Jewish Scholars and Yad Vashem Forced to Deny "Soap," "Lampshades" Horror Stories

At the end of the war it was claimed that the Dachau and Bergen-Belsen camps in Germany had operating gas chambers; and that in camps in Poland, Jews had been killed in "steam chambers" or had been skinned to make lamp shades, gloves and their body fat made into soap.

All of these horror stories have in the subsequent years been refuted by all serious scholars, including the leading Jewish scholar on the issue, Raul Hilberg.

In a lengthy letter to the *Los Angeles Times* of May 16, 1981, Professor Deborah Lipstadt, well-known as an official "Holocaust historian" said, "The fact is that the Nazis never used the bodies of Jews, or for that matter anyone else, for the production of soap. The soap rumor was prevalent both during and after the war. It may have had its origin in the cadaver factory atrocity story that came out of World War I. The letters 'RJF' probably stood for the name of the factory that produced soap. The soap rumor was thoroughly investigated after the war and proved to

Zyklon-B and "Jewish soap" on display in a synagogue in Europe shortly after the war. Allegations that Nazis made Jews into soap, and even shrunk their heads were commonplace—until Jewish scholars and the official Israeli holocaust museum Yad Vashem, were forced to formally repudiate them.

be untrue" (Deborah Lipstadt, "Nazi Soap Rumor During World War II," *Los Angeles Times,* May 16, 1981).

Section 19: What Was Really Said at the Wannsee Conference

The Holocaust storytellers maintain that a conference was held at a Wannsee villa outside Berlin in January 1942, at which the "final solution" was planned.

The minutes to the Wannsee Conference survived the war in full, and are publicly available at the Wannsee Villa museum and elsewhere.

A reading of the Wannsee Minutes shows the following:
– Nowhere in the meeting's minutes is genocide discussed, planned, proposed, or even suggested;
– The Wannsee Conference never discussed gas chambers, shootings, or any of the claims made after the war.
– The Wannsee Minutes reported that there were only 4.5 million Jews under German control (yet 4.3 million Jewish compensation claims have been lodged against the postwar German government);
– The Wannsee Conference was a planning meeting on how Europe's Jews should be deported, via transit camps, to the East; with able-bodied Jews being forced to build roads and other labor intensive tasks in those regions;
– The Wannsee Conference also made allowance for specific exceptions to Jewish evacuation, such as Jewish German World War I veterans; all Jews over the age of 65; and all Jews working in industries vital to the German war effort, to be released from the threat of evacuation, and be allowed to stay in Germany.

There is therefore, no justification for the allegation that the Wannsee Conference was a "master plan for mass murder" and the media, Holocaust institutions and reference books which claim this, are simply lying.

Many of the Holocaust "experts" actually admit that there is no plan for mass murder in the Wannsee Minutes, and try to explain this "problem" away by stating that "code words" were instead used, such as "Labor assignment in the East" and so on. There is, of course, absolutely no justification for any of these claims.

Section 20: What the "Final Solution" Actually Meant: Deportation to the East

The Holocaust Storytellers have deliberately created the impression that the Nazis always used "code words" in order to "hide" their activities. The basis of this suggestion is preposterous.

An undertaking to kill upward of 6 million people—the equivalent of the populations of New Zealand, Cyprus, and Luxemburg, all added together—while fighting a major war against the Soviet Union, Britain, and the United States, would involve the efforts of huge numbers of people, and not just the small number of soldiers, guards, and administrators claimed.

To argue that a project to kill an entire population of that size could be kept "quiet" by using "code words" would be laughable if it were not taken so seriously by the Holocaust storytellers.

So what then, was the true meaning of the *Endlösung* or "Final Solution?" The answer lies within the famous Wannsee Minutes, and is open for all but the willingly blind to see.

In a nutshell, German policy with regard to Jews was divided up into two distinct phases:

1. Before the outbreak of the war, it was their intention to force all the Jews to legally emigrate out of Germany. It was to this end that the cooperation with the Zionists, as outlined above, was based.

2. After the outbreak of the war, practical considerations made these plans void. Increased numbers of Jews fell under German control, and once it was decided to invade the Soviet Union, the decision was taken to systematically deport as many Jews as possible to the Far East, deep into Russia, east of the Ural Mountains.

This then, was the "Final Solution"—the deportation of Jews to the Far East. All German policy from then on was geared toward achieving this objective, as will be detailed below.

Section 21: Hitler's 1939 Reichstag "Threat to the Jews" Speech

One of the most common claims of "proof" of the Holocaust is a speech given by Adolf Hitler before the German Reichstag in 1939. This speech is used to camouflage the fact that there are no written orders from Hitler authorizing or instructing Jews to be killed—an issue which has long perplexed those who believe the extermination story.

The exact words, delivered by Hitler on January 30, 1939, read as follows:

> "If International Financial Jewry within and outside Europe should succeed in plunging the nations once again into a world war, then the result will not be the bolshevisation of earth and thereby the victory of Jewry, but the destruction of the Jewish race in Europe." *(Wenn es dem internationalen Finanzjudentum in und außerhalb Europas gelingen sollte, die Völker noch einmal in einen Weltkrieg zu stürzen, dann wird das Ergebnis nicht die Bolschewisierung der Erde und damit der Sieg des Judentums sein, sondern die Vernichtung der jüdischen Rasse in Europa.)*

These are strong words, but bearing in mind the declaration of war by world Jewry, they are clearly meant to counter the Jewish threat to destroy Germany. Furthermore, the date of the speech, at the beginning of 1939, predates even the most extreme "extermination" claims which allege that the killing of Jews only started in 1942.

What did he exactly mean by the "destruction of the Jewish Race in Europe?" Did he really mean extermination? The answer to this question was, ironically, provided by Hitler himself.

Section 22: What Hitler Said about the "Extermination" Rumors

In the book *Hitler's Table Talk* (Bormann, Martin. ed. *Hitler's Table Talk 1941–1944*. trans. Cameron, Norman; Stevens, Weidenfeld & Nicolson, 1953), which was a collection of round-table discussions between Hitler and his personal entourage, published after the war, he went into details on what he precisely meant:

> "From the rostrum of the Reichstag, I prophesied to Jewry that, in the event of war's proving inevitable, the Jew would disappear from Europe. That race of criminals has on its conscience the two million dead of the First World War, and now already hundreds and thousands more. Let nobody tell me that all the same we can't park them in the marshy parts of Russia! Who's worrying about our troops? It's not a bad idea, by the way, that public rumour attributes to us a plan to exterminate the Jews. Terror is a salutary thing" (*ibid.*, p. 87.).

This quote puts Hitler's speeches into context: in private, he referred explicitly to only resettling the Jews in the east and went on to mock stories of the "extermination" of Jews, specifically dismissing them as untrue.

Section 23: Himmler's 1943 Posen Speech and the Meaning of "Ausrotten"

A speech given by SS Reichsführer Heinrich Himmler at Posen in Poland during October 1943 is also widely claimed to be "evidence" of the Holocaust.

This speech, which was captured on tape, contains the following comments, transcribed here first in German and then in the English translation:

> "Ich meine jetzt die Judenevakuierung, die Ausrottung des jüdische Volkes. Es gehört zu den Dingen, die man leicht ausspricht. 'Das jüdische Volk wird ausgerottet,' sagt ein jeder Parteigenosse, 'ganz klar, steht in unserem Programm, Ausschaltung der Juden, Ausrottung, machen wir.'" ("I am thinking now of the evacuation of the Jews, the extirpation of the Jewish people. It is one of those things that's easy to say: 'The Jewish people will be extirpated,' says every Party comrade, 'that's quite clear, it's in our program: elimination of the Jews, extirpation; that's what we're doing'")—Speech of Reichsführer-SS Heinrich Himmler at Posen, October 4, 1943, Document No. 1919-PS, Nuremberg Trial records.

As with Hitler's Reichstag speech, the meaning of Himmler's Posen speech turns on the English meaning of the German word "ausrotting."

There is no doubt that in modern German, "ausrotting" or "ausrotten" means murder. But in the German of the time, it did not. There are a number of examples of other public utterances by Hitler in particular where he used the

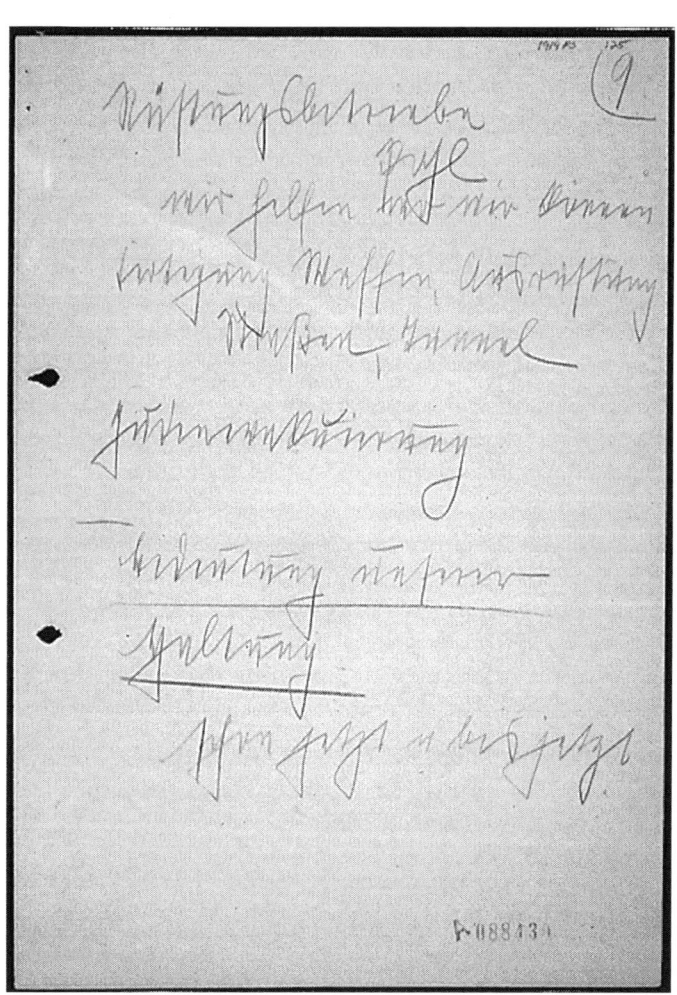

Reichsführer Heinrich Himmler's handwritten notes for his speech in Posen, 1943. The notes specifically referred to "Jewish evacuation" (Judenevakuierung) but in the sound recording of the speech, he used the word "ausrotten." The context of this word has been distorted to mean "murder" but there are numerous other examples of where this phrase was used with no such meaning, as discussed in the text of this work.

word "ausrotting" with reference to people—and these cases have never been taken to mean murder.

For example, in August 1936, Hitler dictated a famous memorandum on Germany's four-year rearmament program, which contains the phrase "if the Bolsheviks succeed in entering Germany, it will lead to the *ausrotten* of the German people" (Akten zur deutschen auswärtigen Politik 1918–1945, *Documents on German Foreign Policy 1918–1945,* series E, 1933-1937, Vol. V, 2. Goettingen, 1977).

This clearly does not mean that if the Bolsheviks invaded Germany it would lead to the murder of all 50 million Germans.

What Hitler said in that memorandum was that the entry of the Bolsheviks would lead to the end of Germany as a national state and an end of the German people.

Hitler also used the phrase to the president of Czechoslovakia, Emil Hácha, on March 15, 1939.

Hácha had just signed the document which led to the German occupation of the Sudentenland, and Hitler said to the Czech president that "It is a good thing that you signed because otherwise it would have meant the *ausrotten* of the Czechoslovakian people."

It has never been taken to mean that Hitler told Hácha that a failure to sign the document would mean the murder of all 8 million Czechs, merely that Czechoslovakia would cease to exist.

It is therefore, a deliberate misinterpretation on the part of the Holocaust storytellers to automatically take the word "ausrotting" to mean extermination.

Himmler's own handwritten notes of his 1943 Posen speech confirm this as well: although he used the word "ausrotting" in the oral presentation, this part of the speech in his notes was marked as "Judenevakuierung," which translates as "Jewish evacuation."

Despite the Holocaust storytellers' best efforts, therefore, no documentary evidence has ever been produced showing senior Nazi leadership orders for any mass extermination policy.

Section 24: Himmler's Personal Correspondence Never Mentions "Extermination" Claims

In late 2013, Himmler's personal correspondence "emerged" from the hands of a private collector in Israel.

The announcement that his personal papers had been "found" provoked numerous articles in the media hoping that there would be some sort of "confession" or at least a reference to the "mass extermination" program attributed to the SS—but these hopes were rudely dashed when the letters were shown to contain not a single word about mass-murders or gassing. On the contrary, the personal correspondence of the leader of the SS in fact underlined the Nazi policy of forcing the Jews to leave Germany.

Section 25: The Bad Arolsen "International Tracing Service" Archives Provides No Evidence of any Mass Murder Program

The International Tracing Service (ITS), situated in Bad Arolsen, Germany, is an internationally governed center for documentation, information and research on displaced persons, forced labor and the "Holocaust," compiled from records all across Europe, run by the International Committee of the Red Cross.

The archive contains about 30 million documents from concentration camps, details of forced labor, and files on displaced persons. Because it contains all the German records, it is regarded as the most significant collection of documents related to all aspects of the Nazi era, holding 25 kilometers of papers which include hand-typed lists of Jews, homosexuals, and other groups detained in the camps, files on children born in the Nazi *Lebensborn* program, and, most importantly, registers of arrivals and departures from concentration camps.

When it was announced in 2007 that the Bad Arolsen archives were to be opened to the public for the first time since the war, mass media reports crowed that this would finally "lift the lid" on the "mass extermination" and "gassing" program.

Once again, just like the Himmler letters, the Holocaust storytellers were deeply disappointed. The records, German and otherwise, contained no evidence whatsoever of any mass genocide program.

According to ITC spokeswoman, Kathrin Flor, as quoted in a Reuters interview, "Only natural causes of death are recorded—heart failure or pneumonia. There's no mention of gassing" ("German Holocaust Archive in Bad Arolsen to Open Fully to Public," *Reuters,* 04/03/2013).

CHAPTER 4: THE NUREMBERG WAR CRIMES TRIALS

Section 26: The Legally-Flawed Nuremberg "War Crimes Trials" Did Not "Prove" the Holocaust

The Holocaust storytellers like to claim that the Nuremberg War Crimes Trials "proved" the mass murder of Jews in open court.

In reality, nothing of the sort was ever proved, and the main charges did not relate at all to the alleged mass murder of Jews.

The actual indictments at the main Nuremberg Trials were as follows:

"1. Participation in a common plan or conspiracy for the accomplishment of a crime against peace.

"2. Planning, initiating and waging wars of aggression and other crimes against peace.

"3. War crimes.

The Nuremberg Trials have been dismissed by all honest legal experts as a farce. People were charged on hearsay evidence, and for "crimes" such as "waging aggressive war." The Soviets, who had invaded Poland, Finland, and the Baltic States earlier in the war, sat on the judges' panel and sentenced German leaders to death for invading Poland.

"4. Crimes against humanity."

In normal legal systems, it is an established legal principle that no one can be charged for a crime that was not a crime at the time the act was committed—in other words, that no one can be charged retrospectively for an act which was not classified as a crime at the time when it was committed.

The Nuremberg Trial indictments are clearly a major abrogation of this principle, a fact which led the famous British General Bernard Montgomery, victor of the Battle of El Alamein, to remark with reference to the Nuremberg Trials that he no longer wished to lead any armies because it had now "become a crime to lose a war."

The legal basis of these main charges aside, the entire Nuremberg Trials process was from the very beginning a mockery because one of the judging parties—the Soviet Union—had, for the first two years of the war, been an ally of Nazi Germany!

For the German leaders to be charged with "waging aggressive war" and "planning, initiating, and waging wars of aggression and other crimes against peace"—and then to be found guilty thereof by judges who included Soviets, is one of the most extreme acts of twisted irony ever seen on the international legal stage.

If Germany could be charged for invading Poland on September 1, 1939 (the main charge of "waging aggressive war"), then why were the Soviets not charged for invading Poland on September 17, 1939—after concluding a secret deal with Nazi Germany over the matter? Why was the Soviet Union not charged with "waging aggressive war" over its invasion of neutral Finland on November 30, 1939?

In addition, nothing was said of the seizure of Lithuania, Latvia, and Estonia by the Soviet Union in June 1940.

The irony of the Soviets sitting in judgment over the Germans on charges of "waging aggressive war" was but only one of the many travesties of justice at the Nuremberg Trials.

The third charge, that of "war crimes" was equally outrageous. According to the definition used at the trials, a war crime was "a serious violation of the laws and customs of war." The mass Allied bombing of German civilians—started by Britain (with the Germans only retaliating after months of nightly bombing)—was certainly a violation of the "laws and customs of war," as were the mass rapes of German women carried out by Soviet soldiers in 1945.

However, these same Allies saw fit to put German leaders on trial for a handful of outrageous acts committed by underlings—none of which were ever sanctioned at senior level, unlike the bombing of civilians, an idea which came from Winston Churchill himself.

The fourth charge, "Crimes against humanity" was vaguely defined by the Nuremberg Trials as acts "committed in execution of, or in connection with, the aggressive war, and therefore constituted crimes against humanity" (Judgment: The Law Relating to War Crimes and Crimes against Humanity, *Judgment of the International Military Tribunal*). In other words, none of the defendants at Nuremberg were specifically charged with the mass gassing of Jews or the operation of extermination camps. They were only alleged to have been "generally responsible."

As a result it is untrue to claim that the Nuremberg Trials "proved the Holocaust."

Even much of the "evidence" produced at those trials has long since been accepted as false. A reading of some of the incredible evidence presented as evidence borders on the laughable if it were not so illustrative of the outrageousness of the "trials." By way of example, some of the "evidence" submitted to Nuremberg under the "crimes against humanity" charge included wild claims of "Jewish soap," "shrunken heads," "lampshades," "gassing by steam", execution by "electrocution" socks made of human hair, and even an astonishing affidavit by a "survivor" which claimed that the SS had killed Jews in one of the Polish camps with a "pedal-driven brain-bashing machine."

All of this was accepted at face value during the court proceedings, even though they have long since been dismissed as lies by all serious historians.

Section 27: The Katyn Massacre—How the Soviets Tortured Nazis to "Obtain Confessions"

A very large number of Nazi "confessions" still regularly used today to "prove" the Six Million came from prisoners held by the Soviet Union—and were obtained under torture.

The best example of this came when the Soviets obtained "confessions" from, put on trial, and executed, Germans who they blamed for the murder of thousands of Polish officers and intelligentsia in the Katyn Forest during the war.

The Katyn Massacre, as it is better known, had been committed by the Soviet Union's secret police, the NKVD in May 1940. Some 22,000 Poles were executed by being individually shot on direct order of the Soviet leadership (an order for the executions was signed by Stalin in person) and the bodies were buried in the Katyn Forest, twelve miles west of Smolensk.

The Germans discovered the graves in 1943. They appointed an international commission consisting of twelve forensic experts and their staff from countries such as Belgium, Bulgaria, Denmark, Finland, France, Italy, Croatia, the Netherlands, Romania, Sweden, Slovakia, and Hungary. In addition, a large number of Canadian, British, and Polish prisoners-of-war were allowed to attend the excavations.

The Soviets blamed the Germans and when they retook Smolensk, appointed a new commission which blamed the Germans, destroyed the Red Cross-built cemetery in the Katyn forest and removed other evidence. Later, two of the twelve forensic experts, the Bulgarian Marko Markov and the Czech Frantisek Hajek were arrested by the Soviets and forced to recant their evidence and blame the Germans.

The accusation that the Germans were responsible for the Katyn Massacre was then entered into the Nuremberg Trial court proceedings, which even specifically named which German army units and officers were responsible

TWO NAZI GENERALS HANGED BY RUSSIANS

LONDON, Dec. 30 (AP)—The Moscow radio said tonight that Lieut. Gens. Friedrich G. Bernhardt and Adolf Hamann and Cpl. Martin Adolf Lemler were hanged in Bryansk four hours after a military tribunal had convicted them as German war criminals. Cpl. Karl T. Stein was sentenced to twenty years in prison, the broadcast said.

All were convicted of atrocities during the occupation of Bryansk.

MOSCOW, Dec. 30 (Reuter)—A German officer in a group facing trial in Leningrad for "nightmare deeds" during the war has admitted Nazi guilt for the massacre of Katyn, in the Smolensk region, where mass graves of about 10,000 persons were found, a Tass dispatch said tonight.

The Germans had alleged that Poles had been murdered by Soviet political police and buried in Katyn in 1939.

The officer, Duere, describing in detail how Russian women, children and old men were murdered by retreating German troops, said that in the Katyn forest 15,000 to 20,000 persons, including Polish officers and Jews, were shot and buried.

A German news agency in April, 1943, asserted German troops had discovered the Katyn graves and blamed the Russians for the atrocity. The Polish Cabinet in London announced four days later that the International Red Cross had been asked to send a delegation to investigate on the spot. On April 25, 1943, Moscow officially severed relations with the Polish exile Government.

Right: Excavation of the bodies at Katyn, 1943. Left: A German propaganda poster distributed in Poland illustrating the method of execution. The Soviets blamed the Germans for the massacre, and, filled with a desire to avenge the exposure of the Katyn crime, went on to invent the first wave of "Nazi war crimes" in the areas of eastern Europe.

for the murders. Finally, in December 1945, in one of a series of "War Crimes Trials" held in Leningrad, a German army officer named Arno Düre was formally charged with participation in the Katyn Massacre.

Düre made a full "confession," explaining in detail how he had seen the Germans shoot and bury thousands of Polish officers. In a tactic which duplicated the defense used by other German war crimes accused, Düre managed to avoid implicating himself directly as a murderer, and was therefore "only" sentenced to twenty years hard labor.

It was only in 1990, with the collapse of the Soviet Union, that the Russian government formally admitted that the Soviets were responsible for the massacre. It was too late for Düre and many other Germans who had already "confessed" to atrocities in the east.

The German "confessions" about Katyn reveal the methodology followed by the Soviets in extracting many of the "confessions" upon which the Holocaust storytellers still rely.

Under these conditions, it is little wonder that the so-called "Nazi extermination camps" all just happened to be located in the Soviet-controlled parts of Europe, rather than western Europe, which were open to inspection by dissenting inquirers.

Section 28: Official "Holocaust" Journal Admits Soviet Torture used to Obtain Nazi "Confessions"

The final word on the Soviet war crimes trials comes from a study on the topic by Alexander Victor Prusin, published in the *Holocaust and Genocide Studies* in 2003:

"In Minsk a member of an execution detail, SS-Unterscharführer Franz Karl Hess admitted that he personally had killed more than one hundred people. His co-defendant Generalleutnant Johann Richert stated, 'horrible and mind-shattering facts were demonstrated in the court.... Now I am a determined opponent of the Nazi regime, and ready to do my share in the antifascist struggle.'

"Hermann Koch confessed to having personally murdered up to five hundred people and emphasized his own initiative in carrying out criminal orders: 'I was a fascist and remain a fascist. I did not simply carry out orders, but I was firmly convinced in the rightness of what I was doing. Racial theory made me a criminal. Much blood is on my hands; I ask for the death penalty for I do not know whether I could ever be able to remedy my crimes.'

"Such self-abasing confessions cast grave doubt on Soviet methods of obtaining evidence, and support the thesis that the proceedings were merely show trials. The conduct of the trials, then, begs a crucial question: do the trials have any value as legal and historical evidence?

"One should look at the interrogation records, which indicate that the defendants were under constant physical and psychological pressure. Sleep deprivation was but one tool used by the interrogators to extract information.

"As a rule, interrogation lasted for hours and often took place at night. Such methods especially affected the health and psyche of the other generals and senior officers, who were on average in their late fifties. Thus, on December 15, 1945, an interrogation of General Richert lasted from nine o'clock at night until two in the morning.

"On December 27, 1945, Jeckeln was subjected to questioning from eleven o'clock in the morning until five in the afternoon, while on January 8, 1946, he was interrogated from ten at night until half past six in the morning. Apparently some defendants were selected for trial because they agreed to cooperate—possibly upon promises of leniency (often unfulfilled), or simply because they were resigned to their fate. For example, there are indications that General Erdsmanndorf was a member of the Soviet-sponsored "Committee for a Free Germany," which carried out anti-Nazi propaganda among German POWs" (Alexander Victor Prusin, "'Fascist Criminals to the Gallows!': The Holocaust and Soviet War Crimes Trials, December 1945-February 1946," *Holocaust and Genocide Studies* 17.1, (2003) 1-30, Oxford University Press).

CHAPTER 5: THE EINSATZGRUPPEN—MYTH AND REALITY

Section 29: Anti-Partisan Warfare—The Real Purpose of the Einsatzgruppen ("Task Forces")

From September 1947 to April 1948, a series of trials took place in Nuremberg known as the "Trials of War Criminals before the Nuremberg Military Tribunals." Better known as the "Einsatzgruppen Trials," these proceedings laid the basis for the allegations that German "Special Action Groups" operating behind German lines in occupied Russia, murdered millions of people, mostly Jews, by mass shootings.

The defendants in the trials were the surviving commanding officers of the Einsatzgruppen, and as many senior officers as could be found—twenty-four in total. All were charged with three offenses:

1. Crimes against humanity through persecutions on political, racial, and religious grounds; murder; extermination; imprisonment; and other inhumane acts

committed against civilian populations, including German nationals and nationals of other countries, as part of an organized scheme of genocide.

2. War crimes for the same reasons, and for wanton destruction and devastation not justified by military necessity.

3. Membership of criminal organizations, the SS, the Sicherheitsdienst (SD), or the Gestapo, which had been declared criminal organizations previously in the international Nuremberg Military Tribunals.

The astute observer will see immediately that the third charge was bogus: The men were put on trial for the "crime" of belonging to an organization which was perfectly legal at the time when they joined, and only declared a "criminal organization" after the war ended.

All the defendants were convicted of this third charge—of course—and so it can be safely said that one-third of all the convictions at the Einsatzgruppen Trial were legally fraudulent.

The evidence prepared on the other two charges was obtained mainly from "confessions" extracted from the accused under torture, as detailed below.

The Einsatzgruppen were set up with two purposes, all of which was openly stated in the authentic and surviving German documentation.

These purposes were, firstly, to physically eliminate the entire Soviet Communist Party Commissar structure in areas occupied by the German army as it advanced eastward; and secondly to coordinate anti-partisan fighting behind the front line so as to ensure that there was as little disruption as possible to German supply lines.

The Einsatzgruppen were therefore active military units mostly engaged in active combat with Communist partisans, and not simply, as the allegation goes, "mobile killing units." In fact, Franz Stahlecker, commander of Einsatzgruppen A in the Baltic region and White Russia, was himself killed by partisans in 1942.

Soviet records claimed that in three years of warfare, from July 1941 to July 1944, Soviet partisans in Byelorussia "eliminated approximately 500,000 German soldiers and officers, 47 Generals, blew up 17,000 enemy military transports and 32 armored trains, destroyed 300,000 railway tracks, 16,804 vehicles and a great number of other material supplies of all kinds" (.S. Telpuchowski, *Die Geschichte des Grossen Vaterländischen Krieges 1941–1945*, Bernard & Graefe Verlag für Wehrwesen, Frankfurt/Main 1961, p. 284.).

These losses, it bears remembering, were in one sector of the Eastern front alone, and therefore give the reader an idea of the scale and intensity of the war behind the German front line.

Given these figures, it comes as no surprise to understand the real nature of the Einsatzgruppen—as anti-partisan units. In fact, the only surprise is how small they were. Each Einsatzgruppen consisted at maximum strength of 900 men, which meant that the total force deployed by all four units in Russia never exceeded 2,700 men—and that at full strength, which was never the actual case.

In spite of their relatively tiny numbers, it is claimed by the Holocaust storytellers that these 2,700 men killed anywhere between one and three million people by shooting them in mass execution style.

The sheer logistics of this undertaking—bearing in mind the Einsatzgruppen only worked from July 1941 to late 1943—should by itself make the mass murder allegations out to be preposterous—but, as the reader will see, all the "evidence" submitted at the trial was compiled under duress—as was later openly admitted by the Chief Prosecutor.

Nonetheless, the order to physically eliminate the Soviet Commissar structure is in fact the closest to the truth that the entire "Holocaust" story ever comes.

There were tens of thousands of Commissars—and, because of the close affiliation between Soviet Jews and the Communist Party, large numbers of these Commissars were Jews. It was therefore to be expected that the Einsatzgruppen would, as part of their activities, execute large numbers of Jews.

Section 30: Benjamin Ferencz, Jewish Chief Prosecutor at the Einsatzgruppen Trials, Admits to Using Forced Confessions and Death Threats

The American Army's Chief Prosecutor at the Einsatzgruppen Trials was not even an American, but a Hungarian Jew by the name of Benjamin Ferencz, who in 1945 had somehow been "assigned" to the job of setting up a war crimes branch and "collecting evidence" for the trials.

In this capacity, he was sent to concentration camps in western Germany which had been seized by the American Army. Ferencz was therefore primarily responsible for the "evidence" presented to the Einsatzgruppen Trial, and it is his "work" which is still today presented as "proof" that the German Task Forces killed vast numbers of people in the East.

In a much later—and rare—candid moment, Ferencz openly admitted that he had used threats of summary execution against civilians to "obtain confessions." In an interview with *The Washington Post* in 2005, Ferencz explained it this way:

"You know how I got witness statements? I'd go into a village where, say, an American pilot had parachuted and been beaten to death and line everyone one up against the wall. Then I'd say, 'Anyone who lies will be shot on the spot.' It never occurred to me that statements taken under duress would be invalid" ("Giving Hitler Hell," *The Washington Post,* July 24, 2005.).

Giving Hitler Hell

By Matthew Brzezinski
Sunday, July 24, 2005

This is the story of a man who has stared evil in the eye and held the fates of mass murderers in his hands. It

While it was perfectly legal under military law to hand over suspects for further questioning to DPs, says Benjamin Ferencz, who was a lead U.S. prosecutor at the Nuremberg War Crimes Tribunals in 1945 and 1947, knowingly delivering suspects for execution was not. And of course the DPs were not interested in extracting information.

Ferencz, who today is 85 and lives in New York, cautions against making sweeping armchair moral judgments. "Someone who was not there could never really grasp how unreal the situation was," he says. "I once saw DPs beat an SS man and then strap him to the steel gurney of a crematorium. They slid him in the oven, turned on the heat and took him back out. Beat him again, and put him back in until he was burnt alive. I did nothing to stop it. I suppose I could have brandished my weapon or shot in the air, but I was not inclined to do so. Does that make me an accomplice to murder?"

Ferencz -- who went on to a distinguished legal career, became a founder of the International Criminal Court and is today probably the leading authority on military jurisprudence of the era -- cannot specifically address Weiss's actions. But he says it's important to recall that military legal norms at the time permitted a host of flexibilities that wouldn't fly today. "You know how I got witness statements?" he says. "I'd go into a village where, say, an American pilot had parachuted and been beaten to death and line everyone one up against the wall. Then I'd say, 'Anyone who lies will be shot on the spot.' It never occurred to me that statements taken under duress would be invalid."

Jewish Chief Prosecutor Benjamin Ferencz addresses the court at the Einsatzgruppen Trial. He later openly admitted to obtaining his evidence by threatening to kill innocent civilians, and by participating in the torture death of an SS man at a concentration camp.

In the same interview, Ferencz also confessed to being at least a passive participant, or observer, in the torturing of captured Nazis at a concentration camp:

"I once saw DPs [Displaced Persons] beat an SS man and then strap him to the steel gurney of a crematorium. They slid him in the oven, turned on the heat and took him back out. Beat him again, and put him back in until he was burnt alive. I did nothing to stop it. I suppose I could have brandished my weapon or shot in the air, but I was not inclined to do so. Does that make me an accomplice to murder?" ("Giving Hitler Hell," the *Washington Post,* July 24, 2005).

These admissions by the Chief Prosecutor in the Einsatzgruppen Trials casts an immediate shadow over the entire proceedings.

Is this the sort of "objective" legal person who can be relied upon to produce evidence at a major trial?

The dreadful irony of a Jewish Chief Prosecutor at Nuremberg threatening to kill German civilians in order to gain "confessions" about Germans allegedly killing Jews, will not be lost upon the reader.

Section 31: The Einsatzgruppen *Ereignismeldungen* ("Event Reports")

The Einsatzgruppen sent irregular reports by radio, known as the *Ereignismeldungen* (EM), back to Berlin on their activities. Once received in Berlin, they were transcribed and edited by civil servants, and distributed in summary format, called the *Tätigkeits- und Lageberichte (TuLBs) der Einsatzgruppen,* to non-SS offices such as the German Foreign Office. In total, there are 194 *Ereignismeldungen*, 7 *TuLBs* der *Einsatzgruppen* and 12 *TuLBs* of Einsatzgruppen B in existence today—all of them copies, and none in the original.

The accuracy and authenticity of these reports has long been open to question, primarily because the originals have never been produced, and secondly because even though the officers charged with transcribing the reports attested to the general report-capturing nature of their work, the actual copies which have been produced show clear signs of postwar additions.

One such typical example, "Einsatzgruppen Report No. 111," contains not only completely garbled wording, but also a clear addition to the end of a paragraph (highlighted in italics below):

"These were the motives for the executions carried out by the Kommandos: Political officials, looters and saboteurs, active Communists and political representatives, Jews who gained their release from prison camps by false statements, agents and informers of the NKVD [National Commissariat for Internal Affairs], persons who, by false depositions and influencing witnesses, were instrumental in the deportation of ethnic Germans, Jewish sadism and revengefulness, undesirable elements, partisans, Politruks, dangers of plague and epidemics, members of Russian bands, armed insurgents—provisioning of Russian bands, rebels and agitators, drifting juveniles, *Jews in general.*"

The authenticity question surrounding the *Ereignismeldungen* and *TuLBs* has been further questioned by researchers because, once again, like so much other "evidence" of Nazi atrocities, the documents emerged from the Soviet occupation zone.

It is a common tactic of Holocaust storytellers to claim that the *Ereignismeldungen* were "captured" or "seized" by the US Army when they "took the Gestapo Headquarters"—but this is another blatant lie, because the Gestapo headquarters were located at 8 Prinz Albert Street in Berlin, and were captured by the Soviets in April 1945.

Even the chief prosecutor at the Einsatzgruppen Trials, the self-admitted forced confession expert, Benjamin Ferencz, admitted in his memoirs that the "copies" of the *Ereignismeldungen* which the Americans had, and which were used in the trial, originated with the copies held by the German Foreign Office—in Berlin, which makes them also originally Soviet-origin papers.

Finally, the trial of German Field Marshal Erich von Manstein, in August 1949, cast further doubt over the accuracy of the *Ereignismeldungen.* Charged with overseeing the Einsatzgruppen activities in his command sector on the Eastern Front, Von Manstein denied all the allegations, and his British lawyer R. T. Paget demonstrated that whole areas which the *Ereignismeldungen* claimed had been "cleared of Jews" (*Judenfrei*) contained many flourishing Jewish communities that were actually fully functional and untouched throughout the entire war.

The trial court accepted this argument—that the *Ereignismeldungen* were unreliable—and Von Manstein was acquitted on that charge.

Nonetheless, the *Ereignismeldungen* are widely regarded as authentic by Holocaust storytellers—even though this claim, if true, raises more problems with the Holocaust narrative then it does to "prove" it.

Firstly, to address the numbers claimed killed by the Einsatzgruppen in the *Ereignismeldungen.* If the reports are genuine, then the total number of killings—due to the intense combat and subsequent executions—is unreliable by virtue of the fact that the surviving reports are incomplete.

Secondly, in accordance with the stated purpose of the Einsatzgruppen, the *Ereignismeldungen* list deaths which were due to both the ferocious anti-partisan warfare as well as executions. For example, by the autumn of 1941, Einsatzgruppen B reported having executed 1500 partisans.

Thirdly, the surviving *Ereignismeldungen* also reveal that by late 1942, there were no more "Jewish Actions" (*Judenaktionen*) taking place—meaning that after that time, no formal anti-Jewish operations took place, and the rest of the Task Forces' existence was taken up with anti-partisan operations.

Section 32: The Babi Yar Massacre in Kiev: Wartime Aerial Photography Exposes the Lie

One of the most infamous atrocities attributed to the Einsatzgruppen (in this case, Einsatzgruppen C) is an alleged mass-murder outside Kiev in the Ukraine, known as the Babi Yar massacre.

The allegation is that after the Germans occupied Kiev, a series of bombs, set off by Communist insurgents, struck the city, killing many civilians and German occupying troops. Much of the city was set on fire as a result of the bombings, and as German troops helped with putting out the blaze, a Jewish insurgent was caught cutting one of the water hoses.

According to the Holocaust storytellers, the arrest of this Jew persuaded the Nazis that all the Jews in Kiev had to be killed, and Einsatzgruppen C rounded them all up over the period of September 29–30, 1941, marched them to a ravine outside the city, and shot them all—some 33,771 individuals.

The "evidence" for this atrocity is contained in one of the disputed *Ereignismeldungen,* where the report specifically gives the figure of 33,771 Jews having been shot in Kiev on that date.

Once again, the *Ereignismeldungen* report is open to question—because the physical facts surrounding the Babi Yar ravine do not support the report's claim. There are today no remains of tens of thousands of bodies to be found at the Babi Yar site, even though a monument now stands on the spot.

The Holocaust storytellers claim that the reason why there are no bodies to be found at the site—even though the story claims 33,771 people were shot there—is because the Nazis sent a special team back to the site in 1943 to exhume, burn, and crush the bones—using, of all things, tombstones from a nearby Jewish cemetery to smash the last of the bones.

Of course, the time, effort and fuel it would take to exhume, stack on iron rails, burn and then crush 33,000 bodies makes the allegation absurd—but nonetheless, this is the given reason why there are no bodies present. The Soviets even produced a compliant German officer, SS-Standartenfuhrer Paul Blobel, to "confess" to having destroyed all the 33,771 bodies within a period of thirty days, from August 18 to September 19, 1943.

The "confessions" remind the reader of those "obtained" by the Soviets to cover up the Katyn massacre, which was also blamed on the Germans. In fact, the parallels with Katyn offer a further valuable insight into the Babi Yar claims.

The mass graves created for the Soviet massacre and burial of Polish officers and intellectuals at Katyn (a crime that for fifty years was blamed on the Germans), as well as the graves used to accommodate the bodies of some 100,000 innocent residents, including children, of Hamburg, Germany, that were slaughtered by Allied bombing, have proven that it takes about a one acre area of excavation material to bury roughly 10,000 bodies.

Wartime aerial photograph of the Babi Yar Ravine, taken at the exact time that the SS was allegedly exhuming, cremating, and crushing tens of thousands of bodies. If the Babi Yar massacre had occurred as claimed, the whole area would have seen massive earth displacements, burning stacks of bodies, and frenetic human activity. Instead, the entire area is completely undisturbed. The photo is available from the US National Archives and is listed as: GX 3938 SG, exposure 105.

Babi Yar would have needed a minimum of three and one half acres for 33,000 bodies. There is, therefore, no possibility that the precision aerial photos available from the period in question would not show such a disturbance in the soil.

Even if the mass grave's depth is increased to sixteen feet, 50,000 bodies would take up about one and a half acres. Approximately 1,600,000 cubic feet of soil would need to be excavated. This would be a major excavation project even for today's modern heavy equipment.

Any claim that it was done in 1941, and once again in 1943 under battle conditions, is pure fantasy. This does not even address the question of where was this equipment obtained on a battle-weary front?

There are a host of other physical problems associated with the Babi Yar massacre story. For example:

– In order to "machine gun" people, it is worth emphasizing that twice as many bullets as the given number of people would be needed. If 33,771 people were shot, then the Germans would have needed at least 67,000 rounds—and probably more—to complete the task.

Such a large amount of ammunition would weigh about 1,876 pounds, or 850 kilograms. Lead is essentially an inert substance which survives practically forever in the soil. That amount of lead should be easily recoverable on the site—if it had been shot out there, but not a trace of it has ever been found.

– Next there is the matter of the fuel needed for cremation of the bodies, which the Holocaust storytellers say took place two years after these "murders" and while the German army was in full retreat in that sector.

The Holocaust storytellers claim that the bodies were burned in the open, with wood, after being piled onto iron rails. Present-day open air cremations, as carried out in India amongst Hindus, require at least 10 hours per body, and 330 pounds (150 kilograms) of wood.

This would mean that the cremation of 33,771 bodies would require at least 11 million pounds (5 million) kilograms of wood. To believe that anyone could cut down and provide that amount of firewood in the face of a rapidly advancing Soviet Army is about as nonsensical as believing that the removal of so many trees in the nearby area could go unnoticed.

– Furthermore, the "mass murder" of Jews at Babi Yar allegedly took place almost four months prior to the Wannsee Conference, where, the Holocaust storytellers claim, the idea to kill all the Jews was first planned. The Babi Yar allegations therefore, fairly typically, raise more questions than answers.

Finally, aerial photography, held in the US National Archives in Washington DC, contains 600 wartime aerial photographs of Kiev, including Babi Yar, taken on over 20 flights over the area. The first photos, taken at 12:23 pm on May 17, 1939, reveal such details as cars and even the shadows of the lamp posts on the streets of Kiev.

More importantly, every large bush and small tree is visible on the slopes and at the bottom of the Babi Yar ravine.

The last aerial photo coverage of Kiev (and Babi Yar) took place on June 18, 1944, about nine months after the city was re-occupied by the Soviets.

These reconnaissance photos show clearly that the foliage and ground cover of the ravine remained completely undisturbed throughout the two years of German occupation, and that there is absolutely no evidence of human activity in the ravine.

The aerial photographs do, however, reveal the existence of ten mass graves in the Ahovtnevyi borough of Kiev and in the general area of Babi Yar, situated closed to a labor camp set up by the German occupiers called Syretz.

Going by their size, these graves likely contain several hundred bodies—but the dead would most likely be those who perished during the two years of German occupation.

In addition, at the nearby Orthodox Lukianivsky cemetery, another, larger mass grave can be seen. This one would appear to contain several hundred victims of the very public German executions of partisan fighters by the Einsatzgruppen.

The already problematic story was further complicated in 2007 when E. Musiyenko, the editor of the *Kiev Evening News* (*Vechirnyi Kyiv*), published a four page story on March 19 of that year which claimed that there was a mass grave at Babi Yar—but that it did not date from the Nazi occupation. Rather, he said, evidence showed that it was a burial field used between 1922 and 1935 for the victims of the Communist secret police, the Cheka/NKVD.

The claims of a "massacre" at Babi Yar Ravine do not, therefore, match up with the physical evidence, and also cast a serious shadow over the reliability of the *Ereignismeldungen*.

Section 33: The "Confession"—and Retraction—of Einsatzgruppen Commander Otto Ohlendorf

SS-Gruppenführer Otto Ohlendorf was the commanding officer of Einsatzgruppen D, which was deployed in Moldova, south Ukraine, the Crimea, and the north Caucasus. Arrested after the war, he was initially not charged with any crimes and instead called as witness for the prosecution in front of the International Military Tribunal in Nuremberg in January 1946.

There, under cross examination, Ohlendorf claimed that his Task Force had killed 90,000 people, Jews and non-combatants, that from the Spring of 1942, women and children had been executed in "gas vans," that the victims were all buried in trenches, and that he had personally been present at two mass shootings.

Ohlendorf giving testimony.

Despite this "confession," Ohlendorf was not charged with any crime until 1948, when he was arraigned as a defendant in the Einsatzgruppen Trial mentioned above.

At the 1948 trial, he completely recanted his 1946 confession, claiming that it had been extracted from him by force. In his recantation, Ohlendorf never mentioned killing children; declared that the Einsatzgruppen were merely engaged in fighting an anti-partisan war; that he knew nothing about gas vans; and reduced the number of executions under his command to 40,000.

Furthermore, Ohlendorf continued, he denied any knowledge of, or participation in, any grand genocide plans, testifying as follows:

[Ohlendorf Direct Examination Testimony. Questions posed by his defense lawyer, Dr Aschenauer.]

Q. Did you know about plans or directives which had as their goal the extermination on racial and religious grounds?
A. I expressly assure you that I neither knew of such plans nor was I called on to cooperate in any such plans. Lieutenant General [Obergruppenführer] Bach-Zelewski testified during the big trial [before the International Military Tribunal] that the Reich Leader SS in a secret conference of all lieutenant generals made known that the goal was to exterminate thirty million Slavs. I repeat that I was neither given such an order nor was there even the slightest hint, given to me that such plans or goals existed for the Russian campaign. This is not only true for the Slavs but this is also true for the Jews. I know that in the years of 1938, 1939 and 1940, no extermination plans existed, but on the contrary, with the aid of Heydrich and by cooperation with Jewish organizations, emigration programs from

Germany and Austria were arranged; financial funds even were raised in order to help aid the poorer Jews to make this emigration possible.

The presiding judge at the 1948 trial rejected Ohlendorf's recantation, and refused to consider it as evidence—effectively convicting Ohlendorf and the others on the basis of the earlier "confession" which had been extracted under duress.

Ohlendorf expressed his bitterness at the refusal to acknowledge that his earlier "confession" had been forced from him, and in his closing statement to the 1948 trial, said the following:

"I have been now in the Palace of Justice in Nuremberg for two and a half years. What I have seen here of life as a spiritual force, in these two and half years, has increased my fear. Human beings who under normal conditions were decent citizens of their country were deprived of their basic conception of law, custom, and morals by the power of the victors."

After he was sentenced to death—on the basis of his forced confession and no other physical evidence—Ohlendorf went into attack mode, telling the Jewish chief prosecutor Benjamin Ferencz that "the Jews in America would suffer for what he [Ferencz] had done" (*Nuremberg Trials and Tribulations, 1946–1949,* Chapter 4, Benjamin Ferencz).

Ohlendorf also publicly attacked the Jewish attorney-general of the "Bavarian State Office for Restitution," Philip Auerbach, who had announced that he was "seeking compensation for eleven million Jews who had suffered in concentration camps." Ohlendorf said that "not the minutest part" of the people for whom Auerbach was

A picture issued by the US Holocaust Museum titled "Members of an Einsatzkommando (mobile killing squad) before shooting a Jewish youth. The boy's murdered family lies in front of him; the men to the left are ethnic Germans aiding the squad. Slarow, Soviet Union, July 4, 1941." This is supposed to be "evidence" of the mass murders committed by the anti-partisan Special Action Groups. However, a cursory examination of the picture proves the caption to be a lie. Firstly, the corpses are all wearing army boots, showing that they were soldiers of some sort, and certainly not a "Jewish family." Secondly, the figure on the left of the picture, supposedly part of the "Jews about to be shot" is actually smiling. This picture is obviously of some war dead, surrounded by curious observers. It is a typical tactic of the Holocaust storytellers to take images and add the most outrageous captions, confident that no one would dare question the "truth."

seeking compensation had even seen a concentration camp. Ohlendorf lived to see Auerbach convicted of embezzlement and fraud before his own execution finally took place in 1951.

Section 34: The Wildly Varying Numbers of Einsatzgruppen "Victims"

The wildly varying numbers of victims claimed for the Einsatzgruppen also reveal much about the "accuracy" of this story.

- In the book *Jews in the Soviet Union,* by Solomon M. Schwarz (Syracuse Univ. Press., Syracuse 1951, p. 220), it is claimed that 3 million people were shot by the Einsatzgruppen.

- In the book *Die Truppe des Weltanschauungskrieges. Die Einsatzgruppen der Sicherheitspolizei und des SD 1938–1942,* by H. Krausnick, H.-H. Wilhelm (Deutsche Verlags-Anstalt, Stuttgart 1981, p. 333), it is claimed that 2.2 million people were shot by the Einsatzgruppen.

- In the book *The Destruction of European Jewry* by "Holocaust expert" Raul Hilberg (Quadrangle Books, Chicago 1961; pb: Harper & Row, New York 1983; 2nd ed., Holmes & Meyer, New York 1985), it is claimed that 1.3 million people were shot by the Einsatzgruppen.

In the *Encyclopedia of the Holocaust,* issued by the US Holocaust Memorial Museum, it is claimed that "over 1 million" people were shot by the Einsatzgruppen. All of these sources claim to quote "eyewitnesses" and "official records." The fact that the number of victims claimed can vary so wildly from 1 to 3 million, shows an obvious flaw in the "proof" available.

Section 35: The Oswald Pohl "Confessions"— Example of the Nuremberg Miscarriage of Justice

The trial, conviction, and execution of Oswald Pohl, the head of the SS-Wirtschafts-Verwaltungshauptamt (the Economic and Administrative Main Office of the SS, abbreviated to SS-WVHA), which ran the administration of the concentration camps during the war, serves as a textbook example of the miscarriage of justice which took place at the Nuremberg Trials.

Pohl went into hiding at the end of the war, and was only captured in 1946. He was taken to Nenndorf where British soldiers tied him to a chair and beat him unconscious. He lost two teeth in repeated beatings (Legal brief for Oswald Pohl, *Grundzüge des Systems der Deutschen Konzentrationslager und Bemerkungen zum Urteil des Militärtribunals II gegen Oswald Pohl,* pp. 23–27.)

During this time, Pohl was forced to sign false and self-incriminating affidavits written by prosecution officials that were later used against him in his own trial, including a bogus admission that he had seen a gas chamber at Auschwitz in the summer of 1944. As he recalled: "Whenever genuine documents did not correspond to what the prosecution authorities wanted or were insufficient for the guilty sentences they sought, 'affidavits' were put together. The most striking feature of these remarkable trial documents is that the accused often condemned themselves in them. That is understandable only to those who have themselves experienced the technique by which such 'affidavits' are obtained" (Written statement by Pohl, June 1, 1948. *Deutsche Hochschullehrerzeitung* (Tübingen), Nr. 1/2, 1963, pp. 21-26.).

American officials also made use of false witnesses at Nuremberg, Pohl wrote: "Whenever these productions [affidavits] were not enough to produce the result sought by the prosecuting authorities, they marched out their so-called 'star witnesses,' or rather, paid witnesses … A whole string of these shady, wretched characters played their contemptible game at Nuremberg. They included high government officials, generals, and intellectuals as well as

Oswald Pohl, bound and photographed before his execution.

prisoners, mental defectives, and real hardened criminals" (*ibid.*).

Pohl also protested that defense attorneys were not allowed free access to the German wartime documents, which the prosecution were able to find and use without hindrance: "For almost two years the prosecution authorities could make whatever use they wanted of the many crates of confiscated documentary and archival material they had at their disposal. But the same access right was refused to the German defendants despite their repeated efforts … This meant a tremendous or even complete paralysis and hindrance of the defense cases for the accused, for those crates also contained the exonerating material that the prosecution authorities were able to keep from being presented to the court. And that is called 'proper' procedure" (*ibid.*).

During his own trial, Pohl freely admitted to being in charge of the entire concentration camp administration system, but denied ever having anything to do with gas chambers. This tactic—of not denying the prosecution's main claim that there was an "extermination program," and merely denying personal participation, was, as will be detailed below, a logical and, under the lynch-mob circumstances, only reasonable defense which any individual could offer.

The forced confessions extracted earlier from Pohl were however used to convict him, and he was hanged in 1951.

Section 36: The Perjured Testimony of Erich von dem Bach-Zelewski

Reference has already been made above to the SOP Order No. 4 at Nuremberg, where witnesses were offered amnesty if they provided evidence against other parties. One extreme case of this was SS General Erich von dem Bach-Zelewski.

A senior officer in the SS, Bach-Zelewski held a number of positions which would have made him a prime candidate for prosecution. These positions included a series of appointments as Higher SS and Police Leader (Höherer SS- und Polizeiführer HSSPF) in Silesia in Poland (where Auschwitz was located); Belarus (where he oversaw the activities of Einsatzgruppen B); head of the anti-partisan operations in Belgium, Belarus, France, the (Polish) General Government, the Netherlands, Norway, Ukraine and Yugoslavia; and head of the German forces which suppressed the Warsaw Uprising in 1944.

Arrested by the Americans when he was in hiding in August 1945, Bach-Zelewski was offered the choice of "confessing" to a multitude of sins and not being prosecuted, or being handed over to the Communist regime in Poland, which was baying for his blood after his suppression of the Warsaw Uprising.

Not surprisingly, Bach-Zelewski took up the "SOP No. 4" offer, and agreed to give evidence for the prosecution in exchange for complete amnesty.

His evidence was—and still is—used to "prove" the alleged activities of the Einsatzgruppen and of many other claims concerning what SS Chief Heinrich Himmler is alleged to have said.

A case in point was his account of Himmler's speech at the SS Castle at Wewelsburg, in March 1941, where his evidence was as follows: "I am of the opinion that this step was closely connected with a speech made by Heinrich Himmler at Wewelsburg at the beginning of 1941, prior to the campaign against Russia, when he spoke of the purpose of the Russian campaign, which was, he said, to decimate the Slav population by 30 million, and that it was in order to achieve this purpose that troops of such inferior caliber were introduced" (*Nuremberg Trial Proceedings Volume 4*, Twenty-Eighth Day, Monday, January 7, 1946, afternoon session).

In fact, what Himmler had actually said was that the coming war in Russia could result in millions of dead, as other accounts of that meeting confirmed. This was not the only deliberate distortion that his evidence included: Other claims were to the effect that the anti-partisan operations of the Einsatzgruppen were a "cover" for the plot to murder both Jews and Slavs (the first and only time a plot to "murder Slavs" was ever made).

Göring denounced Bach-Zelewski to his face for the falsity of this testimony—something that must have had some effect, because in April 1959, Bach-Zelewski repudiated his Nuremberg testimony before a West German court, saying that his all his earlier statements had not the slightest foundation in fact, and that he had made them for the sake of his own survival. The German court, after careful deliberation, accepted his retraction.

CHAPTER 6: THE ADOLF EICHMANN TRIAL

Section 37: Eichmann Only Admitted Deporting Jews, Never Murdering Them

The 1961 trial of Adolf Eichmann, an SS Lieutenant Colonel in charge of arranging the deportation of Jews to the east, has also been touted as "conclusive evidence" of the Holocaust. At his trial, Eichmann in fact specifically denied murdering anyone, although he did say that if anyone had died as a result of the deportations which he had arranged, then he would have been indirectly responsible.

The Jewish journalist Hannah Arendt, in her book *Eichmann in Jerusalem* (Penguin, 1978), wrote that the evidence presented against the SS man was hearsay evidence, "rumours testified to" (p. 208), and therefore without legal validity.

The testimony of all witnesses who had "seen him with their own eyes" collapsed the moment a question was addressed to them.

Arendt also described how Eichmann was placed under severe mental and physical pressure to make statements, revealing how he was kept tied to a bed for eight days after his kidnapping (p. 241).

The Israeli government-paid defense lawyers refused to cross-examine any prosecution witnesses, and *Time* magazine of April 14, 1961 reported that "Eichmann had found it impossible to recruit ex-Nazi colleagues to serve as defense witnesses. Reason: the Israeli government had refused to promise that they themselves would not be arrested if they set foot on Israeli soil."

During the trial, Eichmann claimed that he had seen "preparations in the East for extermination." This was a reference to his earlier claim, made in a taped interview in Argentina, that he had visited a gas chamber in operation at the Majdanek camp near Lublin in "the latter part of 1941" for which a Russian U-Boat motor was used to generate exhaust fumes which allegedly killed Jews.

This claim has always been a subject of dispute because even the Holocaust storytellers claim that there were no gas chambers at Majdanek in 1941.

The Lublin camp was built as a prisoner-of-war camp in 1941 to accommodate some of the thousands of Soviet soldiers captured during the opening offensive of the German invasion of Russia, and the official guide book handed out at the camp museum in 2010 stated that the "construction of the gas chambers at Majdanek started in August 1942 and was completed in October 1942."

This would make Eichmann's claim to have seen a gassing in 1941 impossible. So why did he say this?

Section 38: Eichmann's Doctored "Memoirs"

The reason might be found in the rest of his so-called memoirs, which were published in *Life* magazine in 1960 and which contain so many "mistakes" and contradictions that they give cause for great doubt as to their authenticity.

For example, in the section entitled "The Final Solution: Liquidation," Eichmann claims that the Wannsee Conference took place on "Jan. 10, 1942"—whereas it in fact took place on January 20th (*Life,* Vol. 49, No. 22, November 28, 1960, pp. 24, 101–102). It is unlikely that Eichmann would have made such an error, seeing as he was responsible for organizing the meeting.

Other impossible claims made in Eichmann's "memoirs," which cast further doubt on their authenticity, included a claim that he had witnessed the gassing of 1,000 Jews in buses which "were normal, high-windowed affairs with all their windows closed. During the trip, I was told, the carbon monoxide from the exhaust pipe was conducted

Adolf Eichmann on trial in Israel. He denied killing anybody and his "memoirs" have obviously been altered, as evidence by large inconsistencies in their chronological narrative.

into the interior of the buses. It was intended to kill the passengers immediately."

Apart from the fact that an ordinary windowed bus full of people would never be airtight, there is no possible way that the victims would have not opened or smashed out the windows as soon as the exhaust fumes entered the interior.

This version also contradicts the Holocaust storytellers' claim that the "gas buses" used by Nazis were specially constructed machines with no windows.

All in all, there is good reason to doubt the Eichmann "memoirs" as accurate. Furthermore, the only thing which was proven at Eichmann's trial in Jerusalem was that he had been in charge of deporting Jews to the east—something which had never been under dispute.

CHAPTER 7: THE JOHN DEMJANJUK TRIALS

Section 39: John Demjanjuk—Acquitted in Israel!

In 2011, much media attention was given to the conviction in Germany of Ukrainian-born John Demjanjuk on charges of having been a guard at the Sobibór concentration camp during 1943.

The Demjanjuk case serves as one of the best examples of the sort of lies and distortions which have characterized almost every single "war crimes trial" since 1945.

The Demjanjuk story began in October 1975, when a list of names of alleged Nazi war criminals was circulated amongst members of the US senate. The list originated with the Soviet Union's KGB, allegedly out of material captured by the Soviet Army at the end of World War II.

One of the names appearing on the list was that of John Ivan Demjanjuk, who had immigrated to the US in 1951 and who was living in Cleveland, Ohio. The KGB document alleged that Demjanjuk had been a soldier in the Red Army who, after falling into German captivity, had volunteered for service in the SS. Demjanjuk, had, said the Soviet document, undergone training at the SS camp in the town of Trawniki, Poland. He had, continued the document, served from March 1943 as an SS guard at the Sobibór camp, and later at the Flossenbürg concentration camp.

Acting on this information, the US government started proceedings to strip Demjanjuk of his citizenship, based on his alleged concealment of his Nazi past from the Immigration and Naturalization Service. In addition, the US Government instructed its Department of Justice to start a full investigation into the allegations contained in the Soviet document, in preparation for a deportation hearing to send Demjanjuk to Israel for trial.

In February 1976, the American government requested the Israeli government's cooperation in finding Israeli citizens who were survivors from the Sobibór camp who might be able to identify Demjanjuk.

The source of identification was passport photographs submitted by Demjanjuk to the INS during his application for citizenship in 1950, with the logic being that Demjanjuk would still appear relatively similar to how he had looked in 1943.

During 1976, the Israeli police identified a number of Jews who were on record as having been rescued or escaped from the Treblinka or Sobibór camps. These "survivors," when shown the photographs of Demjanjuk, identified him as a guard called "Ivan the Terrible" who had allegedly operated the gas chamber at Treblinka.

Despite the American government actually having identified Demjanjuk as having been a guard at the geographically separate Sobibór camp, the "eyewitness survivors" placed Demjanjuk at the Treblinka camp, and of being the gas chamber operator there.

The next year, 1977, the INS instituted denaturalization proceedings against Demjanjuk. After an extended legal battle, Demjanjuk was deported to Israel in 1986 to stand trial.

The State of Israel's application for extradition was based on the testimony of these "eyewitnesses" and an SS identification card, allegedly issued to Demjanjuk upon completion of his training at the Trawniki SS camp.

This card, which became known as the "Trawniki certificate" was a pivotal piece of evidence, as it contained Demjanjuk's photograph. The card had been provided to the prosecution directly out of Soviet records.

Along with the identification card, the prosecution produced five "eyewitnesses" who all testified that Demjanjuk was "Ivan the Terrible" who operated gas chambers in Treblinka.

Demjanjuk's defense was that he had been captured by the Germans and had remained in their captivity throughout the war, never serving with the SS. The prosecution dismissed his defense, producing eyewitnesses identifying

---

THE CITIZEN   Tuesday 24 February 1987

Gas chamber worker tells of horrors

JERUSALEM. — A tearful survivor of a Nazi death camp told a packed Israeli courtroom yesterday that alleged war criminal John Demjanjuk was a notorious guard "Ivan the Terrible" who beat and killed prisoners and ordered one to have sex with a teenage girl who had survived a gas chamber.

Dozens of spectators clapped when Pinhas Epstein (62) pointed an index finger at the Ukrainian-born Demjanjuk and told the three-judge court: "That's him."

Epstein said he saw a photograph of "Ivan the Terrible" in an album shown him in 1978 by Nazi-hunting Israeli investigators.

"I was shown an album and my attention was drawn to one picture, and I identified it as that of Ivan," Epstein said.

"I said the photo was not particularly sharp. It was older than the Ivan I knew but still it was him. The frame, the round face, the short neck, the wide shoulders and the protruding ears. I told them this is the Ivan I remember," he said.

— Sapa-Reuter.

The Argus, Thursday February 26 1987

'This man is a killer'

Witness identifies 'Ivan the Terrible'

JERUSALEM. — A man accused of being sadistic death-camp guard "Ivan the Terrible" has stunned an Israeli courtroom in the most dramatic moment of his week-old trial by greeting a prosecution witness with an offer to shake hands.

The witness, a Treblinka camp survivor, backed away in horror from the outstretched hand of alleged nazi war criminal John Demjanjuk and called him a murderer.

Eliyahu Rosenberg spurned the unexpected greeting and accused Mr Demjanjuk of being "Ivan the Terrible", the sadist who operated Treblinka's gas chambers.

Mr Rosenberg testified that Mr Demjanjuk once gave him 30 lashes for stealing bread, and then forced him to say "thank you".

"This man is Ivan, without a shadow of a doubt — Ivan from Treblinka, from the gas chambers — the man I am looking at now," he said.

He told the court he and his family were transported from the Warsaw ghetto to Treblinka, where at the age of 12 he was forced to remove bodies from the gas chambers and bury or burn them.

"We soon discovered that women and children burned quicker than men. The Germans would tell us: 'Throw in the children first because they burn faster'," he said. — Sapa-Reuter.

him personally, and an SS-identification card with his photograph.

Section 40: "Survivor" Testimony Identifies Demjanjuk—But Israeli Supreme Court Dismisses them as Liars

The first "survivor" to testify, Pinhas Epstein, took the stand on February 23, 1987, and told the court that "I am convinced that opposite me sits Ivan the Terrible of Treblinka" (*Gas Chamber Worker Tells of Horrors,* Reuters, February 23, 1987).

The next "survivor eyewitness," Eliyhau Rosenberg, then told the court on February 25, 1987: "This man is Ivan, without a shadow of a doubt—Ivan from Treblinka, from the gas chambers—the man I am looking at now" (*This Man is a Killer,* Reuters, February 25, 1987).

To no one's surprise, the Israeli Court found Demjanjuk guilty on April 18, 1988, and a week later, sentenced him to death. The conviction had been obtained based primarily on the SS identification card and the eyewitness accounts which identified Demjanjuk as the gas chamber operator at Treblinka.

The defense immediately appealed, citing numerous irregularities in court procedure, rules of evidence, and other issues. At a critical juncture in the appeal process—when Demjanjuk's life hung in the balance—fate intervened. One of the appeal judges had a heart attack, and the case was postponed.

During the postponement, in 1990, the Soviet Union suddenly collapsed. As a result, the KGB archives on the case were opened. In the KGB file dealing with Demjanjuk, the shocking truth was revealed: the Trawniki certificate had been forged to frame the Ukrainian as part of a campaign against Ukrainian nationalists.

Faced with the exposure of the Trawniki certificate as an outrageous forgery, the Israeli Supreme Court, to its credit, acknowledged that the entire case against Demjanjuk had been fabricated from start to finish, and acquitted him in July 1993, stating that there was no evidence to show that Demjanjuk was indeed "Ivan the Terrible."

On September 22, 1993, John Demjanjuk was finally released and allowed to return home to Cleveland, Ohio, after spending seven years in an Israeli jail because of a KGB forgery and a pack of fabricated evidence from "holocaust survivors."

Implicit in its dismissal of the case against Demjanjuk, the Israeli Supreme Court tacitly acknowledged that all of the eyewitness accounts which placed Demjanjuk at Treblinka, were false. For this reason, the John Demjanjuk case serves as an outstanding example of just how unreliable "holocaust survivor eyewitnesses" are.

The Argus, Wednesday February 25 1987

You're Ivan the Terrible, says camp survivor

TEL AVIV. — A Jewish survivor of a nazi death camp has told a packed Israeli courtroom he is convinced John Demjanjuk was the sadistic gas chamber operator "Ivan the Terrible" in spite of the alleged war criminal's denials.

Mr Pinhas Epstein, the first survivor of Treblinka death camp to testify at Mr Demjanjuk's six-day-old trial, shouted: "I am convinced that opposite me sits Ivan the Terrible of Treblinka."

"I would go to the gas chambers to take out the corpses... he would stand and look at the result of his handiwork — the stabbing of girls, the gouging of eyes, the pieces of girls' breasts ... this would occur metres from me," Mr Epstein said, his voice choking.

For if the Israeli Supreme Court could not bring itself to believe them—and that institution, of all, would be the most likely to take their word —then this serves as an indication of just how false these accounts are.

Section 41: German Court Ignores Israeli Decision

Astonishingly, this was not the end of the persecution of John Demjanjuk. In 2009, he was deported to Germany to stand trial once again on charges of being a guard at Sobibór. The prosecution's chief document was once again the Trawniki certificate.

Perversely, the German court ignored the Israeli Supreme Court's ruling and a 1985 report from the Cleveland office of the FBI which specifically said that

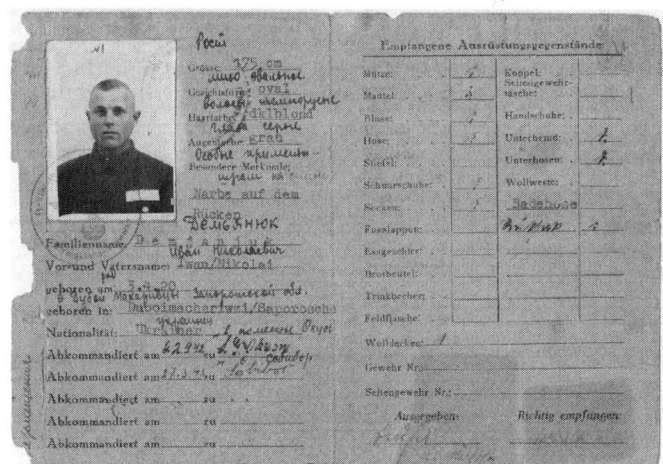

The "Trawniki Certificate," an SS identification card bearing John Demjanjuk's name and photograph. Supplied by the KGB, it was a critical piece of evidence in Demjanjuk's first trial in Israel in 1987, and ensured his conviction. It was only with the collapse of the Soviet Union that the KGB file on Demjanjuk was released and it was revealed that the card was a forgery. The Israeli Supreme Court then overturned Demjanjuk's conviction and set him free.

the Trawniki certificate was "quite likely" a KGB forgery. Demjanjuk was convicted in 2011 and sentenced to five years' imprisonment. He died while appealing against the sentence.

The last word in the Demjanjuk trial was had by Christiaan F. Rüter, Professor of Law at the University of Amsterdam, who is the world's acknowledged expert on National Socialist trials in Germany.

He was quoted in the German media as saying that "it is a complete mystery, how anyone who knows the German jurisdiction up to now, would be able to assume that Demjanjuk could be sentenced based on the given evidence."

CHAPTER 8: THE PSYCHOLOGY OF CONFESSIONS

Section 42: Why Would Anyone "Confess?"

Guards and commanders from several camps faced trial from the end of the war right through to the early 1970s. Most of the important ones are dealt with below under the chapters dealing with the camps.

Here it is however valuable to ask the pertinent question: Why would anyone accused of mass murder at any of the camps "confess" to such heinous crimes at these trials? The researcher Paul Grubach has written extensively on this topic and is worth quoting in full here:

"Long before the enactment of the present laws in Germany that criminalize any 'denial' of the Holocaust, there were still social and political pressures that induced German officials on trial for alleged war crimes to 'confess' to the 'truth' of the extermination of the Jews.

"The 'Nazi extermination camp' mythology was declared 'historical truth' at the Nuremberg trials, and it was then used as an ideological cornerstone for the Allied installed governments in postwar Germany. Since the German government is based upon the 'Nazi gas chamber' ideology, to dispute it in a German court is virtually impossible.

Indeed, in April 1999, the German Federal Foreign Minister Joschka Fischer stated: 'All democracies have a basis, a cornerstone. For France it is 1789, for Germany it is Auschwitz.' In the highly respected German daily *Frankfurter Allgemeine Zeitung*, Patrick Bahners put forth a founding belief of the present German government. If one 'denies the murder of the Jews, he repudiates the legitimacy of the Federal Republic.'

"Is it any wonder that former German soldiers who served at Sobibór 'confessed' that there were 'gas chambers' at the camp? From a legal standpoint they had no choice but to give credence to this legend. The tribunals that these German military men and National Socialist officials faced were committed to the dictum that there was a Nazi plan to exterminate the Jews, and it was done with the use of 'gas chambers.'

"It was out of the question for them to contest this in court, so they simply built their defense strategies accordingly. In a word, it was simply in their best legal interests to simply 'admit' the 'truth' of the orthodox Jewish extermination story and then build their defense strategy around it—thus falsifying the historical record along the way.

"The late Dr. Wilhelm Stäglich, a former judge who was punished by the German government for his 'Holocaust denial,' expressed this dilemma when he stated: From the outset, the defendants in the 'Nazi Crimes of Violence' trials knew that it was utterly pointless to dispute all or part of the picture of the mass murder of the Jews in which they were accused of having taken part, since that picture had been inculcated into the public mind long before the trials began.

"To the defendants it must have seemed the most expedient course not to dispute that the alleged murders occurred, only that they were involved in them. Particularly if they lacked an airtight alibi, the defendants had to secure the goodwill of the court. In short, they had but one aim in mind: their own acquittal.

"Evidence in favor of this view is provided by Holocaust expert Christopher Browning. One of Browning's key pieces of evidence for alleged mass exterminations at Belzec is the postwar testimony of former SS Sergeant Josef Oberhauser. Buried in a footnote, Browning provides us with a reason to be skeptical of Oberhauser's testimony. He accuses Oberhauser of falsifying the dates of events in order to create an adequate defense at the 'Belzec trial' in Germany in the 1960s.

"Specifically, he writes that Oberhauser is guilty of 'clearly falsifying chronology to give the impression that until August 1942—i.e., for the period for which he was on trial—only a small number of test gassings were being carried out in a single gas chamber capable of holding 100 people.'

"Why didn't Oberhauser claim that until August 1942 (the period for which he was on trial) he never witnessed or operated any homicidal gas chambers? This would have been the best defense, would it not? No, because of the nature of the German legal system that he was entrapped in, it would have been hopeless to attempt to repudiate the Belzec gas chamber story.

"So, it was simply in Oberhauser's best legal interests to 'confess' to the existence of 'gas chambers,' and then claim that there were only a small number of 'gassings' while he was in the camp. Professor Browning also admitted that even the memoirs of Adolf Eichmann contain 'calculated lies for legal defense.' This would not be the first time that a German officer in a postwar statement falsely claimed that there was a Nazi policy to exterminate Jews in order to create a defense at his upcoming trial. Browning's colleague, *Final Solution* historian Ian Kershaw, pointed this out in his book.

"Kershaw concedes that some postwar court testimony of German military officers about the existence of an order from Hitler to exterminate the Jews is bogus: 'The early postwar testimony of Einsatzkommando leaders about the prior existence of a Führer order [to mass exterminate the Jews] has been shown to be demonstrably false, concocted to provide a unified defense of the leader of Einsatzgruppe D, Otto Ohlendorf, at his trial in 1947 [p.258].

"We see a similar legal defense strategy in regard to the Germans who stood trial for alleged crimes committed at Sobibór. Karl Werner Dubois, who was sentenced to three years imprisonment at the 1966 Sobibór trial for his alleged involvement in mass murder, explained an overall defense strategy: 'What should be taken into account is that we did not act on our own initiative, but in the context of the Reich's Final Solution to the Jewish problem.'

"At the present time, it is impossible for anyone to contest the traditional extermination story in a German court. Revisionist historian Robert Faurisson profiled the situation perfectly when he pointed out that 'Holocaust denial' is 'an offense which is punishable with up to five years imprisonment. In Germany, no exonerating evidence may be introduced in such trials, since the same evidence would constitute *denial* as well and would merely lead to another criminal indictment of the defendant and his lawyer.'"

This was in fact what happened to the lawyer who defended well-known Holocaust revisionist Ernst Zundel in a German court, Sylvia Stolz. In 2008, Stolz was sentenced to three and a half years in prison and banned from practicing law for five years after declaring in court during the Zundel trial that the "Holocaust was the biggest lie in world history" (Deutsche Welle, *German Neo-Nazi Lawyer Sentenced for Denying Holocaust,* 14.01.2008).

In a climate where one will be sentenced to prison just for saying that the Holocaust is untrue, is it any wonder that the accused on trial for alleged war crimes would "confess" to the existence of "gas chambers" but then try to claim that they were personally not involved?

This is in fact, what many (but not all) of those put on trial did.

Section 43: The Suchomel "Confession" in Claude Lanzmann's "Shoah" Movie

It is often claimed that a "confession" by a former SS man, Franz Suchomel, made in the 1985 documentary film Shoah (directed by the French Jewish producer Claude Lanzmann) "proves the existence of the Treblinka gas chambers.

There are two aspects to the Suchomel "confession" which bring it into question, namely the technical aspects of Lanzmann's film, and secondly, the factual details of the "confession".

(a) Technical aspects: Firstly, Suchomel is quoted in the film as asking Lanzmann not to use his name or attribute anything he says to him. Lanzmann told the *New York Times* (October 20, 1985, page H-17) that the interview was secretly filmed with a single camera hidden in a canvas held by a female assistant.

This, Lanzmann explained, was the reason why the Suchomel interview is of poor black and white blurred quality—as opposed to the rest of the movie, which is all in sharp, clear color.

In actual fact, the clip showing the "confession" is not even original film, but was filmed off a TV screen, as can be seen by the characteristic horizontal lines and flicker of the filmed interview (caused by a difference in the scanning frequency between the TV and the camera making the film).

It is highly suspicious that Lanzmann would record such a supposedly important interview by filming it off a TV screen when he would have the original film material to hand. The only potential explanation for this would be that tampering is far less easy to detect in a "poor quality" film than raw original material.

In this regard, a viewer of the film will also notice that while the image quality of Suchomel is extremely poor, the sound quality is perfect, something which is out of step with the overall production.

It is strange that the "interview" with Suchomel is the only part of the entire nine-and-a-half hour Shoah film which is blurred, indistinct, and so fuzzy that it is nearly impossible to even positively identify the person being interviewed.

Most importantly however, the interview with Suchomel was clearly done with more than one camera—directly contradicting Lanzmann's claims in the *New York Times.* A stationary, hidden camera in a bag would only show one angle of a "secret" interview—but instead, as can be seen from the screen shots below, there are at least four different camera angles, each taken at differing focal lengths and perspectives—something that would be impossible with just one "hidden camera."

In one scene, the camera shows Suchomel actually standing next to a display board allegedly showing the Treblinka camp layout, and holding a pointer stick picking out different locations in lecture style—an arrangement which is obviously highly unlikely for an interview which was supposedly not filmed.

There are other physical anomalies in the "confession": although the viewer is expected to believe that Suchomel was not aware of the "hidden" camera in the bag, more than once he turns his head and looks directly into the camera.

However, when he adopts his (standing up) lecturer mode, and taps on the set-up board with the Treblinka map, the camera moves in to only a few inches away from the board, and clearly shows his pointer stick.

It is far-fetched to believe that anyone holding a "hidden camera in a bag" could hold it so close to the board under such circumstances without being obvious.

(b) Secondly, it is clear from Suchomel's own words in the film—presuming that the film is genuine (and as the facts outlined above show, there is good reason to doubt that)—that there are serious errors in his memory and his recounting.

The Suchomel "confession" in Claude Lanzmann's Shoah *film: made with at least four different camera angles, and not just the "one hidden camera in a bag" as claimed by the film producer. Note also the distinctive distortion and horizontal stripe caused by filming off a TV screen. In fact, the curvature of the screen can be seen in the top left hand side of the first image.*

Camera angle 1: Set up behind Lanzmann (left) and Suchomel (right).

Camera angle 3: Suchomel and the "lecture board" – supposedly not to be filmed.

Camera angle 2: Suchomel standing up, lecture-style, holding a pointer next to a handily-set up board with a supposed map of Treblinka—a highly unlikely arrangement for an interview that was not even supposed to be filmed.

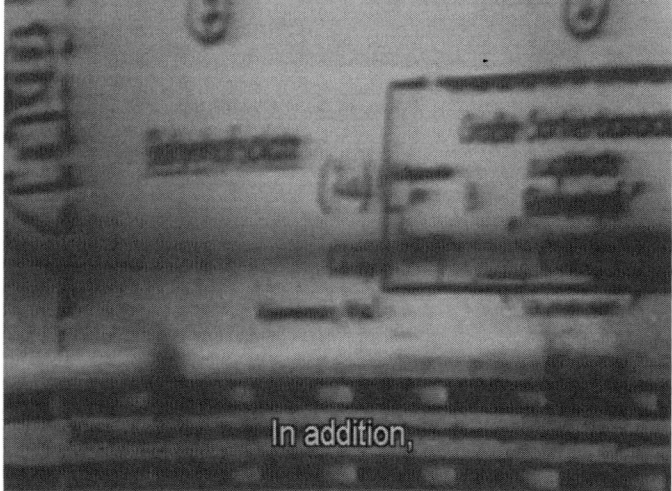

Camera angle 4: The camera moves to a few inches away from the "lecture board." It is impossible, as Lanzmann claimed, for one camera, hidden in a bag, to have produced all of these camera angles.

Firstly, it should be borne in mind that Suchomel had been arrested and tried during the 1965 Treblinka Trial at Düsseldorf.

At that trial, he confessed to being in charge of or organizing the tailor shop at Treblinka. In line with the (already outlined above) common defense tactic used by the accused of not denying the "mass murder" program—which is illegal under German law anyway, and would have therefore only landed him in even further trouble—Suchomel only claimed that he had had nothing to do with it. In a superb example of how this defense tactic worked, Suchomel was only sentenced to six years in jail—and released just over two years later, in December 1967. This by itself was a sure indication that there was indeed no direct evidence linking him to any "gas chambers" or "mass murder program" at Sobibór.

In the Lanzmann "confession", Suchomel is quoted as specifically saying that he only saw the "gas chambers" at Sobibór once during the entire time (August 1942 until late October 1943) that he was there.

His account, as contained in the Lanzmann confession, is typically vague, and follows precisely the already completely discredited—and as outlined above, physically impossible Holocaust Storytellers' version of mass gassings in minutes, bodies falling "like potatoes" and then mass cremations in a tiny area of space, with no provision for fuel—or even a single crematorium!

It is clear from this narrative alone, that even if Lanzmann did not tamper with the fuzzy film "interview", all that Suchomel said was the typical "do-not-deny-it-happened-but-just-deny-that-I-was-involved" type confession which was the only way to avoid being caught up in further legal trouble in post-war Germany.

Finally, it is of great significance that Suchomel died in 1979—that is, six years before the film was released, and thus never saw his "confession," and was never able to deny or refute anything which Lanzmann had attributed to him.

CHAPTER 9: "DEATH CAMPS" VERSUS "LABOR CAMPS"

Section 44: The Distribution of the Concentration Camps

One of the biggest misconceptions which is avidly promoted by the Holocaust storytellers is that there were a large number of German concentration camps which had been set up specifically with the purpose of gassing Jews and other people.

This view is still widely held and repeated by the media *ad nauseam,* so it comes as a shock for many people unfamiliar with the topic to discover that it is claimed that there were only six camps which were designated as "extermination camps." These camps are, in order of their infamy, as follows: Auschwitz–Birkenau, Treblinka, Sobibór, Belzec, Madjanek (Lublin), and Chelmno.

All these camps, bar Chelmno, were located in what was then occupied Poland, called the Central Government under German administration. (Chelmno, located near the city of Lodz, was also in Poland in 1939 but for the duration of the war was incorporated into Germany. It was returned to Poland in 1945.)

The other well-known camps, such as Bergen-Belsen, Dachau, Sachsenhausen, Buchenwald, and Ravensbruck were located inside Germany's borders. Although it was claimed at the end of the Second World War that gassings had taken place at these camps as well, the allegations were quickly dropped as the evidence was completely lacking.

The "extermination" story then focused on the camps in Poland, which, fortuitously hidden from public view by the Iron Curtain and Soviet control, could be embellished as time went on. In this way, it comes as another shock for people unfamiliar with the topic to hear that many of the "gas chambers" and installations which are on view today at the "extermination camps" are in fact "reconstructions" built by the Soviets after the war.

For many years, this shocking fact was concealed from the public, but is now freely admitted to by the museum authorities at the camps, as any person visiting the sites can ascertain for themselves. The revelation that there were "only" six "extermination camps" cast even further doubt upon the ability of these limited number of facilities to hold, murder, and dispose of literally millions of persons.

Furthermore, it is claimed that the "gassings" occurred in a period of little more than two years, from 1942 to late 1944. Considering that the "Six Million" number is a figure which is higher than the individual populations of at least forty nations in the world today (including Ireland, Norway, New Zealand, Togo, Costa Rica, and many others), the impossibility of murdering millions in "only" six camps in little more than two years should, by itself, refute the mass extermination story.

A map showing the location of the most famous Nazi concentration camps. Nowadays it is claimed that the only "extermination centers" were in Poland.

CHAPTER 10: AUSCHWITZ-BIRKENAU

Section 45: Auschwitz Founded as a POW Camp for Polish Soldiers in 1940

Media coverage has ensured that Auschwitz has become central to the entire Holocaust story and mass gassings—the camp has become the embodiment of the Holocaust.

The first camp at Auschwitz was called Auschwitz I, and was started as a prisoner of war camp to hold some 10,000 Polish soldiers captured during the campaign of 1939.

Captain Rudolf Höss was sent to Auschwitz to open the camp in April 1940, and within one month he had converted a number of dilapidated former barracks, set around a large square used for the breaking of horses, into a passable prison camp. It is this camp which has the infamous "Arbeit Macht Frei" (Labor is Freedom) sign which has become a Holocaust icon.

The "reconstructed" nature of Auschwitz's Crematorium I is obvious to even a casual observer. These photographs of the rear of Crematorium I, as presented to the present-day tourist, show that the "reconstructed" chimney is not even connected to the building whose ovens it is supposed to have served. The chimney is actually an empty separate structure, connected to nothing and deliberately built after the war to bolster the "extermination" legend to unsuspecting tourists.

A photograph of the alleged gas chamber at Auschwitz I which is shown to visitors today: note the non-airtight opening door. If this room had been used to mass gas thousands of people, it would have been smashed out in an instant by the victims, especially if they were, as the story goes, packed into such facilities hundreds or thousands at a time.

A close-up of the "gas chamber door" seen above, showing the ordinary "door handle" (!) and the pane of glass (!) which the Holocaust storytellers actually want visitors to believe kept "thousands" of people inside as they were "gassed."

There is even a manhole and a drain in the "gas chamber" floor. The existence of a drain is conclusive proof that the building could never have been used as a "gas chamber" because the gas would have seeped into the rest of the building and into the "crematorium" (also reconstructed!) next door.

The "doorway" between the "gas chamber" and the "crematorium" was, as the camp museum has now admitted, created when postwar "reconstruction" work smashed through the wall with hammers. The view is from the "gas chamber" into the "crematorium" room—an attempt to create the impression that bodies could be moved from the "gas chamber" to the crematorium this way.

Auschwitz was then selected as a major industrial site for a large IG Farben center and an oil-from-coal Buna rubber factory. Labor for these industries was supplied from the prison population, and soon Höss found himself with a camp population in excess of 30,000.

The increase in the camp size brought additional problems for Höss's administration, including the issue of controlling disease amongst the rapidly expanding prison population. After the invasion of the Soviet Union, tens of thousands of Russian soldiers captured as prisoners-of-war were also brought to Auschwitz to work in the factories.

As natural deaths amongst the prison population mounted, Höss ordered the building of a crematorium in Auschwitz I.

Here it is worthwhile to add that almost all the German camps were equipped with crematoria. The existence of a facility to hygienically dispose of bodies is, therefore, by itself no "proof" of an intention of mass murder. Most present-day prisons and hospitals also have in-house crematoria, which is a standard practice in any area of concentrated population.

Section 46: Auschwitz "Gas Chamber" Shown to Tourists Is Officially Admitted to be Fake

The crematorium in Auschwitz I was built out of an old munitions bunker and came into operation in August 1940. It is now claimed that in August 1941, this crematorium's morgue chamber was converted into a "temporary gas chamber" in which "experimental gassings" were carried out until July 1943, when, it is claimed, the gassings were moved to a secondary camp located at nearby Birkenau.

Auschwitz I's "gas chamber," the Holocaust storytellers say, was then converted into an air raid shelter. Tourists visiting present-day Auschwitz are shown camp I's

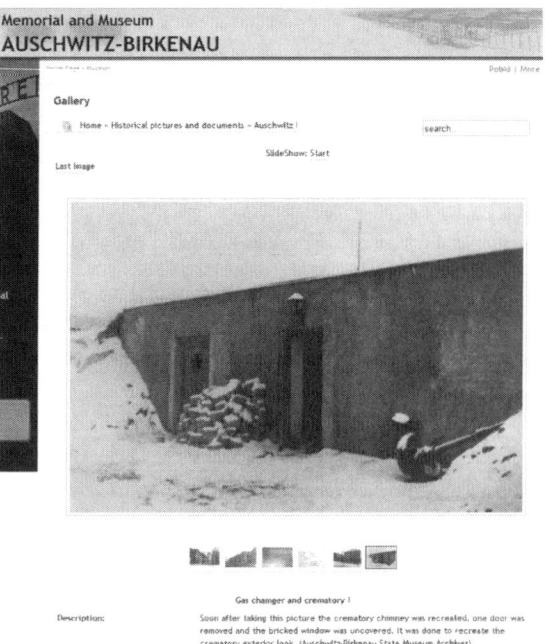

Left: The 2006 confession by the Auschwitz Museum, as announced on their website, that the "chimney," "two incinerators" and the "openings in the gas chamber roof" were "reconstructed" after the war. This was the first time that the Holocaust storytellers ever formally admitted that the "gas chamber" which they still show to tourists, was actually built after the war. Right: A picture of the "Gas Chamger[sic] and Crematory I" in Auschwitz, as replicated on the Auschwitz museum's official website in 2012. The caption reads: "Soon after taking this picture the crematory chimney was recreated, one door was removed and the bricked window was uncovered. It was done to recreate the crematory exterior look (Auschwitz-Birkenau State Museum Archives)." This was the second time that the Auschwitz museum admitted in public that the "gas chamber" shown in Crematorium I had been "reconstructed" after the war.

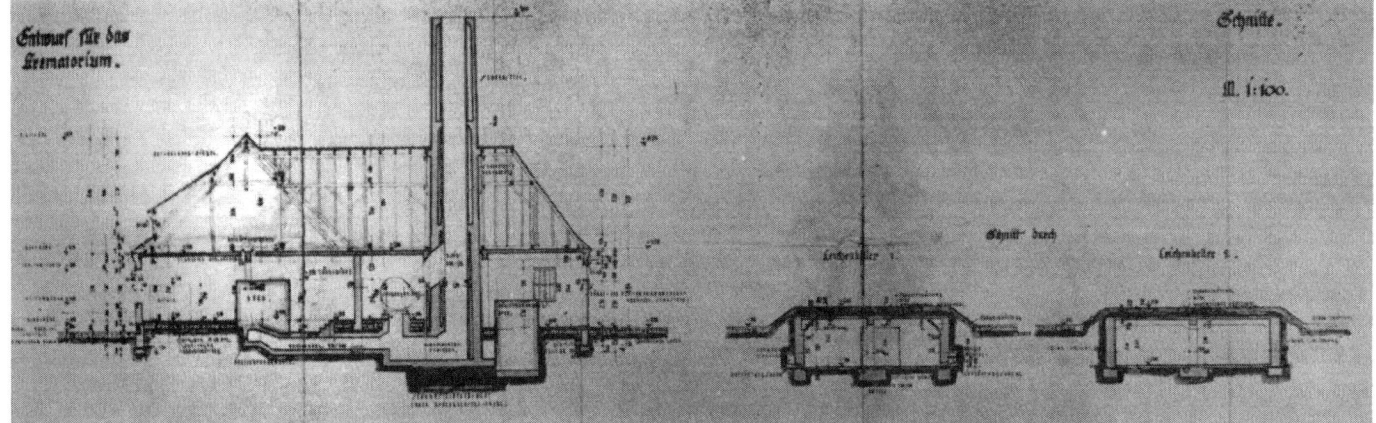

The original German architectural building plans for Crematorium II at the Auschwitz-Birkenau camp, on public display in the camp museum today. According to this original plan, there is no gas chamber. It is claimed that the underground structures, marked very clearly as mortuaries ("leichenkellers") were used as gas chambers.

crematorium building and told that the morgue was a "gas chamber." However, the first objective visitors to the camp after the fall of the Communist regimes in 1990 quickly spotted the following inconsistencies with this "gas chamber:"

– The large chimney which dominates the "gas chamber" stands by itself a short way from the building and is not even connected to the ovens on display inside;

– The "gas chamber" has two non-airtight doors which would have resulted in the deaths of anyone standing around the building had it been used to gas people;

– One of the "gas chamber" doors leads directly into the room which contains the two "reconstructed" ovens. Gas from the "gas chamber" would have leaked or been heated from the crematorium and would have exploded, making the entire complex unusable as a place of execution;

– The "openings" in the roof for the introduction of "cyanide gas" are crude wooden flap boxes of flimsy build which are also not airtight. The use of these holes to introduce poison gas into the chamber below would have resulted in the death of the guards and of the people in the surrounding buildings (as the "gas chamber" is in the middle of a very built-up part of Auschwitz I). Despite these obvious inconsistencies, the Holocaust storytellers continued to maintain that this was a real "gas chamber" and ensured that this lie was repeated *ad infinitum* in the world's media. This farce is maintained to the present day even at the camp itself, where visitors are still informed that this was a "real gas chamber" and are only told the truth if they actually ask.

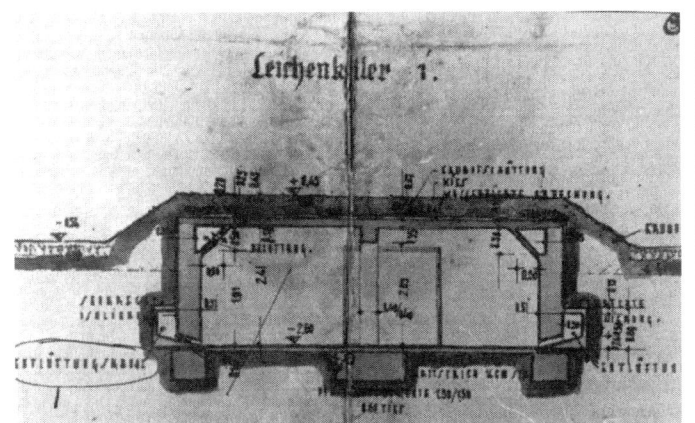
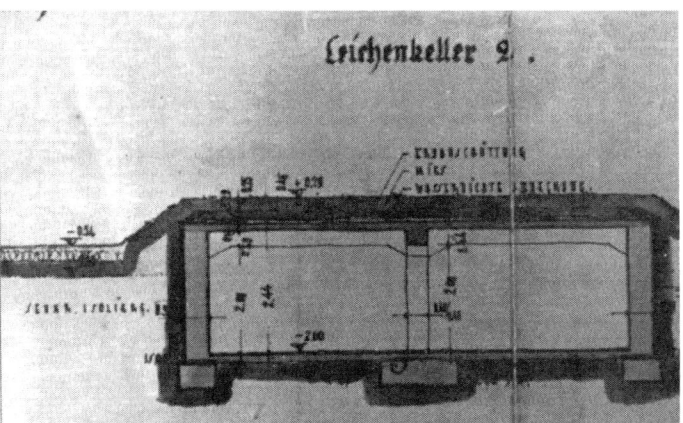

Details of the architectural plans from the previous page, which show the mortuaries marked as "leichenkellers" (mortuaries). Nowhere on the original architect's plans are there homicidal "gas chambers." The only facilities mentioned on the plans were delousing chambers for disinfecting prisoner clothing to counter lice-born typhus— a measure meant to prevent human deaths, not cause them.

A model on display at the Auschwitz Museum. This is how the Holocaust storytellers claim that the underground mortuaries were used as "gas chambers." They claim that the first mortuary room (left) was an "undressing room," and the mortuary on the right was the actual "gas chamber." The ovens were on the ground level. There are multiple obvious flaws in this theory: firstly, it is well-known that people lose control of their bowels upon death as muscles relax. To "gas" thousands of people at a time in an underground room would cause the area to be flooded with human sewage. It would quickly become impossible to even enter such a room. Secondly, if, as the storytellers claim, thousands of bodies were piled on top of each other in the "gas chamber," then extracting them and dealing with the residue "gas" would be an impossible task, given that there was only one small door leading in and out of the room. Finally, the immense logistical difficulties in removing thousands of bodies through a small single door and transporting them on an elevator—designed to take one or two bodies at a time—back up to the ground level for cremation, makes the claim of "systematic mass gassings" impossible both physically and in terms of the time it would take to fill and empty such a chamber—if it were even feasible in the first place.

The layout of Crematorium II, as seen from the air, from which the layout of the two underground mortuaries is visible. It is claimed the shorter of the two mortuaries was actually a "gas chamber" and that Zyklon B was introduced into this room through metal mesh tubes protruding down from its roof. This theory is flawed in several respects: firstly, the single door entrance/exit to the room makes removing thousands of corpses at a time nearly impossible, and secondly, the lack of drainage facilities would mean that human excrement--a natural release upon death-- would soon flood the entire underground structure, if, as is claimed, "thousands" of people were killed there every day.

Section 47: Auschwitz Museum Finally Admits that "Gas Chamber" Was Built After the War

Finally, however, too many people started asking questions, and an article in the French magazine, *L'Express*, of January 1995, proved to be a turning point.

In an article, the journalist Eric Conan stated to a shocked readership that the "gas chamber" shown to tourists was built in 1948 by Polish communists.

"The Auschwitz staff now admits this," Conan wrote. "Tout y est faux"—Everything in it is fake" (Eric Conan:

Crematorium II as photographed in 1943. Note the open terrain, making its operations visible to all. The "short" underground mortuary is clearly visible in front of the building. It is claimed that there were a number of identical buildings to Crematorium II, all using their underground morgues as "gas chambers." Below is a photograph of, for example, Crematorium IV, also built to the same plans and in which it is also claimed that gassings were carried out.

«Auschwitz: La mémoire du mal,» *L'Express,* Paris, 19 janvier 1995).

It took the Holocaust storytellers another ten years before they finally admitted that the "gas chamber" in Auschwitz I had indeed been built after the war, although

Prisoners taking a shower in the Auschwitz shower rooms. It was from these facilities that the story of "gas chambers in shower rooms" originated. The showers can still be seen at the camp today. Photograph from the Auschwitz camp museum archives.

The same shower room in the picture left, as it appeared at the camp in 2011. Note that the shower-heads have mysteriously been removed, just one of many "alterations" carried out at the camp after the war. The story of "gas showers" comes from installations like this.

the word they used was "reconstructed." In 2006, the Auschwitz camp museum admitted in its official literature (and on its website) that

"After the war, the Museum carried out a partial reconstruction. The chimney and two incinerators were rebuilt using original components, as were several of the openings in the gas chamber roof" (Gas Chamber and Crematorium I, Auschwitz Museum website, May 2006).

In 2011, the Auschwitz Museum website had changed the wording to read

"Two of the three furnaces and the chimney were reconstructed (from original parts), and several of the holes in the roof of the gas chamber were reopened."

Despite the obvious problems which would have made it impossible for this building to have been used as a gas chamber, the museum administration maintains to this day that "experimental" gassings took place in the crematorium's morgue, and the building is still presented to thousands of tourists as a real "gas chamber."

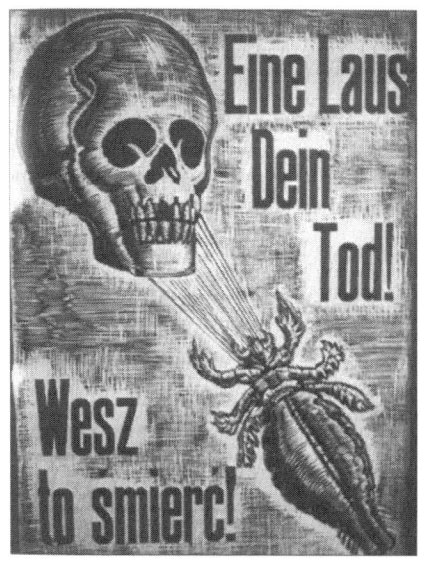

A poster, with wording in German and Polish, distributed at Auschwitz for the inmates, which warns that "One Louse is Your Death." The idea that Nazis would warn inmates that disease could kill them is directly contradictory with the allegation that those same Nazis were trying to kill the inmates.

Left: The Auschwitz camp employed a number of delousing stations, which used steam and Zyklon-B to kill lice in prisoner clothing. This picture shows autoclave number 2, seen from the "dirty" clothing side. Infected clothing was put on hangers attached to a trolley and pushed inside the chamber. Dirty clothes were put on hangers on a trolley which was pushed into the chamber on two short rails. The disinfection stations were constructed with double doors so that the infected and cleaned clothes would not be mixed together. This picture was taken while the camp was operational. Right: This same autoclave today, a picture taken in 2011.

Left: A battery of three autoclaves, showing prisoners at work in the camp. The steam arrived through the light colored pipe above the autoclaves, and the dark pipe connected the pressure vessel to the hot water tanks. An electric motor enabled the steam to be rapidly evacuated at the end of the cycle (to the left of each autoclave). On the table a prisoner is filling in the operating report and there is a clock for timing the sterilization cycle. The two short rails in front of each autoclave are to receive the trolley carrying the effects to be disinfected. Note also the healthy condition of the camp inmates. Right: These same autoclaves, a picture taken in 2011. Note that the surrounding equipment and piping has been removed, another of the many "alterations" carried out at the camp after the war.

Left: Prisoners at Auschwitz working in one of the larger clothing disinfestation chambers in the camp. They worked in much the same way as the autoclaves, with "dirty" and "clean" sides. The peepholes in the doors could be closed by raising the flap and blocking it with a catch. These were opened at the end of a disinfestation cycle to allow fresh air to enter as soon as the extractor fans were switched on. Photographs from the Auschwitz museum archive. Right: The delousing station of above, as it can be seen at the present time. Note that the doors have been removed, another one of the "alterations" carried out at the camp after the war.

Section 48: Auschwitz II: Architect's Plans Show No "Gas Chambers"

The Holocaust storytellers then claimed that the big gas chambers were actually located in the second camp at Auschwitz, built close to the Auschwitz I, on a site called Birkenau.

This camp, known officially as Auschwitz II, was originally constructed to house Russian prisoners-of-war who worked as laborers in the industrial complex called Auschwitz-Monowitz (where the IG Farben factory was located). Here, it is claimed, no less than four large gas chambers were built as part of a "killing complex" and began operations in March 1943.

The Holocaust storytellers claim that the two of the gas chambers, at Crematoria II and III, were located underground next to the building housing the ovens, while the other two, at crematoria IV and V were situated aboveground.

The original German architectural building plans for Auschwitz II have survived and are on display at the camp museum to the present day.

Although it was claimed that the facilities were "purposely built" as gas chambers, the original plans show no sign of this at all. This is a problem for the Holocaust storytellers.

The specialist airtight and fume extraction machinery and construction which would be required to build chambers capable of killing thousands of people at a time, as is claimed, would make it impossible for the architect's plans not to have shown such details.

In reality, the original architect's plans only show morgues, which are marked up on the papers as "leichenkellar," the German word for morgue.

The Germans were meticulous record keepers, even to the point where invoices for dog food are still available for inspection at the camp's museum archives. Yet there is not one plan, drawing, or discussion paper outlining the construction of "gas chambers." The reality is that there are no German plans for "gas chambers" in existence.

The only "evidence" for mass gassings in these "gas chambers"—which were actually morgues—comes therefore from "witness testimony," which is dealt with below.

Section 49: Real Showers in Auschwitz and the "Gas through the Shower-head" Legend

The story of the "shower" gas chambers, at Auschwitz in particular, is derived from the fact that there were indeed mass shower facilities at the camp.

Ironically, the Germans took special care to ensure that all camp inmates were regularly bathed to try and prevent the spread of disease, which would have severely impacted the available labor supply for the industries around the camp. The Auschwitz museum's archives provide a wealth of evidence for the existence of these showering facilities, and some of the available material is produced here.

The shower rooms, which were just that, are the origin of the "gas chamber shower" stories, and also one of the reasons why so many "survivors" claimed to have been taken to the "gas chambers" and survived—because they were in reality taken to the showers for cleaning.

Section 50: Steam Disinfection Stations for Prisoner Clothing as Part of the Anti-Typhus Measures

Typhus, borne by lice, as a continual threat to life in all the camps. The most common source of infection was to be found in clothing, and hence all the camps had extensive delousing installations. These delousing installations all had chambers in which lice were killed either by steam or by an insecticide called Zyklon-B, manufactured by the Degesch company. It is from these delousing stations that the Holocaust storytellers have developed the stories of "gas chambers," "execution by steam" and "execution by Zyklon-B."

Section 51: Delousing Chambers Used in All Camps

There were "real gas chambers" at all the camps, Auschwitz included. These chambers were not built, or used, to kill people, but were actually small, airtight chambers, usually no larger than big cupboards, in which prisoner clothes were deloused with Zyklon-B (which was, and still is to this present day, sold under that brand name as an insecticide). These delousing chambers were used in all the Nazi camps, including those in Germany and Poland. As a result, Zyklon-B was distributed to all camps, including those not claimed as "extermination centers."

What a real gas chamber looks like: The Kanada I delousing station in Auschwitz. From left to right, the main entrance door, two extractor fans and their control boxes, and the gas-tight door of the room in which prisoner clothing was deloused—using Zyklon-B.

This picture was taken shortly after the end of the war by a Soviet photographer, and is now in the Auschwitz Museum archives, available to any researcher who asks to see it.

The building was knocked down at the same time that the (now admitted to be) fake "gas chamber" in Auschwitz I was built. Observers have suggested, based on the photographic evidence, that the bricks from this real delousing chamber building were used to build the bogus "chimney" which now stands next to the "symbolic gas chamber" shown to tourists to the camp. This conclusion is based upon the type of bricks used in the Kanada I building as compared to the "reconstructed" chimney."

Section 52: Photographs of Auschwitz's Kanada I and Its Clothing Delousing Installation Gas Chamber in Action

Auschwitz has "gas chambers" which used Zyklon-B, complete with airtight doors and peepholes–but they were used for disinfecting clothes. The disinfestation center was in the Kanada I section of the camp.

Left: The arrival of trucks loaded with effects at Kanada I. They are unloaded around the only post fitted with a lamp for night work. Right: The unloading of effects and initial sorting takes place under the watchful eye of the SS.

Right: In the yard behind building 164, which contained the clothing delousing gas chamber, non-textile objects are separated. Left: Linen is sorted out at the end of the yard between huts 1 and 2.

Right: The provisional baggage depot. Note the building marked "164." This was where the Zyklon-B was stored for use in the delousing chamber next door. Note also the delousing chamber next door, with a ladder leading up to an extraction ventilator three quarters way up the wall. Left: Another view of the provisional baggage depot.

Left: Unloading linen and clothing to be deloused outside the gas chamber with the gas-tight door open. The extraction fan ventilator from the delousing chamber is clearly visible above the ladder. Right: The same scene a few moments later. The photographer is positioned alongside the wall of building 164.

Building 164, where the delousing Zyklon-B was stored. When the Soviets occupied the camp, a number of empty Zyklon-B cans were found here. It is now claimed that the contents of these tins were used to kill people, even though, as the Kanada I photos show, they were actually used in the clothing delousing process.

Right: Russians inspect the Zyklon-B storage room, hut 164 in Kanada I in 1945. Note also the healthy state of the prisoners. Left: A Russian holds a gas detector box. Behind him is the gas-tight door of the delousing chamber.

Two views of the delousing chamber door. Pictures of these doors are often claimed by Holocaust storytellers to be the "doors to the gas chambers" in Auschwitz. The image on the right shows the view into the delousing chamber.

A picture taken in 2011 of the exterior wall of a still-standing part of the delousing station at Auschwitz. Note the extensive staining (blue-colored) from the Zyklon-B used inside the room to delouse the clothes.

All Nazi documentation relating to "gassing equipment" which has been found in camp records refers specifically to the delousing chambers, and it has been one of the most dishonest tricks played by the Holocaust storytellers to proffer these completely innocent documents as "proof" of homicide.

Architectural plans for delousing chambers exist (but are never shown as the "chambers" are far too small to be have been used as "mass gassing facilities").

There are also invoices for airtight doors, gas masks, Zyklon-B, extractor fans, clothing racks, and other supplies essential to delousing procedures.

Despite the clear and obvious link between these items and the delousing chambers, the Holocaust storytellers have deliberately presented such documentation as "evidence" of homicidal gas chambers. The Germans were aware that lice infestations meant the outbreak of the deadly disease typhus, and that if that disease took hold, it could easily kill their precious labor force. They therefore took great

A close-up of the clothing chamber delousing door, next to building 164, Kanada I. The notice on the door reads "Toxic gases! LIFE THREATENING DANGER on entering this room." The presence of gas-tight doors, peep-holes, gas-tight equipment, Zyklon-B insertion devices and all documentation which mention such articles, refers to these delousing stations. The Holocaust storytellers claim that all these items and documents actually refer to "homicidal" gas chambers—but the facts speak otherwise.

The astonishing level of the postwar "reconstruction" of Auschwitz is visible in this 2011 photograph of one of the "guard watch towers" on the camp perimeter. The "watch tower" is clearly fake—it does not even have a ladder or any other way to enter the top part, and has no door or trapdoor either.

precautions to prevent the outbreak of typhus, which included regular disinfections of the camp barracks.

Auschwitz had a complex and well developed delousing system, consisting of a sophisticated series of larger disinfestation rooms called "autoclaves," which used steam to kill lice in clothing.

The autoclaves were remarkably efficient, and were obviously the source of far-fetched allegations in some Holocaust storyteller books of "executions in steam chambers" which occasionally make the rounds.

Dirty clothes were on a hanger rack and then rolled into one end of the double-door autoclave. Once the clothes had been disinfected, the rack was rolled out on the "clean side" of the autoclave, with the division being necessary to ensure that infested clothing did not come into contact with the clean clothes.

The idea that the Nazis would go through so much trouble to keep Jewish prisoners' clothes clean in Auschwitz is completely at odds with the claim that they were simultaneously trying to kill millions of Jews.

Surviving bills of lading for Zyklon-B, which are available for public inspection at the National Archives in the United States, show very clearly that Zyklon-B was shipped to all camps, and not just to the alleged gas chamber camps.

The bills of lading in the US National Archives run from February 16 to May 31, 1944, and reveal that the cases of cyanide crystals (Zyklon) are numbered in sequence (Nos. 50,053 to 50,210); each shipment consisted of thirteen cases, totaling 195 kg; and identical shipments—six each—went to Auschwitz and Oranienburg concentration camps.

Oranienburg is situated in Germany, and not even the wildest Holocaust exaggeration has ever claimed that there was a homicidal gas chamber at that camp.

The existence of proof of shipping of Zyklon-B to be used as a delousing agent to Oranienburg, is conclusive evidence of the real purpose for which that chemical was actually used in the camps.

Section 53: The Real Auschwitz Gas Chambers—The "Kanada I" Delousing Chambers

The delousing station in Auschwitz I was located in a part of the camp named "Kanada."

These chambers were used exclusively for disinfecting items not handled by the autoclaves and were specifically kept for the clothes of new arrivals, which were the most likely to be infected with lice.

The Kanada delousing station contained Zyklon-B disinfestation chambers, complete with airtight doors and peepholes.

The parallels between the real clothing delousing station and the alleged "human gas chambers" are so close that it is clear the homicidal gas chamber story was developed from the real clothing delousing system.

Section 54: Forensic Investigation of "Gas Chamber" Ruins Reveals No Evidence of Gassings

The crematoria at Auschwitz-Birkenau were destroyed by the retreating Germans as the Soviets swept westwards following the defeat of the Reich's armies.

This has conveniently allowed the Holocaust storytellers to maintain the claim that the morgues at crematoria II to IV had been used as gas chambers, especially given the fact that no proper access was permitted to independent western observers until after the collapse of the Communist regimes in 1990.

The obvious step for anyone wishing to prove the use of cyanide in these alleged "gas chambers" would be to take forensic samples from the ruins and analyze them for traces of the poison gas.

The Holocaust storytellers refused to even consider such a forensic examination, and it was up to the Holocaust revisionists to take the first steps in this regard.

The first forensic examination of the alleged "gas chambers" at Auschwitz II was conducted in 1988 by the American Fred Leuchter, who had earlier designed and built many of the execution methods (such as lethal injection) still used in America. Leuchter's report, published in 1989, consisted of an analysis of forty samples collected directly from the ruins of the alleged "gas chambers" which were then sent for forensic and chemical analysis to a number of reputable American laboratories. These laboratories found no significant residues of hydrogen-cyanide compounds except in one structure, which was commonly agreed to have been the building in which the slave laborers' clothing was fumigated with Zyklon-B. As was expected, there were massive quantities of the poison residue still impregnating the brickwork.

It has since been alleged that Leuchter's samples were invalid because they were ground up with brick and plaster which had not been exposed to Zyklon-B. This allegation is without foundation, as the test results, undertaken by an independent laboratory in the USA which had not been told the samples' origin, found the differentiation in traces of cyanide gas to be constant from site to site.

Thus, even if non-contaminated material had been mixed in with the original, the differences between the area where delousing had taken place and where alleged mass killings had taken place, were still identical, despite all the samples having been subjected to the same mixing process.

In other words, it is the difference between the samples themselves which is the revealing part of the Leuchter Report: the scale of differentiation remained constant, even in the sample from the clothing delousing chamber, where the use of Zyklon-B was never under dispute.

Disturbed by the Leuchter Report, the director of the Auschwitz museum and archives, Franciszek Piper, secretly commissioned a new Polish forensic laboratory report on the camp to double check Leuchter's results. This independent Polish government investigation, which the Auschwitz museum authorities have yet to release, was dated September 24, 1990. It showed that while there were substantial concentrations (between 9 and 147 micrograms per 100g) of cyanide residues in ten samples taken from the walls of the rooms and chambers where cyanide gas was used for disinfecting the slave-laborers' clothing, there were none whatever in ten samples taken from rooms identified in countless war crimes trials as the lethal gas chambers. Only a "vanishingly small trace" was found in one column in Birkenau, which is perfectly compatible with routine disinfestation operations. Forensic tests on human hair samples kept in the Auschwitz museum were also negative.

Section 55: Rudolf Report Confirms Forensic Evidence

Criticism of the Leuchter Report led a German chemist and employee of the Max Planck Institute for Solid State Research in Stuttgart, Germany, Germar Rudolf, to conduct a new forensic investigation of the alleged "gas chambers" at Auschwitz II.

His conclusions were even more definitive than Leuchter's: "Under the physically possible conditions of the mass-gassing of humans with hydrogen cyanide, traces of cyanide must be found in the same range of concentration in the rooms in question as they are found in the disinfestations structures, and the resulting blue discoloration of the walls should likewise be present.

"In the walls of the supposed 'gas chambers' the concentrations of cyanide remnants are no higher than in any other building taken at random. On physicalchemical grounds, the mass gassings with hydrogen cyanide (Zyklon B) in the supposed 'gas chambers' of Auschwitz claimed by witnesses did not take place."

The Rudolf Report, as it is known, remains the most scientific forensic analysis yet undertaken at the Auschwitz site.

Section 56: The Auschwitz "Gas Chambers" Change Location

Confronted with the above impossible-to-explain contradictions and forensic investigations, some of the Holocaust storytellers have reacted by simply changing the location of the Auschwitz "gas chambers" once again.

Despite having told the world for decades that the "gassings" had taken place in Auschwitz II's mortuary rooms, the "new" Holocaust story now maintains that the gassings actually took place in two outbuildings located away from Auschwitz II. The astonishing about-face was first made by the managing editor of the German magazine *Der Spiegel,* Fritjof Meyer. Writing in the politically

Faced with the revelation that the "gas chamber" shown to tourists in the Auschwitz I camp is a "reconstruction," along with the physical impossibility of "mass gassings" in the underground mortuary buildings, some Holocaust storytellers have decided to claim that the gassings actually occurred in two outbuildings, called Bunker 1 and Bunker 2. Absolutely nothing remains of these so-called "Bunkers," as can be seen above—which conveniently makes any sort of forensic examination impossible.

mainstream journal *OstEuropa* in May 2002, Meyer said that "new" research made it clear that there had indeed been no gassings in the mortuaries of the crematoria (as claimed by "eyewitnesses" and all the forced "confessions" obtained from SS-men). Instead, he wrote, the gassings had actually taken place in the sites now called "Bunker 1" and "Bunker 2," a distance away from the crematoria buildings.

These buildings were allegedly two small Polish farmhouses which had their windows and doors bricked up to act as "gas chambers." The bodies of the victims were allegedly buried in nearby open pits, Meyer wrote.

As the outbuildings where the "gassings" are now supposed to have taken place were quite small, Meyer was forced to reduce the number of victims once again, and, citing "official sources," said that some 356,000 people were gassed at the outbuildings.

"[A]ttempts in March/April 1943 to use the mortuaries for the mass murders, after the crematoria were completed in the early summer of 1943 . . . obviously failed, because the ventilation was counterproductive, and because the expected mass of victims did not arrive in the following eleven months," Meyer wrote in *OstEuropa*.

"The real genocide probably took place mainly in the two converted farm houses outside the camp; the foundations of the first house, the 'White House,' or 'Bunker I,' have only recently been unearthed." Most conveniently, both the outbuildings which Meyer and others now claim to have been the "real gas chambers" no longer exist, and therefore cannot be forensically examined.

Meyer's study provoked a hysterical response from many of his fellow Holocaust storytellers, and in particular from the curator of the Auschwitz Museum, who had been a particularly strong proponent of the "mortuary gas chamber" story.

Section 57: Auschwitz's Real Purpose: A Labor Camp

The lack of "gas chambers" raised the next obviously pertinent question: What was the point of the Auschwitz camp? The answer to this is startlingly obvious: Auschwitz was a large industrial area and contained factories from major industries which supported the Reich's war effort.

A third camp, known as Auschwitz III, contained a large number of important factories, which included the Buna rubber plant, the IG-Farben factory and many others. They manufactured everything from clothing to medical supplies. Jews—and others—were sent to Auschwitz to work as forced laborers.

The use of inmates at Auschwitz as laborers also explains why the Nazis would have found it necessary to tattoo identification numbers on prisoners' arms. If it was their intention to gas all Jews sent to Auschwitz, it would have made no sense to go through the trouble and expense of identifying and tattooing them first.

The true reason for the existence of the Auschwitz camp is revealed in this little shown picture of the Monowitz industrial complex, where most of Auschwitz's inmates were put to work in a variety of heavy industries.

As the Soviet army advanced westward, the Nazis closed down the Auschwitz camp and forced all able-bodied inmates to evacuate westward with them.

This once again contradicts the mass murder theory. If the Nazis had indeed wanted to kill all the inmates of Auschwitz, there would have been no logical reason to take Jews with them back into the Reich.

The obvious intention in evacuating all able-bodied inmates was to keep using them as laborers at other locations, once again underlining the real purpose of the Auschwitz complex.

Section 58: Photographs of Auschwitz Inmates Belie Mass Gassing Allegations

The evacuation of all able-bodied inmates from Auschwitz by the Nazis meant that only the elderly, children, or sick remained behind in that camp when it was overrun by the advancing Soviet army.

Herein lies another interesting but suppressed fact: as the pictures below show, the inmates of Auschwitz, as photographed shortly after the camp was overrun in

Inmates at Auschwitz-Birkenau, as photographed by Soviet soldiers upon the camp's liberation in January 1945. Note that they are warmly dressed, reasonably fed and do not resemble the emaciated corpses which are almost universally portrayed as evidence of Nazi "extermination programs."

The fact that so many women, children, and infirm were still in the camp, and had not been "gassed," is yet another factor against the veracity of the "mass gassing" allegation.

If the story were true that those too sick to work, or too young, were "gassed upon arrival," then there would not have been so many young and infirm in the camp when the Soviets arrived.

January 1945, were the sickest and most disabled of all the prisoners—yet they all look in relatively good health.

Section 59: The Rudolf Höss Memoirs

The "confession" of the former camp commandant, Rudolf Höss (published in English as *Commandant of Auschwitz*, London, 1960) was first published in Polish as *Wspomnienia* by the Soviet-installed Communist government of Poland. His "memoirs" illustrate another important point, about how much of the "evidence" regarding the Six Million stems from Communist sources.

"Holocaust expert" Gerald Reitlinger, in his book *The Final Solution*, acknowledged that the Höss testimony was a catalog of wild exaggerations.

For example, Höss's memoirs include the claim that Auschwitz disposed of 16,000 people a day, which would mean a total, at the end of the war, of over 13 million.

Instead of exposing such estimates for the Soviet-inspired frauds they obviously are, Reitlinger and others prefer to think that such ridiculous exaggerations were due to "pride" in doing a professional job.

Ironically, this is completely irreconcilable with the supposedly authentic Höss memoirs, which make a clever attempt at plausibility by suggesting the opposite picture of distaste for the job.

Höss is supposed to have "confessed" to a total of 3 million people exterminated at Auschwitz, though at his own trial in Warsaw the prosecution reduced the number to 1,135,000. Immediately after making this "confession," Höss was hanged by the Soviets in Auschwitz, thereby preventing him from ever being able to recant.

It is worthwhile to point out that he made a number of different statements in German and English, in which the numbers allegedly killed at Auschwitz fluctuated wildly, from 2.5 million to 4 million.

This latter figure is however universally acknowledged as being too high, especially as Höss was relieved of his command of Auschwitz in 1943, long before the camp was closed down, and as such would not have been able to tell with any certainty how many Jews passed through its gates by August 1944. Finally, even the official Auschwitz museum has reduced the death toll at the camp to less than half of Höss's smallest numbers, yet another indication of the exaggerated and forced nature of his "confession."

Section 60: The Auschwitz Swimming Pool

One last notable point to make about Auschwitz I is that there is a swimming pool—for prisoner use—within the camp grounds. The location of this swimming pool is marked in the diagram below, from which it can be seen that it was clearly intended for use by prisoners. Note also that there was a library (!) and, just outside the main camp fence, a hospital, which overlooks the "reconstructed" gas chamber (the one with the fake chimney, as portrayed on the right hand side of the drawing, just below the "Hospital" lettering).

Section 61: The Frankfurt Auschwitz Trial of 1963

In 1963, some 22 people were put on trial in Frankfurt for their roles as guards or administrative staff at Auschwitz. Much is made of this trial by the Holocaust storytellers but none of the evidence showed evidence of any mass gassing, and none of the defendants were actually charged with gassing anybody.

Of the 22 put on trial, 5 were acquitted completely and the rest sent to varying terms of imprisonment.

The only defendant who did not appear at the Frankfurt Auschwitz Trial was Richard Baer, the successor of Rudolf Höss as commandant of Auschwitz.

Though in perfect health, he died suddenly in prison before the trial had begun, "in a highly mysterious way," according to the newspaper *Deutsche Wochenzeitung* (July 27, 1973).

Baer's sudden demise before giving evidence is especially strange, since the Paris newspaper *Rivarol* recorded his insistence that "during the whole time in which he governed Auschwitz, he never saw any gas chambers nor believed that such things existed," and from this statement nothing would dissuade him.

Baer's timely death was once again highly fortuitous for the Holocaust storytellers.

CHAPTER 11: THE AKTION REINHARD CAMPS

Section 62: Details Unknown for Decades

The outrageous lies told about the Auschwitz camp's "gas chambers" should be enough to convince the objective observer that the Holocaust storytellers have engaged in a hoax of truly staggering proportions.

Nonetheless, a brief overview of the other camps is necessary to provide a complete picture.

Operation Reinhard, or in German, Aktion Reinhard, is the name popularly given to the camps of Belzec, Sobibór, and Treblinka, established in the far east of Poland following the Wannsee Conference's decision to implement a mass removal of Jews to the east.

Aktion Reinhard was named after Fritz Reinhard, Staatssekretär in the Finance Ministry. He was the one who drew up the logistical plan by which the property of those Jews who had been deported to the East (as planned by the Wannsee Conference) was collected and sent back to the Reich Finance Ministry. The Holocaust storytellers have seized upon the near total destruction of these three camps to claim that they were the "most deadly" of the

A photograph of the swimming pool, taken in 2011. Note the steps leading up to the now removed diving board. The existence of a swimming pool within the camp perimeter—obviously meant for inmate use—is so discordant with the Holocaust story (why would the Nazis build a swimming pool and a library for people they are going to kill?) that they have invented the most fantastic excuses for it.

A sign put up next to the pool by the camp claiming that it is a "fire brigade reservoir built in the form of swimming pool." (!) This is an utterly ludicrous "explanation" which would be laughable if the situation was not so serious.

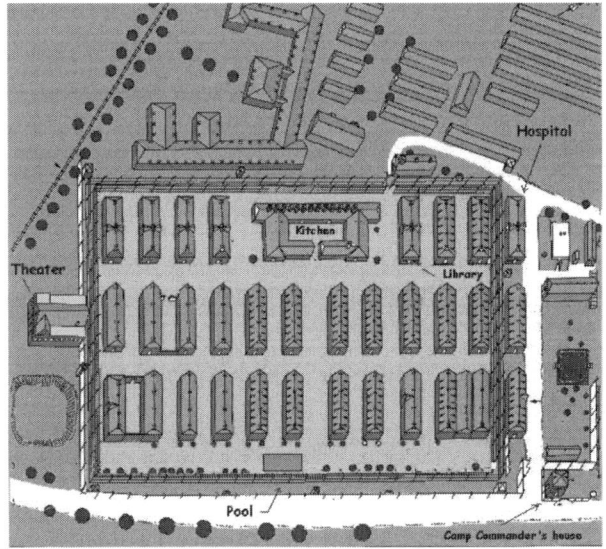

"extermination centers." In addition, the camps at Chelmno and Majdanek are often added to the list of "Reinhard" camps, even though they predate the program.

Although Auschwitz dominated the "extermination" propaganda for many years, the thorough debunking of that camp's facilities has forced the Holocaust storytellers to claim vast numbers of deaths in the alleged "extermination camps" of Aktion Reinhard to make up for the ever-diminishing number of Auschwitz "victims."

In fact, it is even possible that once the Auschwitz legend collapses completely, the Holocaust storytellers will be forced to claim that the "extermination facilities" only really existed in the Reinhard camps.

For many years, the Aktion Reinhard camps were shrouded in secrecy and largely unknown. "Survivor" testimonies ranged from the plausible to the absolutely outrageous, and the claimed methods of execution varied between electrocution, drowning, chlorine gas, unidentified "toxic fluids," mobile gas chambers, railroad cars sprinkled with quicklime, steam chambers, vacuum death chambers, and finally Zyklon-B cyanide gassing.

The number of Jews killed also varied greatly. "Death tolls" for Treblinka varied between 3 million and 870,000; Sobibór between 2 million and 250,000; and in Belzec, between 3 million and 600,000.

The vast differences in the number of deaths claimed (8 million versus 1.7 million) should by itself be major cause for concern, yet discrepancies such as these are routinely ignored by the Holocaust storytellers.

Section 63: The Höfle Telegram

A document released by the Public Record Office in Kew, England, in 2000, helped shed some light upon the real number of Jews transported to the Reinhard camps.

Known as the Höfle Telegram, this document was a German communication sent in January 1943 from SS Sturmbannführer Hermann Höfle in occupied Poland to Adolf Eichmann in Berlin, as intercepted by British intelligence.

The Höfle Telegram provided exact figures for all deportations to the main Reinhard camps, which it identified by their initials, up to and including the end of 1942, as follows:

L (Lublin Majdanek): 24,733;
B (Belzec): 434,508;
S (Sobibór): 101,370;
T (Treblinka): 713,555.

This gives a total of 1,274,166, a figure which is now most often claimed as the number of "victims" of the four camps. The Holocaust storytellers have claimed that the Höfle Telegram "proves" mass murder. Of course, it does nothing of the sort. All it does is give an indication of the number of Jews moved to the East for labor and resettlement purposes, which was spelled out in detail at the Wannsee Conference.

Section 64: Problems with "Gassing by Diesel"

The foremost problem with all of the Reinhard camps is the method of execution which is claimed to have been used. While the story of Zyklon-B cyanide gas is well-known and propagated by the media as the primary method of "killing Jews" during World War II, far less attention is given to the claim that carbon monoxide gas was used in all the Reinhard camps.

According to the Holocaust storytellers, more Jews were killed with carbon monoxide than with Zyklon-B.

They claim that nearly 2 million Jews were killed in the Reinhard camps, almost all of them by carbon monoxide produced by diesel engines, whereas few "official" accounts now ascribe more than 1.1 million to Auschwitz.

If carbon monoxide was therefore the primary method used to kill Jews during the war, why is this not more widely known to the public?

Why has the emphasis always been on Zyklon-B?

The answer to this obvious—but ignored—question is simple. As any chemist will confirm, gassing by diesel fumes is nearly impossible except under the most extreme circumstances.

Numerous tests have shown that a full hour's exposure to diesel fumes in a confined space only produces nausea and a headache in humans.

The problem first came to public attention in 1992, when Walter Lüftl, the president of the Austrian Federal Chamber of Engineers, issued a paper titled *Holocaust: Beliefs and Facts.*

Drawing upon his expertise as an engineer and chemical expert, Lüftl showed that mass murder with diesel exhaust is a "sheer impossibility."

Lüftl went on to point out that "What the Holocaust writers have obviously overlooked is the fact that diesel motors are particularly unsuited for the efficient production of carbon monoxide." He said that diesel-filled airtight chambers would actually take longer to kill people than "normal" asphyxiation.

Referring to diesel exhaust, Lüftl wrote: "The amount of carbon dioxide (CO_2), which is also poisonous gas, is less, the amount of carbon monoxide (CO) is negligible, and the amounts of oxygen and nitrogen are nearly the same. Just what does this mean in plain language?

"It means that nobody can be gassed with diesel exhaust. Instead, victims would more readily suffocate from using up the oxygen in the 'gas tight' chambers. In fact, if diesel exhaust gas is introduced into the chamber, the people inside would actually receive more oxygen than they would from breathing the air in the closed chamber after it passed twice through their lungs! The victims—who would otherwise die quickly—would easily live longer as a result of 'gassing' with diesel exhaust, because of its high oxygen content. This means that the diesel engine is not suited for quick killing, assuming this could be done at all." Further research proved the accuracy of Lüftl's work. Given a normal oxygen content of the air, an average carbon monoxide concentration of 0.4% and above, is needed to kill people in less than one hour of continuous exposure. Concentrations of 0.15%/ vol. to 0.20%/vol. are dangerous, which means they might kill some people in one hour, especially if those people have, for example, weak hearts. But, to commit mass murder in a gas chamber one would need a concentration sufficient to kill not merely a portion of any given group of people but rather, sufficient to kill all.

According to the Holocaust storytellers, gassing with carbon monoxide at the Reinhard camps was always completed within a half hour. This means that the carbon monoxide levels must be at least twice as high (0.8%/vol)—something which under normal circumstances is nearly impossible. It would require the diesel engines to be run at high speeds for inordinately long periods of time, would consume massive amounts of precious fuel and would lead to continuous breakdowns.

Gassing by diesel engines, while theoretically possible, is in fact the least efficient method of killing large numbers of people. The likelihood that the Nazis would have chosen this method over, for example, the large number of gasoline, woodchip, or gas burning engines available to them (all of which would have been far more efficient and produce much higher carbon monoxide levels), is highly unlikely.

Section 65: The Purpose of the Reinhard Camps

The location of each of the Reinhard camps was chosen so as to be close to important factory projects, and, in many cases, large Jewish ghettos.

These ghettos were not policed or surrounded with walls or barbed wire, as for example the Warsaw ghetto was, but were complete towns specifically created for Jewish resettlement.

In this way, for example, the major resettlement location near the Belzec camp was the ghetto of Rawa Ruska, situated some twenty miles from the internment camp.

In mid-July 1941, a *Judenrat* (Jewish Council) was established at Rawa Ruska as the number of Jews increased in the town. Similar settlement areas were created near all the other camps, with the intention of moving the Jews on once again as the Soviet Union was conquered.

The plan to resettle the east with Jews was however unable to be fulfilled due to the defeat of the German army in Russia. Further eastward movement became impossible, and increasingly, the Jews of the temporary resettlement areas and camps came to be used as forced labor.

Overcrowding, disease, and individual acts of brutality took their toll, and a large number of Jews who had been moved east died in appalling conditions.

There is, however, a major difference between deaths under these conditions and a deliberate extermination policy, both in numbers and intent.

However, the reality is that the three main camps—Belzec, Sobibór and Treblinka—were "intake centers" for the forced-labor and resettlement programs, and this was part of the "real" Aktion Reinhard program.

Before the Aktion Reinhard camps are discussed in detail, it is first necessary to review the Chelmno camp, because it is also often classed with the other three.

CHAPTER 12: CHELMNO AND "GAS VANS"

Section 66: Chelmno—"Operational" for Eighteen Months

Chelmno was identified as a "death camp" by the Communist "Main Commission for the Investigation of German Crimes in Poland" in May 1945.

This commission, set up by the Soviet Union's administration, produced a report, kept in the Warsaw archives, and which contained photographs of a "gas van," still used today by Holocaust storytellers including Israel's Yad Vashem, amongst others.

According to the Communist report, Chelmno was established in December 1941 with the purpose of killing all the Jews in the Warthegau area.

The Holocaust storytellers claim that the camp began operations on December 7th, 1941 and had achieved its aim by March 1943, when it was closed down, only to be reopened from April to July 1944 to kill Jews from the Lodz ghetto.

The Chelmno camp was, therefore, operational for eighteen and a half months in total.

Allegedly, all gassing executions at Chelmno were done with three "gas vans" which were produced by the Magirus-Werke running on a Deutz-type diesel engine.

Prisoners were allegedly undressed, divided up into groups of 50, and made to walk down a corridor of a building into the back of the van, whereupon the doors were closed and the diesel engine started.

After being asphyxiated, a process which the Holocaust storytellers say took ten minutes, each load of the bodies were allegedly driven into a nearby forest and buried. It is claimed that between 150,000 and 300,000 Jews were killed in this fashion. There are a number of obvious problems with this story.

Firstly, as mentioned above, gassing by diesel fumes is nearly impossible except under the most extreme circumstances.

Numerous tests have shown that a full hour's exposure to diesel fumes in a confined space only produces nausea and a headache in humans. The claim that 50 people could be killed in ten minutes by diesel fumes is simply impossible. Secondly, the timing of the "execution" process makes the Chelmno story impossible.

According to the Holocaust storytellers, only one truck could be loaded at a time. Moving a trainload of people from the railway station, putting them up overnight (as the story claims), undressing them, dividing them into groups of fifty, putting them into the vans, gassing them, driving half an hour to the "forest graves," unloading the bodies and burying each van load would collectively take over two hours for every 50 people so killed.

Working on the claim of 300,000 people killed at Chelmo, this means that a total of 12,000 hours would be required of continuous operation to murder and dispose of that number of people.

There are only 720 hours in an average month of 30 days, and, given that Chelmno was supposedly only operational for 18 and a half months (11,160 hours) this would have meant that "gassings" with the diesel vans would have had to continue nearly 24 hours per day, every day, for a year and half, without even a break to refuel the vehicles.

Even if it were possible to kill people with diesel fumes in ten minutes–which it is not–such a killing rate would be utterly impossible to maintain.

Staff would need breaks, the logistical process required to maintain such a system would have been immense, and the resources consumed would have been vast.

Furthermore, the labor and territory required to bury and hide 300,000 bodies would make such a mission nearly impossible.

Despite all these obvious problems, Chelmno has become "famous" as the "very first extermination camp."

Section 67: Yad Vashem's Gas Van That Wasn't

Worst of all, the Communist report on Chelmno, upon which most of the story is based, has been completely discredited due to its central claim of "gas vans."

According to that report, its commissioners received information that one of the Chelmno gas vans had been found in the grounds of a factory at the nearby town of Ostrowski.

"Witnesses" identified the van, which was then photographed and included in the commission's report.

The "gas van" of Chelmno, as claimed by numerous Holocaust storytellers. This picture is from the Soviet's postwar report on "Nazi crimes in Poland" and specifically says that this van, which was inspected by their officers, had only been identified as "similar" to the "gas vans" allegedly used at Chelmno. The report went on to state that the van had been inspected and no signs could be found that it had been adapted or used to kill people. Nonetheless, this photograph is still circulated as "evidence" of the "gas van" story. A real "gas van" has of course never been found nor has any firm evidence ever been produced that they actually even existed.

These photographs are now the most widely distributed and used "evidence" of Nazi "gas vans" and have appeared in displays and websites set up by Israel's Yad Vashem and numerous other official Holocaust storyteller organizations.

One of these photos was reproduced in the book *Hitler and the Final Solution* (Gerald Flemming, University of California Press, 1987), with the caption that it was a "gas wagon" used in Chelmno.

However, the Ostrowski van was never a "gas van," as a detailed reading of the Commission's own report reveals.

The testimonies of Polish "witnesses" kept in the same archives of the Main Commission (collection "Ob", file 271 and others) only described the van as "similar."

The inspection of the vehicle in the photograph, carried out on November 13, 1945 by Judge J. Bronowski, found no evidence to show that the van had been fitted out to kill people, and this conclusion was contained in the report. Despite the inclusion of this important information, the photographs of the Ostrowski vehicle have now entered Holocaust legend as the Nazi "gas vans."

Section 68: Walter Rauff and the "Gas Van" Story

The only other evidence proffered for the "gas vans" are two documents, claimed to have been sent to SS-Obersturmbannführer Walter Rauff in Berlin which specifically mentions gassing in sealed trucks. These letters, of which the originals have never been found, are obvious forgeries. There are three major clues indicating that these documents have been tampered with:

1. The signatures of the alleged authors differ widely from other contemporary samples.

2. There are numerous differing copies of the letters, each one varying in content.

3. Many of the "copies" also contain grammatically incorrect German and numerous spelling errors, which are not seen in genuine documents of the time.

One example of a spelling error is the misspelling of the word "Sauer" (allegedly one of the types of gas vans used–the correct German word is in fact "Saurer").

In addition, the type of vehicle mentioned in the main document (dated June 5, 1942) as being a "gas van" had not been produced by Saurer since 1912. This was thirty years prior to their alleged manufacture and use as "gas vans" in 1941.

Walter Rauff always denied the authenticity of the letter and was forced to live out his life in exile in Chile.

Rauff only ever mentioned "gas vans" once, in a deposition made in 1972, in which he said that he had "heard" that vans were used for the "execution of sentences and for the killing of Jews." He also claimed to have been shown two such vans parked in a yard, but never saw them operational or had any idea of their technical workings.

Despite this, Rauff is claimed to have been the mastermind behind the "gas van" project, a claim which he always denied. In the climate of persecution, false witness, exaggeration and hysteria, his denials were ignored, as is the fact that gassing by diesel fumes is virtually impossible.

Section 69: Forensic Digs Contradict "Official History" by Finding "Crematoria" in Chelmno

In 1986, the Polish government allowed Dr. Lucja Pawlicka-Nowak, on behalf of the Konin Museum, to make the first of three major excavations in Chelmo.

The second excavation was conducted in 1997, and the third in 2003 ("Gilead, I, and others, Excavating Nazi Extermination Centers," *Present Pasts,* Vol. 1, 2009).

Apart from a number of personal items and grave sites, which would be expected at a camp of that size, the excavation team also claimed to have found the remains of eight structures which it announced were four "field furnaces" and four "crematoria."

According to the report, in "three out of the four crematoria, fragments of concrete pipes, used to let fresh air into the furnace and chamotte bricks were also found."

Furthermore, the report said, it "appears that the crematoria were located in closed structures and the field furnaces were open air pits."

The major problem with this finding is, of course, that nowhere in the official history, "witness" statements or "confessions" linked to Chelmno, was any mention made of crematoria.

In fact, it was always specifically maintained that the camp did not have crematoria, and relied instead on burning bodies in open pits.

The contradiction has been ignored by the Holocaust storytellers, because it means either that the archaeologists are lying or the camp's "official history" is untrue.

It is more likely, of course, that the latter is the case, given the other vast inconsistencies.

Section 70: The Chelmno Trials

It took until 1962 for the first trials to take place of Chelmno SS personnel. At the Bonn court proceedings, 12 former SS members were put in the dock.

The "evidence" against them consisted exclusively of "survivor" testimony, and all the accused specifically denied any participation in mass murders.

The paucity of the evidence saw none of the accused found guilty of operating any "gas vans," and the main charges were either for arranging deportations to Chelmno or for just being staff at the camp.

In this regard, merely being present was taken as "guilt" in having "assisted in the murder of Jews."

Because this accusation was so vague, not even the lynch-mob court could find all of the accused guilty, and three were acquitted outright.

The remaining nine were sentenced to imprisonment terms ranging from 13 months to 13 years—the sentence lengths being a sure indicator that none of them were found guilty of "mass murder."

CHAPTER 13: BELZEC

Section 71: The Belzec Camp—Given Little Prominence Because of Unbelievable Allegations

Belzec had been established in mid-1940 as a work camp to supply labor for defenses along the border with the Soviet Union.

The camp was not large, and remained relatively obscure, at least in the eyes of the Holocaust storytellers, for nearly two years until March 1942, when it was suddenly transformed into a "killing center."

According to the Holocaust storytellers, the camp only operated from March 1942 to June 1943—a total of 15 months.

During this time, it is claimed that between 430,000 and 500,000 Jews were killed in the camp, along with an unknown number of Poles and Gypsies.

The short lifespan of the camp shows its true purpose: a temporary holding center rather than an "extermination camp" but this obvious point aside, the real problem occurs when the simple mathematics is done.

If the camp operated for 15 months (10,800 hours) and killed 500,000 people, this would have meant that 47 Jews would have been murdered every hour, 24 hours per day, round the clock for all 15 months.

This is of course not feasible, as it would have required a staff of thousands, a massive logistical backup, and, most importantly of all, an incredibly advanced execution method. Just as importantly, the Belzec camp was never equipped with crematoria, which would have been critical had it been meant as an extermination center.

In fact, none of the Reinhard camps had crematoria, a fact which is ignored by the Holocaust storytellers.

Section 72: Belzec's Incredible Execution Methods: Electrocution and Drowning in Excrement

The alleged method of killing at Belzec is yet another incredible story. The first reports to appear about the camp claimed that Jews were electrocuted on steel plates. Another version claimed that prisoners were submerged in water up to their necks and then electrocuted.

In 1954, a "survivor" claimed that the main form of execution was drowning in excrement: "Jews were arrested every day, forced to dig a deep and narrow ditch and were then thrown into it one at a time. Then each prisoner was forced to go to the toilet on the head of the victim. Anyone refusing received 25 lashes. In this way, they went to the toilet all day long until the victim finally suffocated in the faeces" ("Kronika life-span niezanego autora," in *Biuletyn Zydowskiego Instytutu Historicznego,* Warsaw, no. 54, January–June 1954, p. 307).

The allegations of murder became more incredible and bizarre, but were reported in the *New York Times* in 1944 as "fact."

In 1944, Dr. Abraham Silberschein, a member of the Polish parliament and delegate of the World Jewish Congress, published, in Geneva, a series of mimeographed brochures entitled *Die Judenausrottung in Polen* (The extermination of Jews in Poland), in which he included even more incredible stories from "witnesses." In one paper, titled *Die Hölle von Belzec* (The Belzec Hell), he reported as follows: "Jews deported to Belzec were ordered to undress, as if they were going to take a bath. They were, indeed, taken to a bathing establishment able to contain several hundreds of people. However, they were executed *en masse* by means of an electric current. A boy who managed to escape from such an establishment told me what happened after the electrocution: The fat from the corpses was drained in order to make soap from it. The remnants of the corpses were then thrown into anti-tank ditches which had been laid out along the Russian border by the arch-henchman Major Dollf (A. Silberschein, "Die Hölle von Belzec," in *Die Judenausrottung in Polen,* vol. V, Geneva 1944, pp. 21f).

Needless to say, the "soap from Jewish fat" story has been thoroughly rejected as a hoax, even by Israel's Yad Vashem (Bill Hutman, "Nazis never made human-fat soap," *The Jerusalem Post –International Edition,* week ending May 5, 1990).

The "death by electrocution" charge formed an official part of the Nuremberg Trial proceedings and was entered into the court records by the Soviet Prosecutor L.N. Smirnov on 19 February 1946 (document USSR-93, IMT, vol. VII, pp. 576f).

Finally, it was claimed that the fiendish Nazis smeared chlorine and lime inside train transports, so that by the time the unfortunate deportees arrived at Belzec, they were already dead.

Despite the electrocution method being officially entered into the records, the Holocaust storytellers realized that "death by electrocution" or "drowning in feces" was too far-fetched even for the most gullible believers.

By the 1960s, the method of execution had been changed to a Soviet diesel tank engine which pumped fumes into several "gas chambers" which could then allegedly be opened by large side doors for the removal of bodies.

Once again, it is necessary to point out that it borders on the impossible to murder large numbers of people with diesel fumes alone, and this claim should by itself be reason enough to question the Belzec story.

In addition, there were apparently no survivors at all, and only four (!) SS guards (according to a 1959 statement by a "witness," W. Pfannenstiel).

Fortuitously for the Holocaust storytellers, the commander of the Belzec camp, Christian Wirth, was killed in action in Croatia in May 1944 (his Belzec command was as short-lived as the camp).

Another fortuitous "fact" for the Holocaust storytellers is that there are absolutely no official German documents, plans, papers or even any descriptions of exactly what the camp looked like—despite the claim that its "gas chamber system" was duplicated at the other Reinhard camps.

Furthermore, the alleged designer of the "gas chambers" (which, it will be recalled, supposedly used highly ineffective diesel fumes), SS-Hauptscharfuhrer Lorenz Hackenholt, also "vanished" after the war, never to be seen again.

Section 73: The Belzec Trial

An attempt to bring eight former SS guards at Belzec to trial in January 1963 failed when seven of the accused were acquitted almost immediately for lack of evidence. This occurred despite some of them making statements in which they accepted that there had been murders at the camp, but that they were not personally involved.

As discussed earlier, such "confessions" were not unusual at the time, and would in fact have been a perfectly reasonable defense to raise in order to protect oneself: not to deny a crime, but to say one had nothing to do with it.

Almost no other evidence was led at the trial (the only "eyewitness survivor" was unable to identify any of the accused) and as a result, one defendant was sentenced to a mild four and a half years in prison because hearsay evidence implicated him in some extra-judicial executions.

Section 74: Forensic Digs at Belzec Contradict "Official" History and Fail to Find "Gas Chambers"

In 1997, the Polish Council for Safeguarding the Remembrance of Struggle and Martyrdom, together with the United States Holocaust Memorial Museum of Washington, DC, commissioned a team of archaeologists led by Professor Andrzej Kola from the Nicolas Copernicus University of Torun to excavate the Belzec site in an attempt to discover more of the camp layout and structure.

Kola wrote a paper on the diggings entitled *Belzec: The Nazi Camp for Jews in the light of archaeological sources: Excavations 1997–1999.*

The excavations involved drilling 2,227 holes in the ground some 18 feet (about 5 meters) apart. Kola claimed to have found 33 grave sites in two separate areas, and published the results of analysis of 137 of the 236 soil samples taken.

These results showed that there were bodies buried at the site, which would not be out of the question given that at least 434,000 people passed through the camp before it was closed. Kola was unable to give a precise determination of the number of human remains found, but his published results only indicated a few dozen.

Given the size of the camp, this is most likely an underestimate caused by the sampling methods used, but, even if the number were quadrupled to allow for sampling error, the figure would still be dramatically short of the 600,000 "murders" claimed for Belzec by the Holocaust storytellers.

In addition, Kola claimed to have found the remains of the "second" gas chamber built at the camp.

He describes it as follows in his official report: "In the light of the studies no traces of the gas chamber from the 1st stage of the camp functioning were found. The traces of a wooden building [G] in the central part of the camp can be hypothetically regarded as the remains of the 2nd stage gas chamber."

Of course, the official account contradicts Kola's finding, because it is claimed that the "second" or "new" set of "gas chambers" at Belzec were not made of wood, but allegedly of solid concrete with deep foundations.

It is highly significant that Kola failed to find any foundations which matched this "official account" of a concrete gas chamber.

All that Kola found were "wooden" foundations, exactly what would have been expected at a temporary transit camp. It is claimed that the Nazis demolished the camp when it closed down, but it is unlikely that they would have been able to remove all traces of the foundations of a solid concrete gas chamber of such large size.

Once again, the archaeological evidence firmly contradicts the "official" story.

CHAPTER 14: SOBIBÓR

Section 75: Sobibór—A Temporary Camp Which Only Existed for 15 Months

Sobibór was located on the outskirts of the town of Sobibór in the Lublin Voivodeship of occupied Poland. The Sobibór camp was, like Belzec, selected for its locality to the labor camps of Lublin.

Construction of the camp was completed in April 1942, and, according to Holocaust "expert," Raul Hilberg, a diesel engine was installed by the same people who built the "gas chambers" at Belzec to run a killing center very similar in design to that of Belzec (Raul Hilberg, *The Destruction of the European Jews,* Holmes & Meier, 1961 p. 229.).

Hilberg based his claim of a diesel engine on "survivor accounts," but it is significant to note that other Holocaust "experts" have claimed that it was a gasoline engine.

This claim has most probably emerged after the problems inherent in diesel gassing methods were realized by the Holocaust storytellers. As a result, considerable debate still persists amongst "official" Holocaust historians over this point, and it has never been finally settled.

It is claimed that the first mass gassing took place in Sobibór in May 1942, and that the operation was so successful that a "new" set of "gas chambers," modeled exactly on Belzec, were built in September 1942.

The camp ceased operation in October 1943, which meant that it was only operational for 15 months.

Once again, just like Belzec, the shortness of its lifespan militates strongly against the idea of a "killing center" and in favor of it being a transit and dispersal camp to the surrounding factories and resettlement areas.

Section 76: Chlorine and Electricity: "Survivors" Claim Bizarre Execution Methods in Sobibór

Despite the "official" version of the gassing procedure being one of carbon monoxide poisoning in gas chambers, a number of "survivor eyewitnesses" have alleged that chlorine was used to kill prisoners at Sobibór. "Survivor" witness Hella Fellenbaum-Weiss explained how Jews on their way to Sobibór were gassed with chlorine: "The arrival of another convoy distressed me in the same way. It was thought to come from Lvov, but nobody knows for sure. Prisoners were sobbing and told us a dreadful tale: they had been gassed on the way with chlorine, but some survived. The bodies of the dead were green and their skin peeled off"(Miriam Novitch, ed., *Sobibór: Martyrdom and Revolt,* Holocaust Library, 1980, p. 50.).

Another "survivor eyewitness," Zelda Metz claimed that the "victims" entered the "wooden building where the women's hair was cut, and then were asphyxiated with chlorine. After 15 minutes, they had all suffocated. Through a window it was checked whether they were all dead. Then the floor opened automatically. The corpses fell into the cars of a train passing through the gas chamber and taking the corpses to the oven" (Testimony of Zelda Metz, in N. Blumental, ed., *Dokumenty i materialy,* vol. I, Lódz 1946, p. 210).

"Survivor" Leon Feldhendler also claimed that chlorine was the "death-gas" (N. Blumental, ed., op. cit. note 2, p. 204).

Yet another "survivor eyewitness," Alexander Pechersky alleged that some type of "heavy, black substance" was the death-gas (A. Pechersky, *The Sobibór Revolt,* State Edition Der Emes, Moscow 1946, in Yuri Suhl, Edessi si ribellarono. Storia della resistenza ebraica contro il nazismo, Milan, 1969, p. 31).

One Sobibór "witness" claimed the Jews were killed with electricity and gas (Jules Schelvis, *Sobibór: A History of a Nazi Death Camp,* Berg, 2007, p. 215). Finally, some other witnesses claimed that Zyklon-B gas was used.

The mainstream historians of Sobibór have abandoned the "chlorine death gas" and "trap-door-in-the-gas-chamber" stories—once again, an implicit concession that they are both false.

The contradictory nature of the "eyewitness" accounts of the method of execution has never been sorted out, and is unlikely to be so.

The most obvious reason for the widely differing "witness" accounts is that they were probably never actually witnesses, but were merely repeating rumor and hearsay, a common enough event which plagues the entire Holocaust story.

Section 77: Yitzhak Arad's Contradictory Official History of Sobibór

The most widely quoted "official" history of Sobibór is Israeli historian Yitzhak Arad's Belzec, Sobibór, *Treblinka: The Operation Reinhard Death Camps* (Indiana University Press, 1987). In this book, Arad republished a large part of the "Kurt Gerstein document" (dealt with elsewhere in this work), which specifically claims that a diesel engine was used at Sobibór as a gassing instrument.

On page 101 of his book, Arad quotes Gerstein as being told by SS and Police Leader Odilo Globocnik that his duty was to "improve the service of our gas chambers, which function on diesel engine exhaust."

Arad's book then however goes on to quote the (equally dubious) testimony of a former SS soldier Erich Fuchs, who claimed to have operated the engine that Gerstein supplied—except that he identified the machine as a "heavy Russian benzene engine (presumably a tank or tractor motor) at least 200 horsepower (V-motor, 8 cylinder, water cooled)."

Not even the official book on Sobibór can decide for sure if a diesel or benzene engine was supposedly used at Sobibór.

Arad also differed with a number of other accounts on the size and number of the "gas chambers" at Sobibór, as no one, not Jewish "witnesses" or German "confessors" can agree on the exact nature or functioning of the execution facility. This complete lack of uniformity rings alarm bells as to the overall accuracy of the story, as well it should.

The "witnesses" also disagree with each other on every other major issue about the camp. Some say that the bodies were removed from the "gas chambers" by drop trapdoors, while others say they were manually removed.

Some say the bodies were taken away on narrow gauge train lines, while others say they were carried away manually or by cart.

The "witnesses" all disagree on how the bodies were burned, with some saying that kerosene was used, while others say coal and yet more say wood.

Finally, one of the most improbable "witnesses" of all alleges that hammers were used to crush bones on the ground. The incredible nature of that allegation becomes more breathtaking when it is considered that the official account claims that at least 200,000 people were killed at Sobibór. Teeth and bones do not burn completely, even in conventional crematoria, much less in an open fire. To think that the teeth and bones of 200,000 people could be pulverized by hand-held hammers beggars belief—because it is simply unbelievable.

Section 78: Official Documents Show Sobibór's True Function

Fortunately, a few secret documents have survived which explain the camp's function. On July 5, 1943, SS chief Heinrich Himmler sent a personal directive to several top SS leaders. In this directive, Himmler ordered the "Sobibór transit camp in the Lublin District to be transformed into a concentration camp. A center for dismantling captured ammunition is to be established in the concentration camp." Note the use of the words "transit camp"—this order was issued at the same time that Sobibór was supposedly already functioning as an "extermination camp." Himmler's direct reference to Sobibór as a "transit camp" and its request to be turned into a "concentration camp" clearly shows its function at that time.

This was confirmed in a letter dated July 15, 1943 from the head of the SS concentration camp system, Oswald Pohl, back to Himmler which said that a center for dismantling captured Soviet ammunition could be set up at Sobibór without having to transform it into a concentration camp. Sobibór could, Pohl wrote, remain a "transit camp with a special section for dismantling ammunition."

This correspondence, entered in the Nuremberg trial records as document file NO-482, clearly shows that neither Himmler nor Pohl regarded Sobibór as an "extermination center."

In fact, the only documentation which exists at all alleging that Sobibór was an "extermination camp" is the notorious "Gerstein Statement."

Suffice to say here, the Gerstein statement, made after the war, contains absurd allegations about the Reinhard camps, including the claim that the Nazis gassed 25 million people and that 700–800 victims were crammed into gas chambers 25 meters square (in which case they would have died from suffocation first). It also describes a visit by Hitler to an extermination camp which even the "official" Holocaust historians admit ever took place.

Section 79: The Sobibór Trials

It took until 1965 for the commandant of the forced labor camp at Sobibór, Karl Frenzel, to be arrested and put on trial in Germany for his work at the camp.

Like all similar trials, his only real option was not to say that murders had not taken place, but rather to deny any involvement with them.

He was in fact in charge of organizing the labor sections of the camp—a fact which once again reinforces the original purpose of the camp.

Despite his denials and the total lack of any other evidence, Frenzel was convicted of 46 counts of murder and "participation in a further 250,000 counts of murder" (that was the number of victims claimed in the 1960s. That figure has been reduced in the official versions since then). He was released in 1982 and died in 1996.

Another of the accused, Kurt Bolender, had been in charge of the guards at Sobibór, but was accused of "running" the "gas chambers." He was arrested in 1961 and when he finally appeared in court four years later, admitted to being at Sobibór but denied gassing anyone. He committed suicide before the end of the trial.

SS-Unterscharführer Erich Fuchs was accused of building the gas chambers at Belzec, Sobibór, and Treblinka. Despite the enormity of this alleged crime (and Fuchs's compliant statements), Fuchs was sentenced to only four years in prison, being found guilty only of what the court described as "experimental gassings" in which, it was claimed, some 3,000 Russian prisoners were killed.

Franz Stangl, who for a while was chief commandant of Sobibór and later of Treblinka, escaped to Syria and then to Brazil after the war. He was arrested in Brazil in 1967 and sent back to West Germany for trial. At his first hearing at the West German court, Stangl freely admitted to being commandant at Sobibór and Treblinka, but denied outright that he had anything to do with the mass killing of Jews.

His task, he said, had been solely to supervise the collection and shipment of valuables brought into the camp by the victims—a job which was indeed the entire original purpose of Aktion Reinhard. Despite his protestations, he was sentenced to life imprisonment, and died in prison shortly afterwards under mysterious circumstances, conveniently only a few hours after allegedly giving a "full interview" to Jewish journalist Gitty Sereny. The bizarre details of this interview are discussed below under the Treblinka section.

The deputy commander of the Sobibór, Gustav Franz Wagner, was arrested in 1978 in Brazil under an extradition order from West Germany. Wagner declared that there was no truth to the "extermination" story and that Sobibór had only been a work camp. The evidence he presented was conclusive, and the extradition appeal was turned down. Wagner was released and went home—but was murdered on his farm a few months later, knifed in the chest, another "convenient" end to an SS man who denied the extermination claims.

Section 80: Archaeological Digs Fail To Find Sobibór "Gas Chamber"

Archaeological digs at the Sobibór site were carried out in 2001 by a team directed by Andrzej Kola, who had

Excavations at the Sobibór site were carried out by Polish and Israeli experts in 2009. They failed to find any trace of "gas chambers."

earlier excavated Chelmno. Kola's dig found a number of burial sites and a building which he called "E" and took to be the "undressing room" where the clothes and belongings of inmates were supposedly stored ("Gilead, I and others, Excavating Nazi Extermination Centers," *Present Pasts*, Vol. 1, 2009).

A second excavation, carried out in October 2007 by Isaac Gilead and Yoram Haimi from the Ben-Gurion University of the Negev, Beer Sheva, Israel, and Wojciech Mazurek from the Archaeological Division, Chelm, Poland, recovered about 1,000 artifacts which the archaeologists reported did "not seem to be associated with gas chambers."

The report was unable to identify any structure which could have been a "gas chamber," and ended its section on Sobibór with the sentence: "It is obvious that the location of the gas chambers is a complex issue that has to be solved, an important objective for future archaeological research at Sobibór." Once again, the archaeological evidence simply does not back up the "extermination claim."

Section 81: 2014 Archaeological Dig Contradicts Earlier "Gas Chamber" Claims

In September 2014, it was announced that Haimi and his team had discovered the concrete foundations to a building previously covered up by post-war asphalt in the immediate vicinity of a monument at the Sobibór site.

Despite extensive media coverage of the find—and Haimi's claims that these were the "gas chambers" of Sobibór, there is in reality no evidence that the unearthed foundations are anything else but a building at the camp.

In fact, the unearthing of the foundations created more problems for the Holocaust Storytellers' narrative than anything else. Previously, it had been claimed that there were three, four, or six "gas chambers" at Sobibór—but the September 2014 "discovery" announced that there were now "apparently" eight "gas chambers"—this based purely on the number of rooms unearthed in the foundations.

Photographs of the 2014 excavation results shows an irregular-shaped building with at least seven differing sized rooms, as can be seen in the image below, released by the researchers.

This layout completely contradicts all previous narratives of the Sobibór "gas chambers", which all claimed that the execution chambers worked with a two-door system and floor extensions on either side of the building. These "gas chambers" were, according to the "old" narrative, all the same size (four meters square). On the one side of the "gas chambers," the Holocaust Storytellers claim, there was a ramp type affair used by the supposed victims to enter the "gas chambers" and, on the other side were supposedly larger doors through which the bodies were removed. As can be seen, the unearthed foundations bear no resemblance to this narrative.

The total lack of any confirming evidence was highlighted by media reports which were careful enough to put in their coverage that the archaeological team had unearthed what they "thought" were the "gas chambers."

For example, the Israeli *Haaretz* newspaper quoted Haimi as specifically saying that the unearthed foundations "apparently" served as gas chambers: "We have finally found the building that *apparently* served as the gas chambers," said Israeli archaeologist Yoram Haimi, who has been coordinating excavations at the site for the past eight years" ("Archaeologists uncover remnants of Sobibór gas chambers", *Haaretz*, Sept. 17, 2014).

Israel's *Y-net News* also quoted Haimi as saying only that he "*believed*" he had uncovered the gas chambers: "Up until now, we've been waiting for the asphalt to be removed for the construction of the new visitors center, and as soon as it was removed we found this big structure, that we believe housed the Sobibór camp's gas chambers" ("Sobibór's last survivor: There was no time to fear, only to live", *Ynet News*, 09.18.14).

The foundations unearthed at Sobibór in September 2014: an irregular-shaped building with a number of rooms of different sizes, completely contradictory to the official Holocaust Storyteller narrative of "four square meter chambers." The irregular size of the rooms is clearly visible in this photograph.

In its coverage, the *Reuters* news agency also pointed out that the archaeologists "*believed*" they had found the "gas chambers": "Archaeologists excavated beneath the road and found lines of bricks, laid four deep, where they *believe* the walls of the gas chambers used to stand" ("Archaeologists uncover buried gas chambers at Sobibór death camp", *Reuters,* Sep. 18, 2014).

The same *Reuters* article then produced another example of how the Holocaust narrative continually changes: it stated that prisoners were killed in "fifteen minutes with carbon monoxide gas," and—incredibly—that the Germans kept geese to hide the screams of the dying from other prisoners (!).

The structure of the unearthed foundations—in a place where no-one disputes that there were buildings in the first place—is therefore totally at variance with the "murder facility" claims.

CHAPTER 15: TREBLINKA

Section 82: Treblinka— Another Temporary Camp Which Only Existed for 15 Months

Treblinka was the last of the "Reinhard" camps in Poland at which, the Holocaust storytellers claim, in just fifteen months (!), from July 22, 1942 to October 19, 1943, at least 850,000 people were gassed and cremated.

The utter impossibility of this claim should by itself be reason enough to be dismissed without further ado. 850,000 "gassed" in 15 months means that the Nazis must have killed an astonishing 56,666 people every month, seven days a week, in order to achieve that figure.

These hundreds of thousands of bodies were, so the story goes, buried in huge pits in the perimeter of the "extermination camp" section, called Treblinka II. Poland's "Central Commission" announced shortly after the war that the burial or "ditches" area where the bodies of Treblinka's victims were buried was about two hectares or five acres (or some 20,235 square meters).

According to a diagram in a book about Treblinka by Jewish Holocaust historian Alexander Donat, the camp's "ditches" area was not more than 80 or 100 meters in length and about 50 meters wide—that is, a maximum of 5,000 square meters or half a hectare (A. Donat, ed., *The Death Camp Treblinka* (1979), pp. 318–319).

By comparison, the mass graves area in the Katyn forest (near Smolensk), which held the bodies of some 4,500 Polish officers who had been killed by Soviet secret police and buried there in 1940, measured about 500 square meters.

It is thus very difficult to accept that anything like 700,000 or 800,000 bodies could have been buried in the minuscule area allegedly set aside at Treblinka for this purpose.

As if this was not enough, the Holocaust storytellers then claim that, in "order to cover up their crime," the Nazis dug up the hundreds of thousands of corpses between April and July 1943, and burned them all with "dry wood and branches" on grids made of rails in batches of 2,000 or 2,500. The residual "ash and bits of bone" were dumped back into the burial pits, and covered with a layer of sand and dirt two meters deep. The amount of wood needed to carry out this task makes the claim impossible. Given that a single corpse requires around 150 kilograms of wood to burn over a 10 hour period, 850,000 bodies would require an incredible 12,7500,000 kilograms of wood—nearly 13 million kilograms (around 28,660,096 pounds).

The absurdity—and practical impossibility—of this claim has not been lost on the Holocaust storytellers. According to Polish-Jewish historian Rachel Auerbach, fuel to burn bodies was not needed at Treblinka because "the bodies of women," which had more fat, "were used to kindle, or more accurately put, to build the fires among the piles of corpses."

Even more incredible, "blood, too, was found to be first-class combustion material," she wrote (Rachel Auerbach, "In the Fields of Treblinka," in: A. Donat, ed., *Death Camp Treblinka*, 1979, p. 38.). Yet, in the fantasy world which the Holocaust storytellers have created, the legend of Treblinka has assumed a major role as an "extermination center."

Section 83: Treblinka I and II—Labor Camp and Transit Area

There were actually two camps at Treblinka, called I and II. Even the Holocaust storytellers admit that camp

All that remains of the Treblinka camp today. Ground penetration radar analysis has failed to detect any of the claimed "mass graves" which are supposed to litter the area. Just like Chelmno, Belzec, and Sobibór—here at Treblinka, "conveniently," everything is gone—a fact which makes it easy to invent all manner of lurid claims without having to even try and justify them.

I was a labor camp which provided a workforce for the nearby gravel pit and irrigation area.

Camp II, however, the Holocaust storytellers claim, was the "extermination" center, located just a few miles from camp I. Most often it is claimed that the "gas chambers" at Treblinka were run on "exhaust fumes from engines of Soviet Red Army tanks which the Nazis had captured."

The location of Treblinka camp II was anything but ideal for mass murder. The train line to the nearest large town of Siedlce ran only 980 feet (300 meters) from the camp, and the closest village of Wólka Okraglik is only 1.2 miles (2 kilometers) away.

It is impossible to murder over three quarters of a million people in that area with no one noticing or without leaving massive evidence behind: yet this is exactly what the Holocaust storytellers would have the world believe. It is claimed that the camp inmates staged an armed uprising in 1943, and after that the camp was closed and all the buried bodies cremated in open pits.

The allegations of mass murder at Treblinka become even more bizarre when it is considered that there were only 50 SS men at Treblinka. To claim that 50 men, with the assistance of a tank engine, could kill 850,000 people in a year and remove all traces is utterly bizarre and an obvious lie.

Section 84: The Famous "Black Book of Polish Jewry" Claims Execution by "Steam" in Treblinka

According to the standard Holocaust storyteller resource, the *Encyclopedia of the Holocaust,* there were three brick "gas chambers, each measuring 13 by 13 feet" and the "gas" was supplied from a diesel engine (Israel Gutman, ed., *Encyclopedia of the Holocaust,* 4 vols., Macmillan, New York 1990, vol. 4, p. 1486).

The "diesel fume" story, as impossible as it is (see above), was not the originally claimed method of execution at Treblinka. The first major story to appear in the West which claimed Treblinka as an "extermination center" originated in a November 1942 Warsaw Ghetto document titled the *Liquidation of Jewish Warsaw.* This was forwarded to the Polish government-in-exile in London in January 1943 and appeared in English as *The Black Book of Polish Jewry,* with the subtitle "Treblinka. Official Report Submitted to the Polish Government."

This *Black Book* has become a standby "source" for the Holocaust storytellers, and is still quoted today even though it claims that steam (!) was used to execute Jews.

The *Black Book* says: "In the walls pipes were installed from which water-steam is supposed to pour into the chambers. . . . Inside the steam-room there is a large vat which produces the steam. The hot steam comes in to the chambers through pipes installed there, each having a prescribed number of vents . . . Due to the steam all the bodies have become a homogeneous mass stuck together with the perspiration of the victims."

Even though the "steam chamber" story was completely fabricated (as even the later Holocaust storytellers have admitted), the *Black Book's* claims of mass murder are still today used as "evidence" for the "extermination" allegation. The *Black Book* also claimed that 2 million Jews had already been murdered at Treblinka before the end of 1942, another claim which is now simply ignored by present-day Holocaust storytellers.

Furthermore, the Communist-controlled Polish government produced a report on Treblinka which was submitted by the Soviets as Document USSR-93 to the Nuremberg Court proceedings which claimed that "When the process of exterminating Jews was initiated, Treblinka became one of the first camps to which victims were brought. They were put to death in gas chambers, by steam and electric current" (USSR-93, English version, p. 44.).

This Nuremberg Court document goes on to claim that soap was manufactured from human fat at Treblinka as well, another claim long dismissed by even the Holocaust storytellers as fiction.

At the trial of the German governor of occupied Poland, Has Frank, charge no. 6 was that the "German authorities acting under the authority of Governor General Dr. Hans Frank established in March 1942 the extermination-camp at Treblinka, intended for mass killing of Jews by suffocating them in steam-filled chambers."

The camp was of course not established in March 1942 and it is no longer claimed that "steam" was used to kill Jews, but Frank was found guilty and hanged in October 1946. Even as late as 1961, at the last Treblinka-related trial in Düsseldorf of Kurt Franz, a witness statement said that Jews were killed with "steam."

Section 85: "Survivors" Claim Execution by "Vacuum Chambers"

Even more incredibly, it was claimed by "eyewitnesses" that Jews were killed at Treblinka by "vacuum chambers."

This astonishing claim was first made by a "survivor," Abe Kon, whose statement claimed that the "steam chambers" were made of cement with a "Star of David" on it. The building was, according to Kon, disguised as a bath and behind the "bath" stood a machine. It pumped the air out of the chambers. The people allegedly suffocated within six to fifteen minutes.

"People were driven into the 'bath' three times a day. In this way 15,000 to 18,000 persons were destroyed each day," Kon claimed (State Archive of the Russian Federation, GARF, 7021-115-11, pp. 33f.).

This "vacuum chamber" execution method was also entered into the official Nuremberg Trial court record as the sole means of murder at Treblinka.

Ultimately, the outlandish claims of "steam chambers," "vacuum chambers" and "electrocution" were dropped in favor of "diesel fume" gassings, only because the latter was (incorrectly) believed to be more possible than the other methods.

Treblinka had no crematoria (a bad oversight for an "extermination center") and it is claimed that almost all of the "gassed" victims were first buried, then later exhumed and burned in open pits.

It was claimed that all the burials took place within the boundary fence of Camp II. Of course, the space required to bury 850,000 bodies is far more than the size of that camp, but that fact has never worried the Holocaust storytellers.

Section 86: First 1999 Forensic Examination of Treblinka Site Reveals No Mass Graves

A detailed forensic examination of the Treblinka site with sophisticated electronic ground radar has however found no evidence of mass graves there.

For six days in October 1999, an Australian team headed by Richard Krege, a qualified electronics engineer, carried out an examination of the soil, using an $80,000 Ground Penetration Radar (GPR) device, which sends out vertical radar signals that are visible on a computer monitor.

GPR detects any large-scale disturbances in the soil structure to a normal effective depth of four or five meters, and sometimes up to ten meters. These devices are routinely used around the world by geologists, archaeologists, and police.

In its Treblinka investigation, Krege's team also carried out visual soil inspections, and used an auger to take numerous soil core samples. The team carefully examined the entire site, especially the alleged "mass graves" portion, and carried out control examinations of the surrounding area. They found no soil disturbance consistent with the burial of hundreds of thousands of bodies, or even evidence that the ground had ever been disturbed. In addition, Krege and his team found no evidence of individual graves, bone remains, human ashes, or wood ashes.

"From these scans we could clearly identify the largely undisturbed horizontal stratigraphic layering, better known as horizons, of the soil under the campsite," Krege said in a later report.

"We know from scans of grave sites, and other sites with known soil disturbances, such as quarries, when this natural layering is massively disrupted or missing altogether."

Because normal geological processes are very slow acting, disruption of the soil structure would have been detectable even after sixty years, Krege noted.

"Historians say that the bodies were exhumed and cremated towards the end of the Treblinka camp's use in 1943, but we found no indication that any mass graves ever existed," he said.

The site of the Treblinka camp in this US aerial reconnaissance photo, taken in September 1944. Cultivated fields of Polish farmers can be seen directly adjacent to the T II camp, suggesting that is was not carefully guarded or closed off. A small part of the Malkinia-Siedlce main road is visible at the upper right. At the bottom, the Treblinka I labor campsite can be clearly seen, just below the quarry area.

Section 87: US National Archive Aerial Photography of Treblinka Shows No Sign of "Extermination Camp"

As was the case with Babi Yar in Kiev (see section 32 above), wartime aerial reconnaissance photography carried out by the US Air force of the Treblinka camp can be found in the US National Archives. It will, by now, come as no surprise to the reader that the site shows no signs of having been anything other than a temporary transit camp.

Section 88: The 2010 Second Forensic Analysis of Treblinka Reveals No "Mass Graves"

The complete lack of any physical evidence at the Treblinka site has long been a great source of concern to the Holocaust storytellers, even to the point where the *Jewish Daily Forward* newspaper admitted in a 2014 article that

Trees and other vegetation seen in this aerial photo of Treblinka II show that the campsite was not carefully closed off from the surrounding area. One of the most remarkable features of the Treblinka "death camp" is its small size. The entire Treblinka II camp area was only 32 or 33 acres (13 hectares), or about one-twentieth of a square mile. Even smaller was the alleged "extermination" area of the camp, which was 200 by 250 meters in size (or five hectares) according to purportedly authoritative sources. Poland's "Central Commission" announced shortly after the war that the burial or "ditches" area where the bodies of Treblinka's victims were buried (before they were supposedly later dug up for burning) was about two hectares or five acres (or some 20,235 square meters). And according to a diagram in a book about Treblinka by Jewish Holocaust historian Alexander Donat, the camp's "ditches" area was not more than 80 or 100 meters in length and about 50 meters wide—that is, a maximum of 5,000 square meters or half a hectare. By comparison, the mass graves area in the Katyn forest (near Smolensk), which held the bodies of some 4,500 Polish officers who had been killed by Soviet secret police and buried there in 1940, measured about 500 square meters. It is very difficult to accept that anything like 700,000 or 800,000 bodies could have been buried in the minuscule area allegedly set aside at Treblinka for this purpose.

the "absence of physical evidence allowed Holocaust deniers to maintain that Treblinka II was a transit, not death, camp" ("Uncovering the Remains of Treblinka," *Jewish Daily Forward,* March 27, 2014.).

Finally, in 2010—fifty-five years after the end of the war—an attempt was made to try and "prove" that Treblinka was an "extermination center" after all (why this could not have been done sooner, is only explained because of persistent questioning by revisionists over the camp's true purpose).

To this end, a British forensic archaeologist, Dr. Caroline Sturdy Colls, from Staffordshire University, was employed to carry out two sets of research into Treblinka. The first foray duplicated the Krege research with ground penetrating radar in an attempt to "disprove" the earlier results.

The findings of this first investigation were trumpeted to the world as "proof" that mass graves had been found in Treblinka—for example, the British Broadcasting Corporation announced on January 23, 2012 that "any doubts about the existence of mass graves at the Treblinka death camp in Poland are being laid to rest by the first survey of the site using tools that see below the ground" ("Treblinka: Revealing the hidden graves of the Holocaust," *BBC,* January 23, 2013).

This headline was, however, misleading to say the least. In reality, no mass graves were found at all, as Colls readily admitted in the article.

The BBC report—which was made into a radio show as well—specifically said that her work had only revealed the existence of "pits"—and, crucially, that no excavations were carried out at all and no graves had been found.

Quoting Colls, the BBC article said that her work "revealed the existence of a number of pits across the site. Some may be the result of postwar looting, prompted by myths of buried Jewish gold, but several larger pits were recorded in areas suggested by witnesses as the locations of mass graves and cremation sites.

"One is 26m long, 17m wide and at least four meters deep, with a ramp at the west end and a vertical edge to the east.

"Another five pits of varying sizes and also at least this deep are located nearby. Given their size and location, there is a strong case for arguing that they represent burial areas.

"No excavation was carried out and the ground was not disturbed, which would be a violation of Jewish law and tradition, banning the exhumation of the dead" ("Treblinka: Revealing the hidden graves of the Holocaust," *BBC,* January 23, 2013).

In other words, despite the headlines proclaiming that mass graves had been found in Treblinka, in reality nothing except an "indication" of some pits had been "recorded" in the general area.

This failure to produce any real evidence, glowing media coverage aside, was greeted with derision by revisionists around the world, and Colls was obliged to undertake a second expedition to Treblinka, this time having obtained permission to carry out digging work.

Section 89: The 2013 Third Forensic Analysis of Treblinka and the "Star of David Gas Chamber Tiles" Hoax

In 2013, Colls returned to Treblinka to carry out the long-awaited forensic digging at the campsite. The expedition was regarded as so important by the Holocaust storytellers that a film crew accompanied Colls to make a documentary—that was aired by the Smithsonian Channel in 2014, titled *Treblinka: Hitler's Killing Machine*.

The Smithsonian and other media gave the documentary a significant amount of coverage and in their official description of the film, the Smithsonian claimed that the "watershed discovery of Star of David tiles confirms the existence of Treblinka's gas chambers and becomes the key to reconstructing the death camp's sinister workings."

In this they were referring to the unearthing of some tiles at the Treblinka site.

The documentary showed Colls and her Dutch colleague Ivar Schute digging in a ditch and finding four pieces of ceramic tile. The narrator of the documentary then announced that "Dutch archaeologist Ivar Schute has just uncovered an orange tile with a Star of David on the base."

The camera then moved to a close-up of Colls and Schute handling the tiles. Schute tells Colls that he has uncovered "four tiles, three yellow ones and one red one."

"As you see, the Star of David on the bottom, which is quite remarkable," Schute tells Colls and the camera, then asking her "But have you ever seen the tiles?"

Colls replies "No" and then Schute goes on to say that these tiles "fit in with the idea that we are in the area of the gas chambers."

Colls then says what "immediately springs to my mind is that witnesses who were allowed in the gas chamber and the area talked about the Star of David on the outside of the gas chamber building to build up the illusion that people were going to somewhere that was safe."

On this basis—that tiles had "Stars of David" on them—the narrator of the video then asserts that "Treblinka eyewitnesses have identified tiles just like these. Now for the first time, Caroline and her team have hard evidence confirming the existence of the gas chambers," the narrator adds. Unfortunately for these Holocaust storytellers, the "Star of David" to which they refer is nothing of the sort.

Firstly, the symbol—a six pointed solid star, with a dot in its center, surrounded by a circle, and with a clear "D"

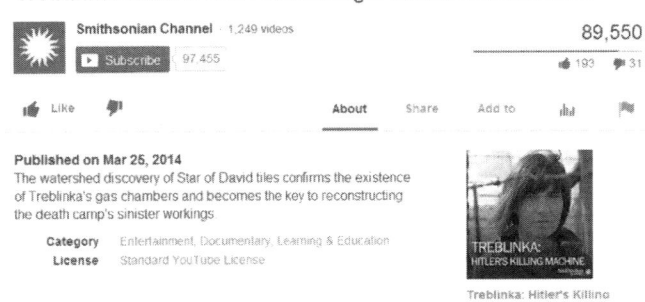

The Smithsonian YouTube Channel announcement that "Star of David" tiles have been found at Treblinka which "prove" the "gas chambers" at the camp.

letter to its right, was imprinted on the back of the tile—which means that wherever it would have been placed, the symbol would have been cemented onto the floor, and would not have been visible.

This makes Colls's claim that the symbol was there to "make people think they were going somewhere safe" out to be complete nonsense. In any event, no "eyewitness" has ever claimed that there were Stars of David "inside a gas chamber" at Treblinka—only that there was a large Star of David over the "front door" of the gas chamber.

Even worse for Colls, Schute, and the Smithsonian, the symbol which they all claimed to be a "Star of David" was in fact not that at all, but a brand mark of the 125-year old Dziewulski i Lange porcelain factory in Poland. That factory still exists, although it was renamed the Opoczno Terracotta Products Factory in 1950 and is today just called Opoczno S.A.

The company's symbol is known in the heraldic world as a pierced mullet star, as is not unusual for porcelain marks and coats of arms around Europe.

It is grossly amateurish for so-called "specialist archaeologists" like Colls and Schute to make such a basic error—and for the Smithsonian to then broadcast it to the world as "proof" of a "gas chamber."

After excavating for hours on end, the "specialist archaeologists" finally unearthed what they claimed were forty bone fragments, which they immediately pronounced as evidence of "three mass graves."

The "specialists" then quickly decide to rebury the bone fragments because, as Colls asserted, all they will do is "find more" (an incredibly poor reason to stop the digging). She then claims that these bone fragments and tiles "prove that [the] Treblinka I camp [was] more than just labor camp."

There is, of course, no evidence to back up this claim. The Höfle telegram (see section 62 above) has already confirmed that in excess of 700,000 people passed through the Treblinka transit and labor camp, and given those numbers and the pressures of wartime evacuations on that scale, it would only be incredible if there were not any graves to be found in the area.

The farcical documentary does not end there: a few hours later, digging in another spot, this time in the "Treblinka II" camp, some brick and mortar foundations are discovered, and, without any further ado, the Smithsonian narrator announces that the team has "confirmed the existence of the gas chambers and [has] confirmed their location."

In reality, nothing of the sort has happened. All that happened was that the "specialist archaeologists" made fools of themselves misidentifying a tile brand mark, found what they claimed to be forty bone fragments, along with a handful of assorted personal items and some foundations.

It is not under dispute that there were buildings in the camp—therefore there would naturally be foundations of some sort. In addition, given the nature of the camp, and the number of people who worked and passed through it, all of these finds would be perfectly normal—and in no way "prove" that Treblinka was an extermination center.

Above: The terracotta tile excavated by Ivar Schute at the Treblinka camp, and wrongly identified by him, Colls, and the Smithsonian as a "Star of David." The symbol is in fact a brand mark of the 125-year-old old Dziewulski i Lange porcelain factory in Poland.

Section 90: The "Evidence" of "Treblinka Guard" Paval Leleko

The Smithsonian documentary referred to in Section 79 above then went on to quote the "testimony" of an individual named as Paval Leleko, who, it was said, was a guard at Treblinka who had made a full confession.

The Leleko "confession" is not often used by the Holocaust storytellers, mainly because it is so contradictory and self-defeating as to be unable to withstand even the most superficial analysis. The reason for Leleko's statement is yet another "confession" extracted by the Soviet Union's SMERSH secret police—the same ones who got the Germans to "confess" to the Katyn Massacre.

What claims to be a transcript of Leleko's "confession" was released in 1978 by the then Soviet Union, in English, in order to assist, among other things, with the railroading of John Demjanjuk. For this reason, many Holocaust storytellers claim, quite incorrectly, that the statement was made in 1978—whereas the transcript clearly shows that it was "made" on February 20, 1945—at the height of the Soviet torturing of German prisoners into making "confessions."

> "EXCERPT from Interrogation of Defendant, February 20, 1945. I, Lieutenant EPPEL, Investigator of the Fourth Department of the "SMERSH" Directorate of Counterintelligence of the Second Belorussian Front interrogated as defendant—LELEKO, Pavel Vladimirovich, born in 1922, native of the village of Chaplinka, Chaplinka District, Nikolayev Region, Ukrainian, citizen of the USSR."

The "confession" follows the pattern of Soviet forced statements, in that it makes a number of now easily disprovable claims about Treblinka.

It is worthwhile reviewing the Leleko confession in some detail, because it illustrates precisely how the Soviet

Left: Some early advertising posters for the old Dziewulski i Lange porcelain factory in Poland, showing the brand mark. It is in fact known in the heraldic world as a pierced mullet star, and is not uncommon in pottery and porcelain marks. Right: Another example of Dziewulski i Lange terracotta tiles which use the same brand mark wrongly identified by Colls and Schute as a "Star of David."

secret police went to work to make up the "facts" of the "holocaust" in the eastern areas.

For example:

1. Leleko changed the order of the camps: Treblinka I became the "death camp" instead of the "labor camp" and vice versa:

"Question: Describe the exterior appearance of the camp?

"Answer: The Treblinka camp is divided into two parts: Camp no. 1, or as the prisoners called it, the "death camp," and the worker's camp, called Camp no. 2. The camps were situated at a distance of some 2–3 km from each other."

2. Leleko's statement continuously makes reference to the Germans as "beasts," (for example: "The Germans who were in charge of the camp were real beasts who found enormous pleasure in the extermination of people. I myself was repeatedly confirmed in this belief.")—something which makes it obvious that the statement was written for him in order to serve Communist anti-German propaganda, given that he was supposedly an individual who had volunteered to join the Trawniki section to fight for the Nazis.

In another part, the "confession" reads like a third rate novel, saying the Germans "smiled cynically:" "Many women begged to be allowed to keep at least some clothing on their persons, but the German, smiling cynically, ordered them to undress "to the end."

3. Similarly, the Leleko statement also repeatedly refers to the "horror" of the camp, (for example, "After the barrack had been camouflaged into a railroad station, the people brought to the death camp did not suspect the horrors closing in on them.")—once again indicating that the statement was written for him to serve propaganda purposes.

4. Leleko's description of the physical "gas chamber" is at great variance with other "eye-witnesses." For example, it is most often claimed that the front door of the "gas chamber" was a solid, heavy door—but according to Leleko's statement, there was no door, only a rug hanging across the opening! (His statement reads: "Flowers grew right by in long boxes. There was no door at the entrance. Instead of it there was a heavy hanging made from a rug.")

5. Leleko's statement also contradicts the official version of the Treblinka story by claiming that the when the bodies were burned, they were cremated in a specially built furnace pit. This contradicts the official story in that it is now claimed that the bodies were burned after being exhumed and stacked up on iron rails, and burned with wood. Leleko's statement reads: "An incinerator from the burning of bodies was situated about 10 meters beyond the large gas chamber building. It had the shape of a cement pit about one meter deep and 20 meters long. A series of furnaces covered on the top with four rows of rails extended along the entire length of one of the walls of the pit. The bodies were laid on the rails, caught fire from the flames burning in the furnaces, and burned. About 1000 bodies were burned simultaneously."

Obviously when this "confession" was made, that part of the story had not yet been thought through.

6. Leleko's statement claims that the hair cut from the women was sent to Germany to fill mattresses! "The women sat on a long bench and the 'hairdressers' cut off their hair.

The cut hair were packed in large bags and sent by trainloads to Germany. One of the Germans told me that in Germany they are used to fill mattresses, also for soft upholstery. He said that this hair makes very good mattresses and the Germans buy them willingly."

7. Yet another example of the blatant propaganda contained in this "confession" comes with the absurd assertion that as the victims marched to the "gas chamber" they shouted "Hail Stalin" and "Hail the Red Army" (!) and that the Ukrainian guards were going to be killed by the Germans.

Leleko's statement reads: "The men walked more quietly down this path. Several times I heard how one, speaking to another, asked: 'Why are you weeping? Do you believe you can arouse compassion in these Germans?' Frequently we could hear cries of 'Hail Stalin!', 'Hail the Red Army!' To us Russian guards, they said: 'Today you exterminate us, and tomorrow the Germans will be killing you'."

8. The absurdity of the claims continues: According to this "confession", the Germans and the Ukrainians competed with each other to see who could commit the most gruesome atrocity and one of the guards had a sword with which he would "cut off the breasts of women." The statement reads:

"The Germans and the motor operators then competed as to atrocities with regard to the people to be killed.[sic] MARCHENKO for instance, had a sword with which he mutilated people. He cut off the breasts of women."

9. The ridiculousness of the "confession" possibly reaches a new height when Leleko claims that the Germans "threw babies in over the heads" of the adult victims standing in the gas chambers!

His statement reads:

"When the chambers were filled to the very limit, the Germans started to throw in the children left by the women either in the undressing place or more frequently outside the gas chamber building. As the ceiling of the gas chambers was very low, the children thrown into the chamber hit the ceiling and then, disfigured, sometimes with broken heads, fell on the heads of the prisoners."

10. Other incredible claims made in the Leleko "confession" included the assertions that the Germans forced the prisoners to put on "comical plays" for their amusement, play in an orchestra "under the window" of

the camp commandant, and stage mock weddings among the prisoners which would end with the Germans shooting both the bride and groom for fun.

11. Finally, the Leleko "confession" says that in one year, no less than two million Jews were killed at Treblinka. The statement says:

"Question: Name the figure for the number of people exterminated in the Treblinka death camp.

"Answer: During my stay in the 'death camp', i.e. during the period from September 1942 to September 1943, no less than two million were exterminated there."

This figure is, of course, not even supported by the official version of the story—but in spite of this, the Leleko "confession" is still used as "proof" of the "extermination camp" of Treblinka—and even in the Smithsonian documentary mentioned in section 87.

There is no indication what became of "Pavel Leleko," but if he did indeed exist, there is little doubt that he met the same end as the German soldiers who "confessed" to the Katyn Massacre.

Section 91: The Franz Stangl Trial and His "Memoirs"

In 1970, the former commandant of Treblinka (and Sobibór), Franz Stangl, was put on trial and found guilty of murder, despite the "eyewitness" accounts often being contradictory, as outlined above. In court, Stangl denied any knowledge of mass exterminations. Despite this, his "memoirs," a set of interviews supposedly conducted with the Jewish journalist Gitta Sereny, appeared in 1970.

Conveniently, as appeared to be so often the case with Nazi "Holocaust criminals," Stangl died a few hours after the interviews were "completed" and thus never saw the finished product or was able to object to any distortions or insertions.

Sereny never taped the interviews, and was thus able to make up anything at all and attribute it to Stangl, safe in the knowledge that no one could "prove" her otherwise. As a result, Stangl's alleged memoirs are thus the most bizarre yet published and full of obvious inventions and distortions.

For example, he claimed that on his first visit to Treblinka he had seen "thousands of bodies" strewn around next to the tracks.

"Hundreds, no, thousands of bodies everywhere, putrefying, decomposing," the "memoirs" claim, and add "in the station was a train full of Jews, some dead, some still alive ... it looked as if it had been there for days."

Other absurdities in the Stangl "memoirs" include a claim that when he got out of his car he "stepped knee deep into money: I didn't know which way to turn, which way to go. I waded in paper notes, currency, precious stones, jewelry, and clothes. They were everywhere, strewn all over the square."

To top this bizarre scenario, Sereny claimed that Stangl had told her that the scene was completed by "whores from Warsaw weaving drunk, dancing, singing, playing music" on the other side of the barbed wire fence.

The conclusive evidence that the "Stangl" memoirs are forged is however to be found in his supposed reply to the question why he thought the Jews were being exterminated: "They wanted the Jews' money," Stangl allegedly told Sereny. "That racial business was just secondary."

Such a clearly ludicrous claim is obviously designed to try and hide the real reason why the Nazis disliked the Jews. A senior SS officer such as Stangl would have known and understood exactly what the ideological reasons behind the Nazi program to expel the Jews would have been. The answer that it was "to get their money" is a blatant insertion by Sereny who would never have admitted the real reasons for Nazi anti-Semitism.

Bizarrely, Sereny also never asked Stangl outright about the "gas chambers," despite this being the most obvious first line of questioning. She later said that she "had not thought about it," which is so outrageous as to be unbelievable.

The more likely explanation is that she did ask him about the gas chambers, and he repeated his earlier denials that there had been none, or if there were, he had nothing to do with them. This did not fit in with the demands of the Holocaust story, and it was easier for Sereny just to leave this part out.

As mentioned earlier, Stangl denied at his first court appearance that there was any extermination program at Treblinka. He was lucky never to have seen what Sereny put out in his name after he died.

CHAPTER 16: MAJDANEK

Section 92: Majdanek, Lublin—Originally Built as POW Camp for Soviet Army Prisoners

The Majdanek camp, situated within eye-shot of the city of Lublin in Poland, achieved brief fame in the Holocaust storytellers' legend immediately after the war, but has since faded away in importance.

The reason for this change in status has primarily been a realization amongst the Holocaust "experts" that the initial burst of propaganda and stories about the camp were so grossly exaggerated that it was damaging to the legend to give Majdanek too much prominence.

Initially called "Prisoner of War Camp of the Waffen-SS in Lublin," Majdanek was built in October 1941 as a prisoner of war camp to help hold the large number of Russian soldiers captured during the invasion of the Soviet Union which began in June of that year.

By March 1942, orders had been given for the camp to be able to hold 250,000 Soviet POWs, although the official records show that the numbers never reached that amount.

Prisoners were put to work in the nearby industrial sites, of which the largest was the Steyr-Daimler-Puch weapons and munitions factory.

It was also built close to the former Polish-Soviet border, and its location meant that when the Soviet armies advanced westward following the defeat of the German invasion, Majdanek was the first German concentration camp to be liberated on July 23, 1944, some nine months before the war ended. The Germans had hastily evacuated the camp, and as a result it was captured almost intact.

The only building which had been destroyed was the wooden housing of the crematoria, which had burned down in a fire a few days earlier.

It is claimed that this fire was deliberate, but, given that nothing else in the camp was damaged and the brick crematoria ovens survived the fire, a deliberate arson seems unlikely. The wooden crematoria building has been completely "reconstructed" at the camp today, a fact which is of great significance, as will be seen below.

Section 93: First Majdanek Soviet Show Trial, November 1944

The Soviets, seeking revenge for the German exposure of Communist crimes such as the Katyn Massacre (where NKVD officers had murdered thousands of Polish army officers and intelligentsia) were delighted with what they found at the camp.

Within a matter of weeks, they circulated stories, faithfully repeated in all the western media, that they had found gas chambers and evidence of the mass murder of one million Jews and at least 500,000 others at the camp.

Six German guards who had been unable to escape in time were put on trial in Lublin in November 1944, and officially charged with the murder of 1.7 million people (Sentencja wyroku. Specjalny Sad Karny w Lublinie, December 2, 1944, "Reasons for Sentence in the Trial of Hermann Vogel et al.", *Archiwum Panstwowego Muzeum na Majdanku,* Archive of the State Museum in Majdanek,

The ovens at the Majdanek crematorium, as they were found by the Soviet army. Previously indoors, the entire building around the ovens burned down before the Soviets arrived, exposing the ovens—and the chimney—to the outside elements.

The extent of the "reconstruction" work at the Majdanek crematorium is evident from these two photographs. Left: The crematorium as it was found by the Soviets. Only the chimney and the crematorium, both made of brick, were left standing after a fire destroyed the surrounding building. Right: How the chimney and crematorium are presented to visitors at the campsite today. The whole wooden building surrounding the crematorium chimney has been added. Although there is no evidence whatsoever that there was a "gas chamber" in the original crematorium building, one has been included in the "rebuilt" wooden house, and is passed off as such to present-day visitors who are not told that the entire surrounding structure was built after the war.

Majdanek Drying Room Air Vent Misrepresented as "Zyklon-B" Insertion Mechanism: A Hoax Still Perpetrated to the Present Day.

THE OPENING IN THE ROOF OF THE GAS CHAMBER THROUGH WHICH "CYCLONE" CRYSTALS WERE POURED

This picture, which was taken by the Soviet commission of investigation into Majdanek in 1944, appeared in the official report titled "Opening through which the substance 'Zyklon' was poured into the gas chamber." It also appeared in The Illustrated London News, *Oct. 14, 1944, p. 442, with the title "The opening in the roof of the gas chamber through which 'cyclone' crystals were poured." In reality, this structure is one of two ventilation shafts of the drying facility of the camp laundry, located in hut 28 of Majdanek Camp section I. The airtight lid allowed the rooms below to keep heated air (provided by piped heaters in another part of the camp) in the room to speed up the drying of prisoner clothes. The Soviet Commission claimed that the laundry section was also a "gas chamber" but this allegation has been quietly dropped by the Holocaust storytellers (Image source: Gosudarstvenni Archiv Rossiiskoi Federatsii, State Archive of the Russian Federation, Moscow, 7021-128-243, p. 7). This image is still to the present-day circulated by Holocaust storytellers as that of a "gas chamber Zyklon-B insertion tube."*

An awful scene awaited the Soviet soldiers in Majdanek: the wooden crematorium building had burned down shortly before they arrived, leaving only the brick ovens standing. Corpses which had been due for cremation were half-burned in the fire, and when the wooden structure had burned away, the skeletal remains of the dead were lying out in the open, as can be seen in this picture. The shocking scene has often been used as "evidence" of mass murder, but in reality the skeleton pictures from Majdanek were only the result of the crematorium building fire. Today, the crematorium ovens are completely enclosed in a building erected after the war—which, as mentioned, also now contains a "gas chamber."

sygn. XX-1, p. 100.). All six were sentenced to death after a perfunctory hearing and executed on December 3, 1944, in a show trial typical of many others run by the Soviets at the time (such as the disgraceful Katyn frame-up mentioned earlier).

The documents entered into the Nuremberg trial record claimed that 1.5 million people had been murdered at Majdanek (IMT, vol. VII, p. 590) and this was for many years the accepted figure.

As such, Majdanek was, for much of the first two decades after the war, the "show camp" for the Holocaust storytellers.

Section 94: Number of Madjanek "Victims" Varies Wildly from 1.7 Million to 79,000

The Soviet claims of 1.7 million were soon disputed, even by other leading Holocaust storytellers. The number of "victims" claimed for Majdanek still varies wildly, according to which source the reader consults:
- 1,380,000 victims, according to Lucy Dawidowicz (Lucy Dawidowicz, *The War against the Jews 1933–1945*, Pelican Books, 1979, p. 191.);
- 360,000 according to Lea Rosh and Eberhard Jäckel (Lea Rosh and Eberhard Jäckel, *Der Tod ist ein Meister aus Deutschland*, Hoffmann und Campe, 1991, p. 217.);
- 250,000 according to Wolfgang Scheffler (Wolfgang Scheffler, *Judenverfolgung im Dritten Reich*, Colloquium Verlag, Berlin 1964, p. 40.);

Fact or Fiction?

The exterior of "hut 41" at Majdanek in the present day, in which it is claimed thousands were gassed. According to the surviving German plans for the camp, it was the delousing building through which all the inmates' clothing was processed to kill lice.

- 200,000 or more according to the West German tribunal which organized the Düsseldorf Majdanek trial (Landgericht Düsseldorf, *Urteil Hackmann u.a.. XVII 1/75*, Band I, p. 90.);
- 79,000 according to Tomasz Kranz, director of the Research Department of the State Museum at Majdanek, in a 2005 article in the official Majdanek Museum journal, *Zeszyty Majdanka* (Kranz, T, Records of deaths and mortality rate of prisoners of KL Lublin, *Zeszyty Majdanka* Tom XXIII, 2005).

The fact that the number of "victims" can casually vary between 1.7 million and 79,000 is a reflection of the fact that there is actually no evidence beyond wild hearsay and speculation about Majdanek.

Little wonder the camp gets so little attention in present-day Holocaust propaganda.

Section 95: "Gas Chamber" Added to Postwar Rebuilt Madjanek Crematorium Building

The state of the camp when captured by the Russians lent itself to anti-Nazi propaganda.

Disease (mainly typhus, which causes extreme weight loss) had killed thousands of inmates, and a shortage of fuel had prevented the camp crematorium from hygienically disposing of large numbers of bodies. The resultant piles of corpses—none of whom had been "gassed"—made horrific viewing. Pictures of these half-decomposed bodies circulated the world along with utterly erroneous claims that they had been gassed or otherwise murdered—and there was no one to say otherwise. In addition, gruesome pictures of skeletons and half-burned bodies lying in front of the crematoria were taken and are still circulated as

An aerial view of the Majdanek camp as presented in 2011, showing its proximity to the city of Lublin. Hut 41—where the Holocaust storytellers claim the "gassings" occurred, is the building on the bottom right-hand side (marked "A"), literally within a stone's throw of the nearest civilian houses—not exactly an ideal location for a "mass gas chamber." Note that the crematorium (marked "B") is located on the far side of the camp perimeter, top left.

"evidence" of mass murder. It is, of course, never explained why the Germans would leave skeletons and half-burned corpses strewn around in front of the crematorium. These horrific scenes are, of course, the product of the fire which destroyed the wooden crematorium building—but that is never mentioned when the pictures are shown.

Some of the camp's buildings were found to be stacked to the rafters with shoes and clothing. This was (and still is) presented to the outside world as belonging to the people who had been "gassed."

The truth was far simpler: Majdanek was the main gathering point for all items seized from deportations to the three Reinhard camps, so the clothing and personal items found there in fact came from four camps, including Majdanek itself.

In addition, section VI of the camp, where the shoes were found, was a cobbler's factory, where worn-out shoes were sent from the Eastern Front for repair. This fact was admitted by Polish historian Zdzislaw Lukaszkiewicz as early as 1948 (Zdislaw Lukaszkiewicz, 'Oboz koncentracyjny i zaglady Majdanek', in: *Biuletyn Glownej Komisji Badania Zbrodni Niemieckich w Polsce,* Vol. IV, Warsaw 1948), but is, of course, ignored by the Holocaust storytellers.

There was even a factory in the Majdanek camp area, staffed by inmates, whose job it was to process the clothing brought in from occupied Poland, clean it, and prepare it for distribution all over the Reich.

This was ignored in the propaganda rush, with the result that to this day, visitors are shown piles of clothing and shoes at Majdanek and told they belonged to "gassed" Jews.

Section 96: The Impossibility of the Majdanek "Gas Chambers"

The claim that Majdanek's disinfection station was used as a homicidal "gas chamber" was first made by the Soviet "commission" which investigated the camp in 1944.

The Communist commission was also the first to make the claim that Jews had been gassed with Zyklon-B and carbon monoxide gas at the camp.

The Soviets found a room with 135 unused cans of Zyklon-B at Majdanek, which can still be seen by the present-day visitor. As was the case with Auschwitz, these cans of Zyklon-B were however used in the "entlausung" ("delousing") section to disinfect clothing.

Ironically, this is not in dispute by the Holocaust storytellers, who merely claim that the insecticide was "also" used to kill people.

Of much greater significance was the claim that carbon monoxide was used to gas people at Majdanek. There is no record, or even a claim, of any of the usual diesel engines being deployed at the camp. Instead, the Soviet

The first room one encounters when entering hut 14 at Majdanek contains a real shower (see shower-heads in the ceiling) and baths (visible at the end of the room) for the prisoners. Incredibly, the Holocaust storytellers admit that the showers and baths are real. When questioned why the Nazis would first give people showers and baths before gassing them, they answer that it was to "warm them up so that the Zyklon-B would work more effectively."

As laughable as that answer is, it is doubly ridiculous because the Holocaust storytellers claim at the same time that carbon monoxide gas was also used to kill people at Majdanek. "Warming" the prisoners would have no effect on that method of execution, which makes a mockery of the "explanation."

commission produced several large gas bottles, which it claimed contained the carbon monoxide gas.

Two of these original gas bottles are on display in the "gas chambers" today—as detailed below—but they are deadly only for the extermination claim, as will be seen below.

According to the Holocaust storytellers, and the official guidebook distributed at the camp in 2009, Majdanek served as a labor camp and an "extermination camp." The latter phase allegedly occurred from September 1942 to October 1943, when at least four "gas chambers" were built on the camp.

As with Auschwitz, the only German plan of the camp does not show any "gas chambers" at all. Instead, just like Auschwitz, the German plans show a "delousing" (German: "Entlausung") section. It is these buildings, which were obviously set up to delouse clothing, which are claimed to have been "converted" into some of the "gas chambers" at Majdanek.

The wooden crematorium building, which burned to the ground before the Soviet army occupied the camp, is also claimed to have contained a "gas chamber." The likelihood of a wooden, impossible-to-make-airtight building containing a "gas chamber" is incredibly far-fetched.

There is of course no documentation whatsoever to support the claim of a "gas chamber" in the crematorium building, but this has not stopped the "reconstructed" building containing a "gas chamber" which is shown to all visitors today.

Leading "Holocaust expert" Jean-Claude Pressac was forced to admit the following about the "reconstructed" gas chamber in the Majdanek crematorium building as follows:

"The vice-director of the museum has written to this author that this gas chamber was used 'little, but really very, very little,' which means that it was not used at all. The fiction is maintained in order not to hurt the popular superstition that every crematorium must have contained a gas chamber ... If prisoners had been murdered with Zyklon-B in that room, its location within the building, between an autopsy room, a corridor and the morgue, would have made an artificial ventilation imperative, but there is not the faintest trace proving that such a ventilation ever existed. In case of a natural ventilation by the draught, it would have been necessary to evacuate the whole crematorium for a period of time difficult to estimate" (Pressac, Jean-Claude, "Les carences et incohérences du rapport Leuchter," *Journal J*, December 1988).

The other "gas chambers" shown to visitors at Majdanek today are located in what is known as "hut 41," also called "barrack 41." This was actually the delousing section at Majdanek which the Germans had clearly marked out on their plans for the camp. There were two huts used to delouse clothing, numbers 41 and 42, and both are right next to each other and still on view at the camp today. However, today, only hut 41 is claimed to have contained a "gas chamber."

If there was any single reason why "hut 41" could not have been used as a "gas chamber," it would be its location.

It is within sight (literally a stone's throw) from the main road which runs past the camp and is physically outside the main camp fence, as can be seen in the overview photograph.

In other words, the "gassing site" would have been in open sight of passersby, civilians, and in fact the whole town of Lublin. The "gas chambers" are also quite a distance from the crematorium building.

This means that the "gassing" would have to be carried out in sight of the public—and then the gassed bodies would have to be transported, under public gaze, to the crematorium—located on the outer perimeter of the opposite side of the camp—presumably on carts or trucks.

The possibility of such open mass murder makes the "extermination" allegation nothing short of laughable. It is an indication of how biased media coverage and academia has become on the topic that this obvious fact is so blatantly ignored.

Section 97: Majdanek's Real Showers for "Gassing Victims"

A sign at the entrance to hut 41 says Bad und Desinfektion ("Bath and Disinfection"). It is claimed that this was there to lull the "victims" into a sense of security about their fates, an allegation which is astonishing because the first room one enters while touring the building is indeed a room in which real shower-heads and even two baths (!) are installed.

The Holocaust storytellers claim that victims were genuinely showered with hot water and given the opportunity to bathe. When confronted with the obvious question of why one would shower people before gassing them, the Holocaust storytellers claim that this was to "warm them up" so that the Zyklon-B gas would work more efficiently. If these outrageous claims were not taken seriously, they would be laughable.

There are a series of rooms in hut 41 which are shown to the present-day tourist as "gas chambers." The first is immediately adjacent to the real shower room, and measures 184 ft^2 (17.1 m^2). There are no Prussian blue Zyklon-B stains on the walls of this "gas chamber," so, in order to get round this, the Holocaust storytellers claim that people were murdered here with carbon monoxide gas.

Section 98: Majdanek's "Gas Bottles" on Display are Carbon Dioxide, Not Carbon Monoxide

Two of the gas bottles discovered by the Soviets are now conveniently set up in an adjoining room to this "first" gas chamber.

The bottles are connected to pipes which allegedly run into the "gas chamber" and there is a "peep hole" in the wall through which the SS man who "operated" the gas bottles could allegedly keep an eye on the victims.

This "gassing" operation is however, the final evidence that the whole display is fake.

The sign which accompanies the display says that "carbon oxide" gas was used—while this might be a Polish-English translation error, the truth is that there is no such gas as "carbon oxide."

However, even if the sign meant to say "carbon monoxide," the "lethal" Nazi gas bottles on display are engraved with the name of their contents: carbon dioxide.

As anyone with even basic chemistry knowledge knows, there is a world of difference between carbon *dioxide* and carbon *monoxide*. The latter gas is poisonous, while carbon dioxide is the gas which is used to make sweet drinks fizzy and often added to other foodstuffs.

Carbon dioxide is also used in applications as diverse as wine making, agriculture, refrigerants and a host of others—all of which are ultimately consumed by humans. Carbon dioxide is also the gas that people exhale while

The gas bottles on display at Majdanek camp: the Holocaust storytellers claim they are carbon monoxide (CO) which was used to kill Jews.
The bottles are in fact engraved as follows:

"Dr. Pater Victoria Kohlensäurefabrik Nußdorf Nr 6196 Full. 10 Kg [...] und Fluid Warszawa Kohlensäure [...] Fluid Warszawa Lukowski. Pleschen 10,1 kg CO_2 Gepr."

(The inscriptions are only partly legible.) These gas bottles are actually carbon dioxide (CO_2) which is a completely different chemical most commonly used in the manufacture of foodstuffs (for example to give sweet drinks such as Coca-Cola the "fizz"). It is tragic that such an obvious fraud is taken seriously by anyone. Note also the official sign which claims that the gas is "carbon oxide" (which does not even exist). The sign also claims that the SS men could watch the gassing through a "grated window"—see the picture below for the location of this "grated window" and the "gas bottles."

The peephole supposedly used by SS men to check on the dying prisoners in the "gas chamber" next door to the "gas bottle" room. As can be seen, the "hole" does not even have glass and is completely open. Any poisonous gas released in the "chamber" would have come straight back into the "operator's room." Errors such as these are ignored by the Holocaust storytellers.

A close-up of the open "grated window" through which the Holocaust storytellers claimed that the SS-men could "watch gassings." Any "gassing" undertaken in the "gas chamber" into which this glass-less window looks, would be impossible as the "gas" would disperse through the "observation window" into the next room.

breathing, and which is then absorbed by plants in the photosynthesis process.

It borders on the impossible—even more so than with diesel fumes—to gas large numbers of people with carbon dioxide.

Official tests show that carbon dioxide only becomes fatal to humans at levels above 5% concentration (50,000 parts per million, or ppm) exposure.

The claim that large groups of people could be gassed to death in a room into which carbon dioxide was pumped from bottles is so absurd as to be mad.

To make matters even more ludicrous, the "peephole" through which the SS operator was supposed to watch the victims, is merely an open hole with small iron cross bars.

The "carbon oxide gas chamber" is not airtight, which makes the claim of gassing with any chemical physically impossible.

Section 99: The Anomalies of Majdanek's Second and Third "Gas Chambers"

The second "gas chamber" shown to visitors is the same size as the first, and the walls here contain distinct blue discoloration from Zyklon-B.

In addition, there is an opening in the ceiling through which, it is claimed, Zyklon-B pellets were dropped into the chamber by SS men on the roof.

The third "gas chamber" shown to present-day visitors measures 378 ft² (35.2 m²). Its walls are also stained with "Prussian blue" Zyklon-B marks. However, there is no "Zyklon-B inlet" in this room, which was supposedly the largest of all the gas chambers. The Holocaust storytellers get around the lack of Zyklon-B inlets by now saying that the SS men threw the gas pellets into the room over the heads of the victims before slamming the doors shut.

The largest of the delousing rooms—bearing the characteristic marking of Prussian Blue stains from Zyklon-B use—is presented to the present-day visitor as a "gas chamber." Note the sign which claims that prisoners were gassed using "carbon oxide" and an addendum that "cyclone B was also used." There are no Zykon-B "induction holes" in this chamber, which makes using that chemical as a homicidal gassing method impossible, something which has actually already been admitted by Holocaust "expert" Jean-Claude Pressac.

This is of course, ludicrous, and even Holocaust "expert" Jean-Claude Pressac was forced to admit that "It is frankly unrealistic to imagine an SS-man with a gas mask and a can of Zyklon-B in his hand throwing the pellets into a space of 30 cm between the heads of the victims and the ceiling—the pellets might have fallen on the floor in front of the gas chamber—and subsequently trying to slam the door without the doomed inmates making a desperate attempt to break out" (Pressac, Jean-Claude, "Les carences et incohérences du rapport Leuchter," *Journal J,* December 1988).

Section 100: The Plain Glass Window in Majdanek's Fourth "Gas Chamber"

The fourth and last gas chamber, located next to the real bath in which the victims could wash "before being gassed" (!) measures 1153ft^2 (107.7 m^2).

The walls in this room show "Prussian blue" discoloration as well and there are two round openings in the ceiling through which, it is claimed, the Zyklon B was inserted from above.

This chamber has a large plain glass window, through which a direct view to the outside can be had. The claim that victims would stand by idly while being gassed and not knock out a plain glass window, is as laughably fraudulent as the supposed site of the "gas chamber" itself.

The Holocaust storytellers have attempted to explain the presence of the plain glass window by claiming that it was installed after the war. However, the Zyklon-B "Prussian blue" stains are present on the wooden window frames, which means that it was there when the chemical was deployed in the room.

The idea that people could be gassed in this room without smashing their way out, is impossible.

Yet tourists to the camp are told that this was the single largest "gas chamber" at the camp in which thousands of Jews were put to death.

Furthermore, this "gas chamber" has two doors, both of which open into room. Logically this would be impossible. If, as the "eyewitnesses" claim, the bodies of "gassed victims" were pressed up against the door and walls from the inside, then it would be impossible to open the doors from the outside.

As the scholars Jürgen Graf and Carlo Mattogno have written on the topic of the Zykon-B "insertion holes" at Majdanek:

"The existing openings in Chambers I and II are so small (26 × 26 cm and 29 × 33 cm respectively) . . . were cut through the ceilings in a downright crude manner, especially in Chamber II where there is not even so much as a wooden frame for the hole. All indications are that these openings were hastily added for the Polish-Soviet Commission.

"The following description of Chamber I by Constantino Simonov, a correspondent for the Soviet army paper Red Star who visited Majdanek right after liberation, is of great interest: 'But let us open the next door and enter the second disinfestations chamber, which has been built along completely different criteria. It is a square room, not much higher than two meters, and approximately 6 x 6 m in size. The walls, the ceiling, the floor—all are of gray, monotonous reinforced concrete. There is no rack for clothing such as we saw in the previous room: here, everything is bare and empty. A single large steel door hermetically seals the entrance to the room; it is closed from the outside with strong steel bolts. The walls of this reinforced concrete crypt contain three openings: two of them are pipes entering from outside, the third is a porthole, a square little window barred by a large, thick steel grid solidly anchored in the reinforced concrete. The thick glass is on the outside so that it cannot be reached through the grid.'

"C. Simonov had just left Barrack 42, which he described as follows: 'Then we arrive at the chambers where the clothing taken from the inmates was disinfected. Pipes are affixed in the ceiling, and the disinfestation agent was introduced through these. Then they were closed off, the doors were sealed airtight, and disinfestation proceeded. In fact, the barrack walls, constructed of wooden slats, and the doors, which were not lined with metal, were not nearly solid enough to have served for any purpose other than disinfesting clothing.'

"So if Simonov mentions the openings in the ceiling of the disinfestations chambers in Barrack 42,

One of the "gas chambers" shown to present-day visitors to Majdanek has a plain glass window in the wall. It is, of course, impossible to think that victims would not immediately have smashed out the window, but this obvious flaw is ignored by the Holocaust storytellers and missed by the large number of tourists who visit the camp each year.

but not the opening in Chamber I which he entered immediately thereafter, this can only mean that that opening did not yet exist at the time. To summarize: the delousing chambers of Barrack 42, which are acknowledged to have served exclusively for disinfesting clothing, had openings in the ceiling for pouring in the Zyklon B, even though such openings were not absolutely necessary (the pellets could just as well have been thrown on the floor). On the other hand, Gas Chambers I and III of Barrack 41, which allegedly served only for killing people, were not equipped with any ceiling openings for introducing Zyklon, even though such openings would have been utterly, unequivocally necessary!" (*Concentration Camp Majdanek, A Historical and Technical Study*, Jürgen Graf, Carlo Mattogno, Translated by Victor Diodon Chicago (Illinois): Theses & Dissertations Press, Imprint of Castle Hill Publishers, June 2003.)

It is obvious that "hut 41" was a disinfestation center and nothing else. Inmates were made to undress, shower, or bath while their clothes were disinfected with Zyklon-B insecticide—all in an attempt to control lice and typhus at the camp.

It is bizarre therefore, that the German efforts to keep their prisoners alive through attempting to keep disease under control, is now used as "evidence" of mass murder.

Section 101: The Operation "Harvest Festival" Hoax

Not content with producing preposterous lies about "gas chambers" in Majdanek, the Holocaust storytellers have developed an even more incredible story about the camp, called "Operation Harvest Festival." This was supposed to be the execution, by machine gun, of 17,000 Jews in a single day, November 3, 1943, in the camp.

Bearing in mind that it is now claimed that "only" 79,000 Jews were killed at the camp, this single day's alleged massacre supposedly accounted for nearly a quarter of all "murders at the camp," so it is a significant event in the Holocaust story.

The supposed ashes of the 17,000 people allegedly shot to death on this day now form part of a large open-air (!) dome mausoleum at the Majdanek campsite, which has taken on almost religious significance for the Holocaust story. It is incredible to think that ashes are left out exposed to the elements like that, but this is likely done because they are not ashes at all, as detailed below.

The first problem with "Operation Harvest Festival" is the name itself. The Holocaust storytellers claim that this was the "code name" for an operation to kill all Jews in the area following an uprising earlier in 1943—but the words "Harvest Festival" appear absolutely nowhere in any German documentation, nor is there any order to kill all Jews in 1943 in Lublin. The name has literally been invented out of nothing.

Section 102: The Mußfeldt "Confession"

The second problem with the "Operation Harvest Festival mass shooting" story is that the entire event is based on the 1947 "confession" of an SS-Oberscharführer, Erich Mußfeldt.

All other accounts are based exclusively on his version of events, and this "confession" is so obviously faked that it was clearly extracted from him under duress (in exactly the same way that other Germans "confessed" to the Katyn Massacre, for example). Amongst the many impossibilities of this "confession" are the claims that:

- The "victims" were forced to climb into specially prepared ditches in groups of ten and lay down before being shot. This meant that as the ditches supposedly filled up, the "victims" would soon have to be lying down on piles of corpses. Such a scenario carrying on for eleven hours without interruption is extremely unlikely. Resistance of some sort would have been inevitable, bearing in mind that there were supposedly only 100 SS men present as opposed to 17,000 (!) prisoners, all patiently lining up to be shot.

- A huge stockpile of ammunition would have been necessary to shoot so many people, especially bearing in mind that the SS men were allegedly armed with the standard German automatic weapons which fired 600 rounds per minute. If only four of the SS men fired for two seconds at a group of ten Jews, they would expend up to 160 bullets. Eleven hours of almost continual shooting would have expended 3,600 bullets per hour, or 39,600 rounds for the whole day.

Presuming that there was a brief pause in between each round of shootings, it would not be unreasonable to presume that the operation would have used up at least 30,000 rounds—a veritable mountain of ammunition which would most certainly have alerted the 17,000 prisoners supposedly quietly lining up, naked, in the open field.

- The camp was, as pointed out earlier, in open view of the town of Lublin. To think that an eleven-hour mass execution—by shooting—of this nature could have gone unnoticed by the townsfolk, is unimaginable. Yet no one had ever heard of, or reported the killings, before Mußfeldt's "confession."

- No evidence of the mass 328 feet-long (100 meters) "zig zag ditches" which Mußfeldt claimed had been dug for the bodies, has ever been found.

- Mußfeldt "confessed" to having been ordered to organize the exhumation and cremation of the 17,000 bodies shortly afterward.

This task was allegedly completed by December 1943 by using the crematorium and burning in the open on "wooden boards." The ashes were supposedly reburied in the (never-to-be-found) ditches, but somehow mysteriously have now found their way into the mausoleum located under an open-air dome memorial at the camp.

Here, an important part of the whole story falls down: why, if the decision had been taken to cremate the victims, were they buried in the first place?

Also, Mußfeldt "confessed" that he started the cremations on November 5, and finished the task by December 24, some 50 days in total.

This means that for 50 days, the townsfolk of Lublin would have been subjected to the view of gigantic open air exhumations, huge bonfires, the stench of 17,000 bodies being burned, and huge amounts of smoke. It is an impossible claim.

The Polish government-in-exile, the *Delegatura,* issued a report claiming that there had been a massacre in Majdanek on November 15, based, allegedly on its sources within the camp. This was, however, the same propaganda machine which claimed that there were "gas chambers" at Majdanek as early as December 15, 1942—something which, as the evidence above has clearly shown, was not true.

So what did the *Delegatura* report on? The most likely course of events behind this incident is that there was some type of disturbance in the camp at the beginning of November which possibly even resulted in a shooting incident.

This disturbance could have been an attempted escape—there had, for example, been a breakout of prisoners from the Sobibór camp in late October, so it is possible that there was trouble at Majdanek. Alternatively, it could have been the transportation of a large number of prisoners from Majdanek to Cracow, as reported in the Polish resistance newspaper *Dziennik Polski* (printed in England). That paper's November 1943 edition said that "25,000 Jews were transferred from Majdanek to Cracow, where they were quartered in hundreds of recently constructed barracks. Probably these Jews will have to work in the German factories which have recently been transferred to the Cracow district" (Gajowniczek, Jolanta, "Obóz koncentracyjny na Majdanku wietle 'Dzennika Polskiego' i 'Dziennika Polskiego i Dziennika onierza' z latach 1940–1944," in: *ZM, VII*, 1973, note 446, p. 256).

Such a large number of prisoners being moved about, combined with a potentially unrelated minor shooting incident, could easily create rumors about a massacre involving thousands of people in the camp.

Fed by the *Delegatura's* propaganda, the Soviet occupation army sought out the hapless German Mußfeldt who was forced to "confess" to a staggering crime—and the basis for "Operation Harvest Festival" myth was born.

As to the ashes in the open air dome mausoleum today on display at the camp: repeated requests to independently DNA test this mound to see if it really contains human remains has been turned down by the camp museum authorities. Those who know the true story of Majdanek are not surprised.

Section 103: The Second Majdanek Trial of 1975

In 1975, a major trial of sixteen former SS members was held in Düsseldorf for their alleged involvement in the events at the Majdanek camp.

The outcome of the trial was in itself a condemnation of the "extermination camp" theory.

Of the sixteen accused, two were released "due to ill health," one died during the trial, and five were completely acquitted. The eight who were found guilty were sentenced to varying terms of imprisonment.

The two defendants who were given the severest sentences—life—were accused of "selecting victims for the gas chambers."

They both denied taking part in any such activity—something which was plainly true, given the absence of homicidal gas chambers as detailed above—but in the lynch mob climate which ruled German courts, their denials were ignored.

The absurdity of the court proceedings were summarized in the claim made in the judgment that carbon monoxide had been used to kill Jews:

"The gassing always proceeded in the same way. The inmates marked for death were taken to the barrack, made to undress and then herded into one of the gas chambers. As soon as the door was closed airtight behind them, the carbon monoxide or Zyklon B was introduced into the chamber. As soon as the SS-man in charge of supervising the gassing determined that all the victims had died, the steel doors were thrown open so that the gas could escape. Then the bodies were brought out by a special unit of inmates, loaded onto hand carts or vehicles and either taken to the old or new crematorium to be burned, or to pits or pyres prepared outside the camp in the surrounding forest" (District Court Düsseldorf, *Urteil Hackmann u.a.,* XVII 1/75, v. I, pp. 65f.).

As shown earlier, there were no "diesel" engines at Majdanek, and the only "gas bottles" found there were carbon dioxide, not carbon monoxide.

In addition, the claim that poisonous gas could "escape" simply by the doors "being opened" is patently absurd.

Firstly, gas would be trapped between the bodies, even if such an unlikely scenario could have taken place, and, as pointed out above, some of the "gas chambers" only have doors which open inward.

The verdict was, the court said, based almost entirely on "eyewitness testimony."

The court relied in particular upon the testimony of someone who claimed to be a former SS member, one Heinz Müller.

The court judgment described Müller as "one of the few members of the SS who have not sought to hide their knowledge behind alleged ignorance, inability to remember, disinterest in camp events at the time in question, or other excuses."

Müller "confessed" to having attended "gassings with carbon monoxide," at Majdanek—and was the only one from the German side to have claimed so, as all the others denied it.

Even though Müller was the only one to have claimed to have been present at one of these impossible gassings, strangely enough he was also the only one not to be charged with any crime!

It was a clear and obvious distortion of justice that sixteen people could be put on trial on the "eyewitness" evidence of one person who testified about a physically impossible event—while the eyewitness evidence of the sixteen accused was rejected in favor of the one counter-witness.

Other "evidence" accepted by the court without question were written statements by five Polish and Soviet witnesses who refused to come to court, and an astonishing thirteen witnesses who were long dead, including Mußfeldt.

The court also accepted without question the "Operation Harvest Festival" story and the evidence by another man who claimed to have been in the SS, one Georg Werk.

His incredible testimony included the claim that he had been on the detachment which had carried out the mass shootings—but that "luckily" his gun had "jammed" so he personally, of course, had not actually shot anybody!

As a result, this "witness" was not charged but was of course allowed to give "evidence." The court verdict stated: "According to his statements, the witness Werk was posted to the office in Lublin at that time, and had been detailed to the execution squad, but claims that he did not participate in the shooting but only 'watched' because, (in his own words), 'luckily' his submachine gun malfunctioned. The latter is anything but believable; but the Court has absolutely no doubt that the rest of his testimony is truthful, especially with regard to how the witnesses had to lie down on top of each other like roofing tiles, to be killed with shots to the back of the head or in the neck."

As the revisionist researchers Jürgen Graf and Carlo Mattogno have commented: "It doesn't take much of an imagination to picture how the Court probably bought this witness's incriminating statement: in return for the desired description of the mass murder, Georg Werk was exempted from criminal charges, even though the Court considered his excuse, the malfunctioning submachine gun, to be unbelievable and he would therefore logically have to have been charged as accessory to murder, and convicted.

"SS-man Erich Laurich, on the other hand, who categorically denied any involvement in the executions, was 'exposed' by the testimony of the witness Zacheusz Pawlak, and sentenced to eight years in prison" (*Concentration Camp Majdanek, A Historical and Technical Study,* Jürgen Graf, Carlo Mattogno, Translated by Victor Diodon Chicago (Illinois): Theses & Dissertations Press, Imprint of Castle Hill Publishers, June 2003).

CHAPTER 17: DACHAU

Section 104: Dachau and Its Mysterious "Gas Chamber"

When the Dachau concentration camp, north of Munich, was seized by American troops in 1945, it was widely claimed that a "gas chamber" had been found there.

The Dachau "gas chamber" was described in Document No. 47 of the 79th Congress, 1st Session, Senate Report (May 15, 1945) of the Committee Requested by Gen. Dwight D. Eisenhower to the Congress of the US relative to Atrocities and other Conditions in Concentration Camps in Germany, and entered into the Nuremberg trial proceedings as IMT Document L-159. It reads as follows: "The gas chamber was located in the center of a large room in the crematory building. It was built of concrete. Its dimensions were about 20 by 20 feet, and the ceiling was some 10 feet in height. In two opposite walls of the chamber were airtight doors through which condemned prisoners could be taken into the chamber for execution and removed after execution. The supply of gas into the chamber was controlled by means of two valves on one of the outer walls, and beneath the valves was a small glass-covered peephole through which the operator could watch the victims die. The gas was let into the chamber through pipes terminating in perforated brass fixtures set into the ceiling. The chamber was of size sufficient to execute probably a hundred men at one time" (*Document No. 47 of the 79th Congress, 1st Session, Senate Report,* May 15, 1945, of the Committee Requested by Gen. Dwight D. Eisenhower to the Congress of the US relative to Atrocities and other Conditions in Concentration Camps in Germany. Entered into the Nuremberg trial proceedings as IMT Document L-159.). Visitors to the camp are still told, to the present day, that there is a "gas chamber" in the building housing the camp crematorium—but the information signs there now state very clearly that no one was ever gassed at Dachau and that the "gas chamber" was never used. This, of course, directly contradicts the "evidence" presented to the US Congress, the Nuremberg Trials, and in the numerous "eyewitness memoirs" of the camp. The claim that gas was "let in through perforated brass fixtures" in the ceiling as per the Nuremberg trial document L-159 is of particular interest, because today it is claimed that the "gas" was introduced through slide-open hatches in the wall.

The fact that the room now claimed to have been the Dachau "gas chamber" could never have been designed as, or used for that purpose, is however obvious from the most cursory inspection.

Firstly, the room is not airtight and boasts a loose window. The floor contains no less than four drains which run uninhibited into the entire building's drain system, which includes outlets in every single room. This includes the room which houses the ovens and the alleged "changing room." This arrangement would of course, have been fatal for anyone working in the building, SS guards and prisoners alike. Poison gas would have immediately seeped throughout the entire structure and caused an explosion in the crematorium area, which would have destroyed the building.

The Dachau "gas chamber" is an obvious fake, and was clearly designed for use as a morgue and washing room to hold bodies for the crematorium next door.

In a weak attempt to bolster the "gas chamber" story, very crude fake "shower-heads" have been inserted into the ceiling of the alleged "gas chamber" shown to present-day visitors. These "shower-heads," which did not exist when the camp was liberated, are also postwar additions.

Finally, the "gas chamber" sports a ventilation shaft in the roof, something which makes the gassing claims even more ludicrous. Indeed, some more objective observers have already remarked on this very fact. Stephen F. Pinter, who served as a lawyer for the United States War Department in the occupation forces in Germany and Austria for six years after the war, made the following statement in the widely read Catholic magazine *Our Sunday Visitor*, June 14th, 1959:

> "I was in Dachau for 17 months after the war, as a US War Department Attorney, and can state that there was no gas chamber at Dachau. What was shown to visitors and sightseers there and erroneously described as a gas chamber was a crematory. Nor was there a gas chamber in any of the other concentration camps in Germany. We were told that there was a gas chamber at Auschwitz, but since that was in the Russian zone of occupation, we were not permitted to investigate since the Russians would not allow it. From what I was able to determine during six postwar years in Germany and Austria, there were a number of Jews killed, but the figure of a million was certainly never reached. I interviewed thousands of Jews, former inmates of concentration camps in Germany and Austria, and consider myself as well qualified as any man on this subject."

This tells a very different story from the customary propaganda. Pinter, of course, is very astute on the question of the crematorium being represented as a gas chamber.

This is a frequent ploy, because no such thing as a gas chamber has ever been shown to exist in these camps, hence the deliberately misleading term "gas oven"—aimed at confusing a "gas chamber" with a "crematorium." A "gas oven" is a crematorium which uses gas as a fuel to burn a body—something very different to a "gas chamber." Nonetheless, the term "gas oven" is frequently used to mean "gas chamber" in Holocaust literature. The Dachau crematorium was used for the hygienic disposal of corpses of people who had died from natural causes or from individual judicial executions inside the camp. Sometimes it was even used to cremate bodies from outside Dachau as well.

For example, after the Allied air raids on Munich in September 1944—in which 30,000 people were killed—the city's archbishop, Cardinal Faulhaber, asked the Dachau camp authorities to help in the cremation of the bombing victims. He was told that this was impossible: the crematorium, having only one furnace, was not able to cope with the bodies of the air raid victims. Clearly, therefore, it could not have coped with the 238,000 Jewish bodies which were allegedly cremated there. In order to do so, the crematorium would have to be kept going for 326 years without stopping and 530 tons of ashes would have been recovered.

The entrance to the Dachau "gas chamber" as presented to visitors to the camp in 2010. The room is right next to a set of ovens, and was obviously used as a morgue, and has, just as in the case of Auschwitz, been "turned into a gas chamber" by postwar "reconstruction." In this particular case, the door is not even airtight, as can be clearly seen from this picture.

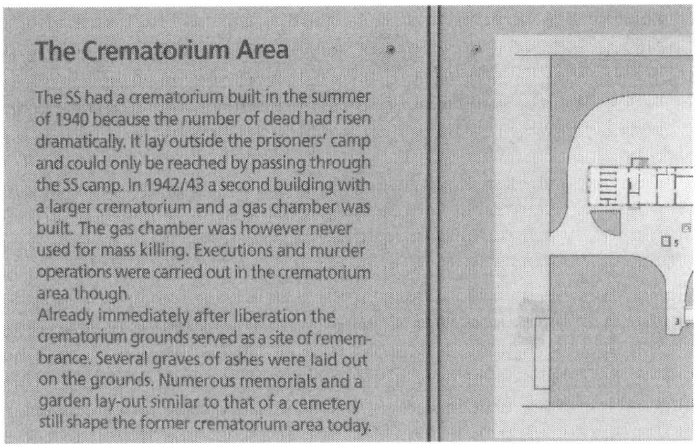

Fact or Fiction? 83

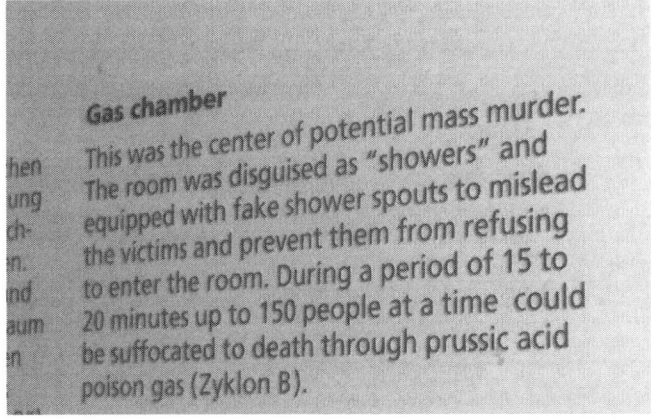

Contradictory signs at the Dachau camp, as presented to tourists in 2010. On the left: This sign is outside the crematorium building, and states that the "gas chamber was however never used for mass killing." Right, the sign inside the building at the door next to what is claimed to be the "gas chamber." It is phrased in such a way as to create the impression that the room was indeed used to gas people.

The interior of the Dachau "gas chamber" as presented to tourists in 2010. The floor contains four drains, directly connected to the other rooms in the building (two of which are visible in this picture). This feature alone would have made "gassings" in the room impossible, as poisonous gas would have leaked throughout the structure and killed everyone else, SS guards included. It is now claimed that Zyklon-B was inserted through the hole in the far wall, but in 1945, the Nuremberg Trial was told that gas was emitted through "brass fixtures in the ceiling." Today there are only crude "fake shower-heads" in the ceiling (visible in this picture), which are another postwar addition. Inset: a close-up of the drain in the floor of the "gas chamber" at Dachau. This open drain system runs throughout the entire building, and if the chamber had ever actually been used as a "gas chamber" the gas would have spread into every room.

Left: This famous photograph of an American soldier outside a "gas chamber" in Dachau which has reached wide circulation. The "gas chamber" is, of course, actually one of the disinfestations chambers, but Holocaust storytellers always omit to say this when the photograph is used. Right: These same disinfestation chambers are clearly signposted today as "fumigation cubicles" and, like the disinfection chambers at Auschwitz and the other camps, also used Zyklon-B as its disinfection agent.

Left: The rear (outside) of the Dachau disinfestation chambers. The double doors on both ends of the disinfestation chambers were necessary to keep clean clothes separate from the contaminated ones—dirty clothes were put in on one side, and clean ones taken out the other—just like in Auschwitz. Right: The genuine Zyklon-B insertion mechanism inside one of the Dachau delousing chambers, also visible in the picture top right. The pellets would be dropped through from a special compartment in the ceiling and automatically released into the basket at the end of the visible tube. Compare this with the "hole in the wall Zyklon-B insertion point" of the alleged homicidal "gas chamber" (see photograph on page 80) in the same building, and it is obvious that the latter is a fake.

Section 105: The Real Dachau Gas Chambers—Delousing Cubicles

The building in Dachau which contains the crematorium and the alleged "gas chamber" does in fact contain a number of real gas chambers.

They are however, now clearly marked as "fumigation cubicles." These are some of the best preserved disinfestation rooms which did indeed use Zyklon-B (the insertion mechanisms are still there) and from which the "Zyklon-B gas chamber" story emerged.

As in all the other camps, the only real "gas chambers" in Dachau were for disinfecting clothing, and were even used for this purpose by the occupying American army as well. The real "gas chambers" at Dachau were the disinfestation chambers located on the western end of the crematorium building. These small chambers were used to kill lice and prevent the spread of disease, and are the best-preserved such chambers in any of the camps.

American soldiers with deloused clothing airing outside the disinfestations chambers, 1945. The disinfestations chambers and Zyklon-B continued to be used after the Allied liberation of the camp, something that the Holocaust storytellers always neglect to tell.

Section 106: Dachau Casualty Figures Officially "Reduced" from 238,000 to 20,000

The figures of Dachau casualties are typical of the kind of exaggerations that have since had to be drastically revised.

In 1946, a memorial plaque was unveiled at Dachau by Philip Auerbach, the Jewish State-Secretary in the Bavarian Government (who was later convicted for embezzling money which he claimed as compensation for non-existent Jews) which read: "This area is being retained as a shrine to the 238,000 individuals who were cremated here."

Since then, the official casualty figures have had to be steadily revised downward, and now stand at "only" 20,600, the majority dying from typhus and starvation only at the end of the war. This deflation, to 10 percent of the original figure, will doubtless continue and one day will be applied to the legendary figure of six million as a whole.

CHAPTER 18: SACHSENHAUSEN

Section 107: Sachsenhausen: Gas Chamber Built in November 1945, Knocked Down in 1952

The Sachsenhausen concentration camp outside Berlin hardly features in the "extermination" legend in present-day Holocaust storytelling, but in the period immediately following the war, it was big news. Located in the Soviet

Left: Female prisoners at Dachau wave at their American liberators. Right: Polish inmates of Dachau celebrate with champagne and cigars upon the arrival of the American troops. The prisoners all look well-fed and healthy. Hence, pictures such as these are rarely used by the Holocaust storytellers, who instead prefer to use pictures of typhus-ridden inmates to represent the concentration camp population.

occupation zone of Germany, it was at first taken over by the Soviet secret police, the NKVD, for the detention and interrogation of German prisoners.

Then, during the 1947 Soviet Military Tribunal held in Pankow, Berlin, the commandant of Sachsenhausen, Anton Kaindl, was put on trial. Kaindl "confessed" to having ordered a gas chamber to be built at the camp in 1943 which used "liquid Zyklon-B."

Immediately after making this "confession," Kaindl was moved to the Vorkuta Gulag in Siberia, where he conveniently died of unknown causes within a few months.

The first indication that there was something untoward with the Sachsenhausen "gas chamber" came in 1952, when the Soviets announced that they had bulldozed the building which contained the chamber.

No one could understand why this supposedly clear-cut "evidence" of Nazi crimes would be destroyed in this manner.

In 1992, however, the truth finally emerged when a long-hidden statement by a German prisoner-of-war, Gerhart Schirmer, was made public.

In his statement, Schirmer revealed that after his capture by the Soviets, he and a number of Germans were taken by the NKVD to Sachsenhausen in October 1945.

There, his statement said, he and seven other prisoners were ordered by the Soviet political officer, Lieutenant-Colonel Kolowantienkow, to rebuild a shower in a building in the "Front Zone" of the camp into a mock gas chamber and execution room.

"When we arrived, the material required for the construction work was already there. Under the directions of Klein, we now connected pipes from outside the building to the water supply pipes. We built an additional concrete cell adjoining the bathroom measuring about 4×2 square meters with an opening into the ante-room of the shower room. The new opening from the ante-room to the newly built so-called 'execution room' [Erschießungsraum] was about 20 cm wide. It was made to look as if the offender who was to be shot would have stood at the entrance facing the concrete wall enabling the person with the gun to fire a shot into the back of his head.

"As we were unable to prevent the construction of the installation, it seemed to make sense to us that we should continue the work and, in this way, learn what was being made there. After completion, at about the end of October 1945, Dipl.-Ing. Dörbeck was brought before the political officer alone and received precise instructions about the explanations he was to give to Soviet groups of visitors. He had to say the following:

'This installation, which was built by the Nazis, served to kill [Vernichtung] Jews and Soviet officer prisoners. Each day some 200 people were gassed and about twenty-five were shot. This went on from 1943 till 1945 (April).'

"From about December 1945 until the end of 1947 an average of two tours a week, each consisting of some thirty to forty Soviet men, mostly soldiers and people from the GPU, and women, were escorted by Dörbeck round the installation.

"There were often officers amongst them who quite openly expressed doubts about the age of the installation because they saw that the concrete was new, that there were no bullet holes from the executions in the concrete wall and that the blood stains (red paint) were very meager and unconvincing."—Signed Gerhart Schirmer, Rastatt, 16.12.86 (Gerhart Schirmer, *Sachsenhausen—Workuta. Zehn Jahre in den Fängen der Sowjets*, Grabert, Tübingen, 1992).

The preposterous "gas chamber" and "execution room" were so blatantly fake that they were torn down only a few years after being constructed, thereby destroying all incriminating evidence. Nonetheless, visitors to Sachsenhausen are still today shown the foundations of the building and told that a "gas chamber" killed thousands there. The Holocaust storytellers are able to continue with the deception about the Sachsenhausen and Dachau "gas

These foundations are shown to present-day visitors to the Sachsenhausen camp outside Berlin as the remains of a "gas chamber." The "gas chamber" was demolished in 1952 after its obviously falsified nature had become an embarrassment. A German prisoner of war revealed in the 1980s that he and seven other colleagues had been forced to build the structure in November 1945 to provide "evidence" for the Soviet's allegations of mass gassing at camps in Germany. Even though no "Holocaust historian" today claims that there were any gassings in Germany (they say they only took place in Poland), visitors to Sachsenhausen are still told that this was a "gas chamber" in which thousands were killed.

chambers" hoaxes in Germany because it is a criminal offence to even say that they were not real.

The German POW Schirmer was prosecuted in Germany just for allowing his sworn statement to become public. He was given the choice of a fine or imprisonment at the age of 90, and chose the fine because he said, he had already served eleven years in a Soviet prison and did not want to die in a German one. This serves as a tragic reminder of how the Six Million lie is maintained.

CHAPTER 19: BERGEN-BELSEN

Section 108: Typhus Deaths—Origin of Horror Images in Bergen-Belsen—No Gas Chambers

The Bergen-Belsen camp in northwestern Germany was originally a prisoner of war camp named Stalag XI-C.

It was "converted" into a concentration camp in 1943 on the orders of SS Reichsführer Heinrich Himmler as a part of a program to exchange Jews for German POWs held by the Allies (Ben Shephard, After *Daybreak—The Liberation of Belsen,* 1945, London, Random House, 2006).

The camp was liberated by the British army on April 15, 1945. Mainly because a large Western media contingent accompanied the British soldiers, and thereby had immediate access to the entire camp, it has never been claimed that there was a "gas chamber" at Bergen-Belsen.

Nonetheless, the pictures of piles of emaciated bodies and mass graves taken at Bergen-Belsen have come to symbolize the entire Holocaust, and more often than not the horrific images are presented as "victims of the Nazi genocide" and, by implication, the "gas chambers." As shocking as the images are, they are not evidence of any mass extermination policy.

The reason for the large number of deaths was simply that a typhus epidemic had erupted in the camp during the closing months of the war, and the Allied bombing of the German infrastructure had made it impossible to bring up sufficient supplies—including Zyklon-B, which was used to delouse clothing and kill the typhus-carrying lice—to combat the disease and to keep the prisoners properly fed.

As the British army approached Bergen-Belsen, the Germans negotiated a truce and exclusion zone around the camp to prevent the spread of epidemic typhus.

The British were forced to implement a strict regime at the camp to stop the disease spreading, and measures taken even included the stationing of armed guards under typhus warning signs at the gates.

According to camp records, some 35,000 inmates died of the disease from January to April 1945, and when the British entered the camp, some 13,000 bodies still lay unburied. It is these corpses which were photographed being buried and bulldozed into mass graves, which have now become etched in the public mind as the "Holocaust."

Some 55,000 other inmates were however saved and removed after being deloused. The typhus epidemic was so bad that once the prisoners had been washed and deloused (by German doctors under Allied supervision), the entire camp was then burned to the ground by flamethrowers mounted on British army Bren carriers to kill the last

A British solder stands guard outside the Belsen camp after liberation. The warning sign is for visiting Allied soldiers not to drive too fast for fear of spreading typhus in the dust. Eventually, the British burned down the entire camp with flamethrowers to end the epidemic.

Allied soldiers supervise a mass burial at Bergen-Belsen. Horror scenes like these awaited the camp's liberators, and these images have come to exemplify the Holocaust. As terrible and as tragic as they were, the truth is that these unfortunate people died of the typhus epidemic which swept through many of the camps during the last months of the war, and not from any mass murder or genocide program. Zyklon-B, which had been used as a delousing agent, had been in short supply due to the Allied aerial bombardment of Germany's infrastructure. It is thus doubly ironic that the German inability to supply Zyklon-B delousing chemicals to Bergen-Belsen contributed to the typhus epidemic which caused these nightmarish scenes.

of the lice. Bergen-Belsen is thus a supreme and awful irony. The lice infestation grew out of control because the Germans were unable to ship enough Zyklon-B to the camp because of Allied bombing. The large number of deaths at Bergen-Belsen are therefore attributable to the lack of Zyklon-B at the camp—something which turns the entire "extermination" legend on its head.

It is also ironic that the awful scenes of death found at Bergen-Belsen were not the result of any "gas chambers" but are nonetheless used by the Holocaust storytellers to "prove" that genocide took place.

CHAPTER 20: "EYEWITNESS" ACCOUNTS

As shown above, the physical evidence for mass exterminations is simply not there, and, as a result, the Holocaust storytellers have relied on "holocaust survivors" and "eyewitness accounts" to bolster the allegations of "mass murder."

We have already seen how the Israeli Supreme Court dismissed all the Jewish "eyewitnesses" at the Demjanjuk Trial in Jerusalem as liars. This tendency to lie, exaggerate, and fabricate is the overriding characteristic of almost all "eyewitness" literature.

Section 109: Simon Wiesenthal's Faked "Memoirs"

One of the world's most famous Holocaust "survivors" was the Austrian Jew, Simon Wiesenthal. He claimed to have been interned at the Mauthausen camp and after the war, devoted his life to hunting ex-Nazis. Wiesenthal had an organization (which is still in existence), devoted to Jewish interests and promoting the mass extermination legend, named after him.

Yet it is a little known fact that Wiesenthal's own personal Holocaust memoirs, entitled *KZ Mauthausen, Bild und Wort* (Concentration Camp Mauthausen, Pictures and Words), published in 1946, contains one of the most blatant forgeries of all Holocaust memoirs.

Wiesenthal illustrated his book with drawings which he allegedly did either while in Mauthausen or from memory thereafter. One of the more famous pictures from his book is of three Jews, in their striped prisoner outfits, who had been shot at the stake by the Nazis.

Although Wiesenthal alleged in his book that the drawing of the three shot Jews occurred in Mauthausen, the pictures were in reality plagiarized from a series of photographs which appeared in *Life* magazine of June 11, 1945.

The title page of "Nazi hunter" and "Holocaust survivor" Simon Wiesenthal's memoirs, KZ *Mauthausen: Bild und Wort (Concentration Camp Mauthausen: Pictures and Words, Vienna, 1946) and an illustration in the book, drawn by Wiesenthal with his signature at the bottom. The illustration purports to be the shooting of three Jews Wiesenthal "witnessed" while imprisoned in the camp.*

Fact or Fiction?

LIFE

TEEN-AGE BOYS

JUNE 11, 1945 — 10 CENTS
BY SUBSCRIPTION: TWO YEARS $8.50

In the death march the Germans walked to the place of execution between MPs. The prisoners are not wearing regular PW clothes but GI denim fatigues that were painted with blue stripes.

Behind cell block prisoners are bound to stakes by MPs. Just before execution, spies were allowed a last request and they chose meal of U. S. Army meat-and-vegetable hash.

FIRING SQUAD
Army executes three German spies who were caught in U.S. uniforms

During Nazi breakthrough at Bastogne last December the Germans managed to smuggle some of their intelligence officers behind U. S. lines. Three of these spies were captured, tried and shot. Last week the War Department released pictures on this and the following pages, taken by LIFE Photographer Johnny Florea, which show their speedy execution.

The Nazis were carefully groomed for their dangerous mission. They spoke excellent English and their slang had been tuned up by close association with American prisoners of war in German camps. Wearing U. S. uniforms, carrying a radio transmitter and receiver, they infiltrated U. S. positions to reconnoiter roads and bridges along the Meuse and to report on the deployment of Allied forces. Under the rules of the Hague Convention these Germans were classifiable as spies and subject to immediate court martial by a military tribunal. After brief deliberation American officers found them guilty, ordered the usual penalty for spies: quick death by the firing squad.

The volley is fired and three white puffs of smoke appear against the wall of the concrete cell block. The initial burst killed all three almost instantaneously. The firing squad, all military police, consisted of three groups of eight men, each with one additional marksman along as a spare. They used carbines capable of firing 15 cartridges without reloading.

CONTINUED ON NEXT PAGE 47

BING CROSBY says:

"I'll be a Glad Dad...
...when my four little shavers give me Personna Blades on Father's Day!"

"Most of the year, our four little tykes are gang-busters at heart. But on Father's Day, they soften up long enough to come across with a present Pop. Being smart little shavers, they can recognize a first-class hint when they get one. So on June 17..."

"**Surprise me** with Personna Blades, our keenness foursome, and life with father will be more melodious than ever! Personna's close, smooth shaves make every morning a beautiful one. Give your Dad Personna Blades, and he'll probably sing like Bing!"

See "THE GREAT JOHN L." a Bing Crosby Production

PERSONNA
Precision Blades

Personna, 599 Madison Ave., N.Y. 22. Available also in Canada.

Firing Squad CONTINUED

Last preparations are carried out. Each prisoner is securely bound, hand and foot, to a stake in front of concrete wall (top). After the blindfolding, a large white paper target is pinned over spy's heart (middle). When prisoner is ready for death (bottom), MPs stand at attention until squad's commanding officer inspects final arrangements.

CONTINUED ON PAGE 50

50

THEY'RE CUT TO FIT...TO FIGHT FATIGUE

"Smartest move I ever made... changing to REIS Scandals"

Treat yourself to Scandals comfort! Enjoy the manly underwear that's scientifically designed and cut to follow male anatomy. Reis Scandals, with the exclusive Dart-stitched pouch, provide the mild, athletic support that helps fight fatigue... keeps you looking and feeling your trim best. Exclusive "Hi-waist" design for perfect fit. Concealed no-gap fly. Seamless seat for extra comfort. Should you find your dealer temporarily out of Scandals—blame the Japs (war needs get first call on our production)—and ask again later.

FULL SEAT Covers you better and seems to sit on.

MATCHING SHIRT absorbs perspiration. Cut to follow leg line of Scandals.

REIS
UNDERWEAR PAJAMAS   SPORTSWEAR NECKWEAR

ROBERT REIS & COMPANY · 2 PARK AVENUE · NEW YORK 16, N.Y.

Firing Squad CONTINUED

After execution, spies lurch back and sag forward from the posts. The cement wall is pocked with bullet holes. The prisoners refused the ministrations of a U.S. chaplain. They kept up their nerve by singing patriotic German songs. After they were officially pronounced dead, the spies were cut down by MPs, carried away and buried.

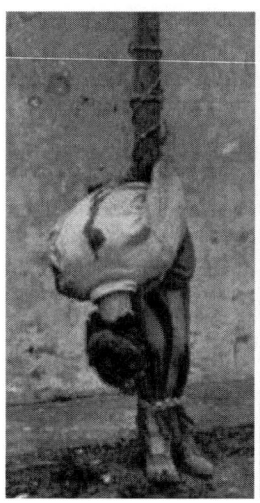

The series of photographs were of German soldiers, captured during the "Battle of the Bulge" wearing American uniforms, and executed by firing squad as allowed by the Geneva Convention.

Wiesenthal copied his picture of "three shot Jews" from this *Life* photo essay, as can be seen in the illustrations on the previous page and above.

Section 110: The *Diary of Anne Frank*—Father Admits "Transcribing" to "Explain" Ball Point Pen Use

One of the most celebrated "Holocaust" books is the so-called *Diary of Anne Frank*, first published in 1947, and supposedly the work of a young Jewish girl written while her family and four other Jews were hiding in a factory during the German occupation of Holland.

Eventually the eight were arrested and detained in various concentration camps. Anne Frank died in Bergen-Belsen of typhus, by which time she was fifteen. When Auschwitz was liberated by the Russians, her father Otto Frank was being treated for typhus in the camp hospital, and he died in 1980.

Life Magazine of August 18, 1958, carried a photograph of Anne Frank on the cover against the background of what is clearly and unquestionably the childlike non-cursive handwriting of a very young girl.

However, other published examples of the handwriting from the diary—including a large poster set up in front of the "Anne Frank School" in Amsterdam, clearly show the handwriting of an adult.

This fact alone showed that the diary was clearly not written by Anne, or at the very least, that large portions of it were written by someone else, most likely her father, Otto.

Eventually, in 1993, Otto Frank was forced to admit in an Amsterdam court that the handwriting was in fact his, and not that of Anne's. He explained that he had "transcribed" Anne's diary before publication, and this was why the handwriting was his. Furthermore, Otto Frank announced, he had actually only published a "novel" called *The Annex: Diary Notes 14 June 1942 —1 August 1944* (in Dutch, *Het Achterhuis. Dagboekbrieven 14 juni 1942 —1 augustus 1944*) and had never called it the "Diary of Anne Frank." The title *Anne Frank: The Diary of a Young Girl* had been given to the book's first English translation.

This "transcription" by Otto Frank finally explained the 1980 report by the German Bundeskriminalamt (Federal Criminal Investigation Bureau, or BKA) which showed that portions of the dairy had been altered or added after 1951. The manuscript was examined on orders of a West German court as the result of a libel action brought by Otto Frank against a German publisher who had claimed the book was a fraud.

The manuscript, in the form of three hardbound notebooks and 324 loose pages bound in a fourth notebook, was examined with special equipment.

The results of tests performed at the BKA laboratories show that portions of the work, especially of the fourth volume, were written with a ballpoint pen. As ballpoint pens were not commercially available until after the war, the BKA concluded that those sections were added after Anne Frank died.

Otto Frank's 1993 admission that he had transcribed the work not only finally explained the ballpoint pen writing, but why the subject matter of the diaries also shows an adult hand at work.

Early in the book, the diary contains an essay on why a 13-year-old girl would start a diary, which is then followed by a short history of the Frank family and a review of the anti-Jewish measures in Holland which followed the German occupation in 1940. To think that a 13-year-old would assemble a factual historical account in a diary is improbable to say the least.

There is no doubt that Anne Frank had a diary. It would however have been a perfectly normal 13-year-old's work. The diary which has been sold to the world as a "witness to the Holocaust" is however, an obvious exaggeration and alteration of the original work by an adult.

Finally, it should be noted that Anne Frank died of typhus and was not "gassed." It is one of the horrific ironies of the war that Anne Frank died due to a lack of Zyklon-B at Bergen-Belsen—and this lack was caused directly by the Allied bombing campaign. The real story of Anne Frank is tragic enough, but the cruel exploitation, exaggeration, and faking of her diary by the Holocaust storytellers is a scandal of epic proportions.

Section 111: Rudolf Vrba's "I Cannot Forgive"

One of the more famous "eyewitnesses" is Rudolf Vrba, who in 1985 was an assistant professor at the Canadian University of British Columbia. Vrba's testimony has formed the basis of most, if not all, descriptions of the gas chambers of Auschwitz.

However, in 1985, during a trial of a holocaust revisionist in Toronto, Vrba testified that his book, *I Cannot Forgive*, which contained all his eyewitness accounts was "an artistic picture" and that he himself had in fact never witnessed any gassings ("Book 'An Artistic Picture': Survivor never saw actual gassing deaths," *Toronto Star*, January 24, 1985).

Pushed on the point, Vrba admitted that he never witnessed anybody being gassed to death and his book about Auschwitz-Birkenau is only "an artistic picture... not a document for a court" (*ibid*). Vrba told the trial that his written and pictorial descriptions of the Auschwitz crematoria and gas chambers are based on "what I heard it might look like."

He said that his 1944 drawings of the "Auschwitz camp layout were inexact."

Vrba, who escaped the camp in Poland in 1944, insisted however he had made an accurate ("within 10%") estimates of 1,765,000 mass-murder victims up to that point.

Section 112: Olga Lengyel's "Five Chimneys"

The blurb on the back cover of Olga Lengyel's *Five Chimneys: a woman survivor's true story of Auschwitz* (Granada/ Ziff-Davis, 1947, 1972), quotes the *New York Herald-Tribune:* "Passionate, tormenting."

Albert Einstein is quoted: "You have done a real service by letting the ones who are now silent and most forgotten [sic] speak."

So what does Lengyel say? "After June, 1943, the gas chamber was reserved exclusively for Jews and Gypsies.

Two images which conclusively prove that Anne Frank did not write the diary which was published in her name. Left, the handwriting of Anne Frank was published on the front page of Life *magazine on August 18, 1958, along with a photograph she had taken of herself. The childish scrawl is in marked contrast to the adult's handwriting of large parts of the diary, as illustrated on the right. The picture is of the front of the Anne Frank School in Amsterdam, where the building facade contains a copy of a page from the diary, allegedly written by Anne and ending with the signature "Anne M Frank."*

was all the time it took to reduce human flesh to ashes, made 720 per hour, or 17,280 corpses per twenty-four hour shift. And the ovens, with murderous efficiency, functioned day and night. However, one must also reckon the death pits, which could destroy another 8,000 cadavers a day. In round numbers, about 24,000 corpses were handled each day. An admirable production record, one that speaks well for German industry" (ibid.., pp. 80–81).

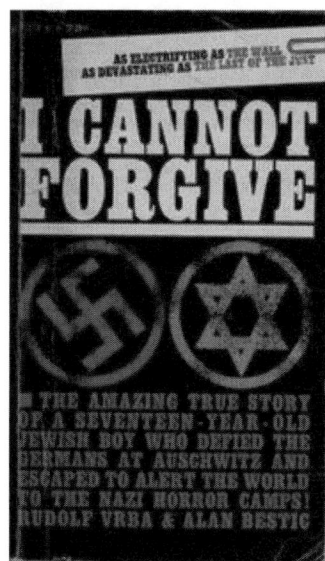

This implies almost 100,000 corpses per four working days, or a million in 40 days, or six million in 240 days (eight months). This is, of course, simply impossible.

Section 113: Kitty Hart's "Return to Auschwitz"

In her book, *Return to Auschwitz* (Granada, London, 1983), Kitty Hart wrote the following: "Working around the clock, the four units together could dispose of about 18,000 bodies every twenty-four hours, while the open pits coped with a further 8,000 in the same period" (ibid., p. 118). This means 26,000 bodies every 24 hours, or 182,000 every week, reaching the magic 6 million figure in an astonishing 33 weeks, or eight months.

Her book deals with "gassing" in just one paragraph on page 112 and in a film version, made especially for television, she claims that she was sunbathing (!) opposite Auschwitz-Birkenau crematorium number 4 when she witnessed an SS man climbing up a ladder and tipping in Zyklon-B, and human ashes coming out "10 minutes later."

The flaws are obvious: what was a Jewess doing "sunbathing" at an "extermination camp" and if the "gassing" story was true, then it would be impossible to kill and cremate people in ten minutes. Despite this, *Return to Auschwitz* is still used as "evidence" of the "Holocaust."

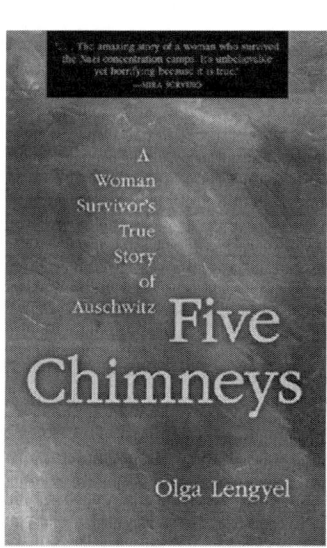

Section 114: Martin Gray's "For Those I Loved"

In addition to the wild exaggerations contained in "eyewitness" survivor memoirs, an entire genre of outright faked accounts have become widely circulated and believed, even though they have all been formally debunked and exposed as such by the official "Holocaust historians."

The book *For Those I Loved* by Martin Gray (Bodley Head, 1973), purported to be an account of the Treblinka camp. Gray specialized in selling fake antiques to America before turning to concentration camp memoirs, although he waited twenty-eight years before producing his "eyewitness" account.

Although it was made into a film and remains a "best seller," the "Holocaust historians" have soundly rejected the book as a fake. In *The New Statesman* magazine of November 2, 1979, "Holocaust expert" Gitta Sereny (who also produced the Franz Stangl "memoirs") wrote in a review of Gray's book: "Gray's *For Those I Loved* was the work of Max Gallo the ghostwriter, who also produced *Papillon*. During the research for a *Sunday Times* inquiry into Gray's work, M. Gallo informed me coolly that he 'needed' a long chapter on Treblinka because the book required something strong for pulling in readers. When I myself told Gray, the 'author,' that he had manifestly never been to, nor escaped from Treblinka, he finally asked, despairingly, 'But does it matter? Wasn't the only thing that Treblinka did happen, that it should be written about, and that some Jews should be shown to have been heroic?'" (Gitta Sereny, "The Men Who Whitewash Hitler," *The New Statesman,* Vol. 98, No. 2537, November 2, 1979, pp. 670–73).

Section 115: Jean Francis Steiner's "Treblinka"

In the same *New Statesman* article, Sereny also condemned Jean François Steiner's book, *Treblinka,* in the following manner:

"Worse again are the partial or complete fakes such as Jean Francis Steiner's *Treblinka* or Martin Gray's *For Those I Loved.* Steiner's book on the surface even seems right: he is a man of talent and conviction, and it is hard to know how he could go so wrong. But what he finally produced was a hodgepodge of truth

and falsehood, libeling both the dead and the living. The original French book had to be withdrawn and reissued with all the names changed. But it retains its format of imagined conversations and reactions—i.e. pure fiction— incredibly remaining nonetheless, in serious bibliographies" (*ibid*).

Section 116: Miklos Nyiszli's "Auschwitz: A Doctor's Eyewitness Account"

The book *Auschwitz: A Doctor's Eyewitness Account* by Miklos Nyiszli was first published in installments by the Hungarian magazine *Vilag* ("World") from February 16, 1947 to April 5, 1947. Its original title was *I Was Mengele's Autopsy Doctor in Auschwitz: A Hungarian Doctor's Diary from Hell*. This book claimed that Auschwitz killed 20,000 people every day in its gas chambers (!) which had been in operation from 1940 to 1944.

At the rate of 20,000 per day, for four years, this would have amounted to an astonishing 29 million dead.

Of course, not even the Holocaust storytellers claim that the gas chambers were built in 1940.

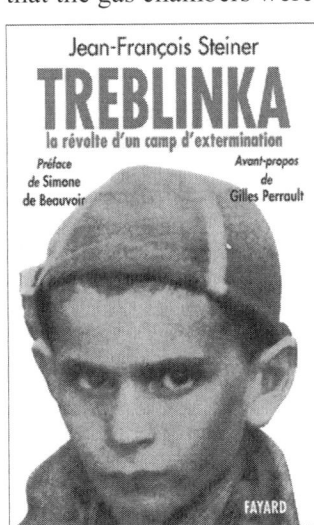

There are also numerous other obvious errors in this "eyewitness account" including a claim that the "undressing room" in which it is alleged that the victims disrobed was "200 yards long" (in fact there is no such building of that size in the crematoria complex); that "four elevators" moved the bodies from the "gas chambers" to the crematorium and that the camp held an incredible 500,000 inmates.

The preposterous nature of the latter claim was quickly recognized, and when the book was translated into English, the 500,000 figure was "edited" down to 100,000.

However, the English version retains to the present day a large number of errors and outrageous claims which reveal that the book is an obvious forgery:

- He claimed (page 23) that Auschwitz is in Germany (it is in Poland);
- He claimed (page 23) that the crematoria chimneys had "enormous tongues of flame" rising from them. (In fact, crematorium chimneys do not belch fire, but only issue smoke.) This "flaming chimney stack" lie has become a firm favorite of the Holocaust storytellers.
- He claimed that Gypsies (!) were used to police the Jews in the camp (chapter 4).
- He claimed (chapter 7) that after gassing, the bodies in the "gas chamber" were piled in a heap to the ceiling and that the "Sonderkommando squad, outfitted with large rubber boots, lined up around the hill of bodies and flooded it with powerful jets of water. This was necessary because the final act of those who die by drowning or by gas is an involuntary defecation. Each body was befouled, and had to be washed."

There is, of course, no drainage system either in the original architect's plans of any of the crematory buildings, or in any of the ruins today, which could cope with the simultaneous defecation of 3,000 people.

The morgue building (which was claimed to have been the "gas chamber") would quickly have filled to the brim with excrement after just one or two "mass gassings." The allegation is patently absurd.

Finally, in chapter 6, Nyiszli said that the Sonderkommando, those Jews allegedly assigned the task of removing the bodies from the "gas chambers," were "never permitted to leave the grounds of the crematorium, and every four months, when they had learned too much about the place for their own good, they were liquidated. Till now such had been the fate of every Sonderkommando since the founding of the KZ; this explains why no one had ever escaped to tell the world what had been taking place inside these grim walls for the past several years."

This last statement is of significance for the next "eyewitness" account, that of Filip Müller.

Section 117: Filip Müller's "Eyewitness Auschwitz: Three Years in the Gas Chambers"

Another Holocaust potboiler is "survivor" Filip Müller's *Eyewitness Auschwitz: Three Years in the Gas Chambers* (Stein & Day, 1979).

This book is quoted as "fact" by the US Holocaust Museum as one of its main sources for descriptions of the Auschwitz "gas chambers." Müller claimed to have been a member of the "Sonderkommando" (a Jewish prisoner detachment which was allegedly tasked with removing bodies from the "gas chambers").

Even though all the official Holocaust storytellers claim that the Nazis routinely killed all Sonderkommando members every few months to "hide their crimes" (see Nyiszli's reference above), Müller claimed to have avoided execution and witnessed "gassings of a million Jews" over an incredible three year period (!) working in the Sonderkommando. The first problem with Müller's book is that despite his unique and breathtaking "experiences," he inexplicably waited thirty years before writing them down.

The second problem is that Müller's book is simply a plagiarism of Nyiszli's book! This is obvious from a cursory overview of portions of the two books, with entire sections repeated verbatim. Some examples suffice to illustrate:

Nyiszli: "Fate has imposed the cruelest duty upon us, to collaborate in the annihilation of our people, before we ourselves become ashes."

Müller: "A cruel and awful fate has forced us to collaborate in the extermination of our people, before we ourselves become ashes."

Nyiszli: "Our eyes, blinded by tears, would seek in vain for our annihilated relatives."

Müller: "We would seek our annihilated relatives in vain."

Nyiszli: "Heaven has not opened, no rain strong enough to extinguish the funeral pyres built by the hands of men has fallen."

Müller: "No miracle has taken place. Heaven has sent no avenging lightning, nor has it let fall any rain strong enough to stifle the funeral pyres built by the hands of men."

Nyiszli: "This is a trial which the Lord has sent us. To seek the reasons is not the business of us humans, who are nothing compared to the Almighty God."

Müller: "With Jewish resignation we must now accept the irrevocable. This is the last trial which Heaven to has sent us. To ask the reasons is not for us, since we are nothing compared to Almighty God."

And so on. It is clear that Müller simply copied Nyiszli's book, added a few parts and claimed to have been a miraculous "eyewitness" to Auschwitz. The parts which Müller added are incredulous, and it is staggering that anyone takes them seriously.

Amongst other things, Müller says that SS doctors would slice off bits of the [dead] gassees' flesh, which would then "jump around in buckets," (p.47); That there was a striptease in the "gas chamber" (p.87);

That the chief gasser, a man he names as Moll, and his dog, were sexually excited by a gassing (p.141);

And that babies were flung into pits of sizzling human fat (p.142).

It is incredible that this book is taken as a serious account of the "gas chambers" and Auschwitz. Or then again, perhaps it is not.

Section 118: Truthful Survivor Books Not Given Prominence

The Holocaust industry continues to churn out ever more "new" Holocaust survivor tales, although they are patently made-up stories based on the first set of "survivor" books outlined above.

Those survivor books which do not support the official line are, by way of contrast, consigned to the rubbish heap.

For example, the book *Under Two Dictators* (London, 1949) by Margarete Buber is a story of a woman unfortunate enough to spend time in both a Russian prison camp and Ravensbrück, the German camp for female detainees, in August 1940.

She noted that she was the only person in her contingent of deportees from Russia who was not straight away released by the Gestapo.

Her book presents a striking contrast between the camps of Soviet Russia and Germany: compared to the squalor, disorder, and starvation of the Russian camp, she found Ravensbrück to be clean, civilized, and well administered.

Regular baths and clean linen seemed a luxury after her earlier experiences, and her first meal of white bread, sausage, sweet porridge, and dried fruit prompted her to inquire of another camp inmate whether August 3rd, 1940, was some sort of holiday or special occasion.

She observed, too, that the barracks at Ravensbrück were remarkably spacious compared to the crowded mud huts of the Soviet camp.

In the final months of 1945, she experienced the progressive decline of camp conditions which she described in detail and which were common throughout the camp system, as outlined earlier.

Another account which is at total variance with popular propaganda is *Die Gestapo Lässt Bitten* (The Gestapo Invites You) by Charlotte Bormann, a Communist political prisoner who was also interned at Ravensbrück. Undoubtedly, its most important revelation is the author's statement that rumors of gas executions were deliberate and malicious inventions circulated among the prisoners by the Communists.

A further shocking reflection on the postwar trials is the fact that Charlotte Bormann was not permitted to testify at the Rastadt Trial of Ravensbrück camp personnel in the French occupation zone.

This was the usual fate of anyone who denied the extermination legend: they were just ignored.

Section 119: Paul Rassinier—The Holocaust Victim Who Argued Against the "Gas Chambers"

One of the most remarkable memoirs which the Holocaust storytellers have deliberately ignored is that of the French historian, Professor Paul Rassinier, who was a Socialist intellectual and anti-Nazi.

From 1933 until 1943, Rassinier was a professor of history in the Collège d'enseignement général at Belfort, Académie de Besançon. During the war he engaged in resistance activity until he was arrested by the Gestapo on October 30th, 1943, and as a result was imprisoned in the German concentration camps at Buchenwald and Dora until 1945.

At Buchenwald, toward the end of the war, he contracted typhus, which so damaged his health that he could not resume his teaching. After the war, Rassinier was awarded the Médaille de la Résistance et de la Reconnaisance Française, and was elected to the French Chamber of Deputies.

Rassinier published his memoirs, titled *Crossing the Line* (Paris: Editions Bressanes, 1949 and 1950), which was an account of his experience in Buchenwald.

It was a best seller of the time and was notable for its revelation that many brutalities in the camp were committed not by the SS, but by the mainly Communist prisoners who took over the internal affairs of the camps for their own benefit.

Rassinier blamed the high death rate at the two camps he saw on their corruption.

The fame which this memoir attracted soon focused his attention on other "survivor" accounts of Buchenwald, all of which claimed that there had been a gas chamber at that camp.

As he was a former detainee, Rassinier knew that these claims were false, and in 1949 published a second book, *Le Mensonge d'Ulysse* (The Lies of Ulysses, Paris, 1949) in which he made short work of the extravagant claims about gas chambers at Buchenwald in David Rousset's *The Other Kingdom* (New York, 1947). Rassinier also confronted another "survivor eyewitness," Abbé Jean-Paul Renard and asked him how he could possibly have testified in his book *Chaînes et Lumières* that gas chambers were in operation at Buchenwald. Renard replied that others had told him of their existence, and hence he had been willing to pose as a witness of things that he had never seen (ibid., p. 209 ff).

French anti-Nazi and resistance fighter Paul Rassinier was arrested by the Gestapo and imprisoned in Buchenwald concentration camp. After the war, he was elected to the French National Assembly and awarded heroism medals. He was shocked to find that others claimed that there were gas chambers at Buchenwald, something he knew was a lie because of his internment there. Rassinier spent the rest of his life exposing the lies behind the "Holocaust" and, as a result, his memoirs of interment at Buchenwald are ignored by the Holocaust storytellers.

Rassinier also investigated Denise Dufournier's *Ravensbrück: The Women's Camp of Death* (London, 1948), and again found that the authoress had no other evidence for gas chambers there than vague "rumors," which Charlotte Bormann stated were deliberately spread by Communist political prisoners.

Similar investigations were made of such books as Philip Friedman's *This was Auschwitz: The Story of a Murder Camp* (N.Y., 1946), and Eugen Kogon's *The Theory and Practice of Hell* (N.Y., 1950), and he found that none of these authors could produce an authentic eyewitness of a gas chamber at Auschwitz, nor had they themselves actually seen one.

Rassinier also mentioned Kogon's claim that a deceased former inmate, Janda Weiss, had said to Kogon alone that she had witnessed gas chambers at Auschwitz, but of course, since this person was untraceable, Rassinier was unable to investigate the claim.

He was able to interview Benedikt Kautsky, author of *Teufel und Verdammte,* who had alleged that millions of Jews were exterminated at Auschwitz. However, Kautsky only confirmed to Rassinier the confession in his book, namely that never at any time had he seen a gas chamber, and that he had based his information on what others had "told him." Rassinier also produced three other books, *Ulysse trahi par les Siens* (1960), which further refuted the impostures of propagandists concerning German concentration camps; *Le Véritable Procès Eichmann* (1962), which revealed the distortions around the Eichmann trial and *Le Drame des Juifs Européens* (1964), in which he exposed the dishonest and reckless distortions concerning the fate of the Jews by a careful statistical analysis. The last work also examined the political and financial significance of the extermination legend and its exploitation by Israel and the Communist powers.

Not surprisingly, Rassinier's eyewitness testimony is never quoted by the Holocaust Industry, even though he was a bona fide victim who could never be accused of being a "Nazi sympathizer."

Section 120: Martin Gilbert's "Auschwitz and the Allies"

Although not a survivor, Martin Gilbert was a well-known Jewish writer and biographer of Winston Churchill, holding a senior and supposedly respected position within the academic community, who also glibly passed off the most outrageous figures with regard to Auschwitz in his book *Auschwitz and the Allies* (Gilbert, Martin, New York: Henry Holt, 1981).

In this book he states: "The deliberate attempt to destroy systematically all of Europe's Jews was unsuspected in the spring and early summer of 1942: the very period during which it was at its most intense, and during which hundreds of thousands of Jews were being gassed every day at Belzec, Chelmo, Sobibór and Treblinka" (ibid., p.26).

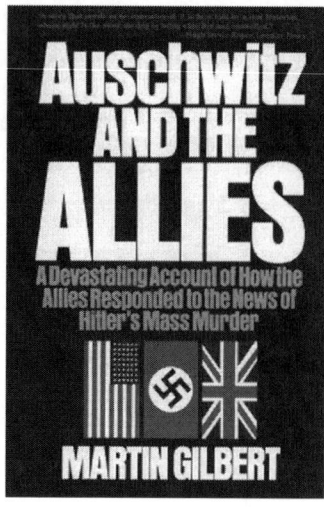

If it is assumed, according to Gilbert's figures, that a minimum of 200,000 Jews per day were being gassed (he says "hundreds of thousands"), this amounts to one million every five days, or six million in thirty days. This is obviously impossible, and makes a complete mockery of the supposed "academics" who claim to be authorities on the Holocaust.

CHAPTER 21: OUTLANDISH HOLOCAUST CLAIMS

By now, the reader should have gained an appreciation of the incredible and quite unbelievable allegations made about the Six Million story. As amazing as it may sound, the allegations already discussed—and refuted—actually consist of the more "sane" accusations made against the Nazis. Herewith follow some of the completely insane allegations, all of which have been made in print by "survivors" who seem to be at liberty to make any sort of claim, expecting not to be questioned at all.

Section 121: Bears and Eagles in Cages Eating Jews; Jewish "Soap Burial" in Atlanta, USA; Sausages Made out of Jews; Mummified Thumbs as Light Switches; "Pedal-driven Brain-bashing Machines"—And More, All in Nuremberg Court as "Evidence."

As the reader will see, the claims are so outlandish that they are not even worth refuting. But remember, these are all allegations which have been made in all seriousness in major publications dealing with the Holocaust Story—including the official records of the International Military Tribunal (*IMT*) of the Nuremberg Trials.

The outlandish claims include:
- A child surviving six gassings in a gas chamber that never existed (Moshe Peer, regarding Bergen-Belsen, in K. Seidman, "Surviving the horror", *The Gazette,* Montreal, Canada, August 5, 1993.);
- A woman survived three gassings because Nazis kept running out of gas (*Montreal Gazette*, February 10, 2000.);
- A claim about a bear and an eagle in a cage, eating one Jew per day (Morris Hubert about Buchenwald,

- acc. to Ari L. Goldman, "Time 'Too Painful' to Remember", *New York Times,* November 10, 1988: "'In the camp there was a cage with a bear and an eagle,' he said. 'Every day, they would throw a Jew in there. The bear would tear him apart and the eagle would pick at his bones.'");
- Mass graves expelling geysers of blood (A. Rückerl, *Nationalsozialistische Vernichtungslager im Spiegel deutscher Strafprozesse,* dtv, Munich 1978, p. 273f.; E. Wiesel, *Paroles d'Etranger*, Edition du Seuil, Paris 1982, p. 86; Wiesel, *The Jews of Silence*, New American Library, New York 1972, p. 48; H. Arendt, *Eichmann in Jerusalem*, Reclam, Leipzig 1990, p. 184; B. Naumann, *Auschwitz, Athenäum*, Frankfurt/Main 1968 p. 214.);
- Erupting and exploding mass graves (Michael A. Musmanno, *The Eichmann Kommandos,* Peter Davies, London 1962, pp. 152f.);
- Soap production from human fat with the imprint "RIF"—"Reine Juden Seife" (pure Jewish soap), solemn burial of soap (This imprint really meant "Reichstelle für Industrielle Fettversorgung," Imperial Office for Industrial Fat Supplies, see S. Wiesenthal, *Der neue Weg* (Vienna), 15/16 & 17/18, 1946; Career affidavit of SS-Hauptsturmführer Dr. Konrad Morgen, National Archives, Record Group 28, No 5741, Office of Chief Counsel for War Crimes, December 19, 1947; Filip Friedman, *This Was Oswiecim. The Story of a Murder Camp*, United Jewish Relief Appeal, London 1946.; the Greenwood Cemetery in Atlanta, Georgia, USA, has a Holocaust-memorial gravestone with the inscription "Here rest four bars of human soap, the last earthly remains of Jewish victims of the Holocaust.");
- The SS made sausage in the crematoria out of human flesh (David Olère, in J.-C. Pressac, *Auschwitz: Technique and Operation of the Gas Chambers*, Beate Klarsfeld Foundation, New York 1989, p. 554, fourth column, lines 17–22.);
- Lampshades, book covers, driving gloves for SS officers, saddles, riding breeches, house slippers, and ladies' handbags of human skin (*International Military Tribunal, Trial of the Major War Criminals*, (*IMT*), Nuremberg 1947, v. XXXII, pp. 258, 259, 261, 263, 265, v. III, p. 515; v. XXX, pp. 352, 355; v. VI, p. 311; v. V, p. 171.);
- Pornographic pictures on canvasses made of human skin (*Ibid.*, v. XXX, p. 469.);
- Mummified human thumbs were used as light switches in the house of Ilse Koch, wife of KL commander Koch (Buchenwald) (Kurt Glass, *New York Times*, April 10. 1995.);
- Production of shrunken heads from bodies of inmates (H. Langbein, *Der Auschwitz-Prozeß*, Europäische Verlagsanstalt, Frankfurt/Main 1965, v. III, p. 516, v. XXXII, p. 267-271.);
- Acid or boiling-water baths to produce human skeletons (F. Müller, in H. Langbein, *op. cit*, v. 1, p. 87; witness Wells in the Eichmann Trial, in F. J. Scheidl, *Geschichte der Verfemung Deutschlands,* pub. by author, Vienna 1967, v. 4, p. 236; Lawrence L. Lange, "Pre-empting the Holocaust", *The Atlantic Monthly,* November 1998, p. 107.);
- Muscles cut from the legs of executed inmates contracted so strongly that they made the buckets jump about (F. Müller, in H. Langbein, *op. cit.*, v. 1, p. 74);
- An SS-father pot-shooting babies thrown into the air while 9-year-old SS-daughter applauds and shrieks: "Papa, do it again; do it again, Papa!" (*IMT*, *op. cit.* v. VII, p. 451.);
- Jewish children used by Hitler Youth for target practice (*Ibid.* p. 447f.);
- Wagons disappearing on an incline into the underground crematoria in Auschwitz (such facilities never existed) (SS-judge Konrad Morgen, acc. to Danuta Czech, *Auschwitz Chronicle*, 1939-1945, Henry Holt, New York, 1990, p. 818.);
- Forcing prisoners to lick stairs clean, and collect garbage with their lips (*IMT*, *op. cit.*, v. VII, p. 491.);
- Injections into the eyes of inmates to change their eye color (H. Langbein, *Menschen in Auschwitz, op. cit.*, pp. 383f.);
- First artificially fertilize women at Auschwitz, then gas them (*IMT*, *op. cit.*, v. V, p. 403.);
- Torturing people in specially mass-produced "torture boxes" made by Krupp (*Ibid.*, v. XVI, pp. 556f.; v. XVI, pp. 561, 546.);
- Torturing people by shooting at them with wooden bullets to make them talk (World Jewish Congress et al. (eds.), *The Black Book: The Nazi Crime Against the Jewish People,* New York 1946, p 269.);
- Smacking people with special spanking machines (*IMT*, *op. cit.*, v. VI, p. 213.);
- Killing by drinking a glass of liquid hydrogen cyanide (which, scientifically considered, evaporates quickly and would endanger those who pouring it into said glass) (Verdict of the Hannover District Court, Ref. 2 Ks 1/60; cf. H. Lichtenstein, *Im Namen des Volkes?* Bund, Cologne 1984, p. 83.);
- Killing people with poisoned soft drinks (*IMT, op. cit.*, v. VII, p. 570.);
- Underground mass extermination in enormous

rooms, by means of high voltage electricity (S. Szende, *Der letzte Jude aus Polen*, Europa-Verlag, Zürich 1945; S. Wiesenthal, *Der neue Weg* (Vienna), 19/20, 1946; *IMT, op. cit.*, v. VII, 576–577, 369, for Bergen-Belsen!; *The Black Book of Polish Jewry*, Roy Publishers, New York 1943, p. 313.);
- Blast 20,000 Jews into the twilight zone with atomic bombs (*IMT, op. cit.*, v. XVI, p. 529.);
- Killing in vacuum chamber, hot steam, or chlorine gas (W. Grossmann, *Die Hölle von Treblinka*, Verlag für fremdsprachige Literatur, Moscow 1947; *The Black Book of Polish Jewry, op. cit.*);
- Mass murder in hot steam chamber (*IMT, op. cit.*, v. XXXII, pp. 153–158.);
- Mass murder by tree cutting: forcing people to climb trees, then cutting the trees down (*IMT, op. cit.*, v. VII, p. 582; Eugen Kogon, *The Theory and Practice of Hell*, Berkley Medallion (NY) 1960, p. 99.);
- Killing a boy by forcing him to eat sand (Rudolf Reder, *Belzec*, Kraków 1946, p. 16; found in Martin Gilbert, *The Holocaust*, Holt, Rinehart and Winston, New York 1985, p. 419.);
- Gassing Soviet POWs in a quarry (*IMT, op. cit.*, v. VII, p. 388.);
- Gas chambers on wheels in Treblinka, which dumped their victims directly into burning pits; delayed-action poison gas that allowed the victims to leave the gas chambers and walk to the mass graves by themselves (Reports of the Polish underground movement, *Archiv der Polnischen Vereinigten Arbeiterpartei*, 202/III, v. 7, pp. 120f., quoted in P. Longerich (ed.), *Die Ermordung der europäischen Juden*, Piper, Munich 1990, p. 438.);
- Rapid-construction portable gas chamber sheds (R. Aschenauer (ed.), *Ich, Adolf Eichmann*, Druffel, Leoni 1980, pp. 179f.);

The "bars of soap" graves in the Greenwood Jewish Cemetery, Atlanta, Georgia, USA. It is has long since been admitted that the Nazis never made soap out of Jews, but the legend persists as part of the broader Holocaust myth.

- Beating people to death, then carrying out autopsies to see why they died (*IMT, op. cit.*, v. V, p. 199.);
- Introduction of Zyklon gas into the gas chambers of Auschwitz through shower-heads or from steel bottles (M. Scheckter and a report of June 4, 1945, written by an officer of the 2nd Armored Division, about Auschwitz; *Französisches Büro des Informationsdienstes über Kriegsverbrechen (ed.), Konzentrationslager Dokument 321*, Reprint 2001, Frankfurt/Main 1993, p. 184, Wolfgang Benz, (ed.), *Dimension des Völkermords*, Oldenbourg, Munich 1991, p. 462.);
- Electrical conveyor-belt executions (*Pravda*, Feb. 2, 1945.);
- Bashing people's brains in with a pedal-driven brain-bashing machine while listening to the radio (*IMT, op. cit.*, v. VII, pp. 376f.);
- Cremation of bodies in blast furnaces (H. von Moltke, *Briefe an Freya 1939–1945*, Beck, Munich 1988, p. 420; cf. P. Longerich (ed.), *op. cit.*, p. 435; *Pravda*, Feb. 2, 1945.);
- Cremation of human bodies using no fuel at all (*IMT, op. cit.*, v. XX, p. 494.);
- Skimming off boiling human fat from open-air cremation fires (R. Höß, in M. Broszat (ed.), *Kommandant in Auschwitz*, dtv, Munich 1983, p. 130; H. Tauber, in J.-C. Pressac, *op. cit.*, pp. 489f.; F. Müller, *Sonderbehandlung*, Steinhausen, Munich 1979, pp. 207f., 217ff.; H. Langbein, *Menschen in Auschwitz, op. cit.*, p. 148; B. Naumann, *op. cit.*, pp. 10, 334f., 443; S. Steinberg, according to *Französisches Büro des Informationsdienstes über Kriegsverbrechen* (ed.), *op. cit.*, p. 206.);
- Mass graves containing hundreds of thousands of bodies, removed without a trace within a few weeks (*IMT, op. cit.*, v. XX, p. 494.);
- Killing 840,000 Russian POWs at Sachsenhausen, and burning the bodies in four portable ovens (*IMT, op. cit.*, v. VII, p. 586.);
- Removal of corpses by means of blasting, i.e., blowing them up (R. Höß, in M. Broszat (ed.), *Kommandant in Auschwitz*, dtv, Munich 1983, pp. 161f.; A. Rückerl, *NS-Verbrechen vor Gericht*, C. F. Müller, Heidelberg 1984, p. 78; H. Grabitz, *NS-Prozesse–Psychogramme der Beteiligten*, C. F. Müller, Heidelberg 1986, p. 28.);
- SS bicycle races in the gas chamber of Birkenau (*Nürnberger Nachrichten*, Sept. 11, 1978.);
- Out of pity for complete strangers—a Jewish mother and her child—an SS-man leaps into the gas chamber voluntarily at the last second in order to die with them (E. Bonhoeffer, *Zeugen im*

Auschwitz-Prozeß, Kiefel, Wuppertal 1965, pp. 48f.);
- Blue haze after gassing with hydrogen cyanide (which is colorless) (R. Böck, *Frankfurt Public Prosecutor's Office*, Ref. 4 Js 444/59, pp. 6881f.);
- Filling the mouths of victims with cement to prevent them from singing patriotic or communist songs (*IMT, op. cit.*, v. VII, p. 475.).

CHAPTER 22: CONCLUSION

Section 122: The "Holocaust"—What Actually Happened

This book has, the authors believe, convincingly shown that the Holocaust story is fiction. It is based upon the flimsiest conjecture which collapses under the slightest scrutiny. So what then, did happen? The facts speak for themselves. The Nazis regarded Jews as a racially-alien subversive element in society, responsible for both Communism and the excesses of Capitalism. As such, it was a central plank of Nazi policy to remove them from Germany, and ultimately from those parts of Europe under German control.

This policy first took on the form of cooperation with the Zionist movement and the encouragement of emigration from Germany to other parts of the world.

The outbreak of the war halted this process for the greatest part, and after the invasion of the Soviet Union it was decided to move the Jews of Europe to the Far East.

Hitler's plans were never to occupy Russia farther west than the Ural Mountains, and the vast expanses of territory beyond those mountains was earmarked as the Jews' final destination.

As the German armies advanced eastward, transit camps were set up in the far east of Poland, some of which doubled as labor camps for the German war effort.

Auschwitz was the largest of these labor camps, while the three smaller camps, Belzec, Treblinka, and Sobibór, served as transit camps.

The defeat of the German armies in Russia marked the end of the plans to move the Jews east, and the plan fell into chaos.

Allied bombing destroyed German infrastructure and supplies were unable to be sent to the camps, resulting in the outbreak of typhus and other epidemics.

These diseases produced the horrific images which are now claimed as "evidence of the genocide."

The Soviet Union, desperate for propaganda to counter the (truthful) revelations about the Communist massacres at Katyn and elsewhere, embarked on a deliberate campaign to generate stories about "gas chambers" in the camps which had fallen under their control.

One of the many faked pictures about the "Holocaust" appeared on the website of the Simon Wiesenthal Center in 1999, with the caption "As these prisoners were being processed for slave labor, many of their friends and families were being gassed and burned in the ovens in the crematoria. The smoke can be seen in the background. June 1944." However the "smoke" from the crematoria was added by hand, and actually emanates from a fence pole in the background. The original photograph can be seen at the left, taken from the Auschwitz Album *(Beate Klarsfeld Foundation, New York, 1978, photo No. 165). The Simon Wiesenthal Center quickly removed the photograph after the fraud was pointed out, but denied that they had faked it, claiming only that a "smudge" had been "misinterpreted."*

To this end torture and forced confessions were extracted and buildings "reconstructed," or, in the case of Sachsenhausen, even altered to fit in with the story.

Over the course of time, the stories which had been invented as anti-Nazi propaganda took on a life of their own, with hearsay, "Chinese whispers" and a climate of hysteria all combined to produce a rash of "survivor" claims, each one attempting to outdo the other in shock and horror value.

Because it is a criminal offence to even question the Holocaust in Germany (and several other countries), dissent on the topic was rewarded with prison and fines, which made an objective debate impossible.

Finally the situation has been reached where any claim can be made about the "Nazi death camps" and it is believed, no matter how outrageous, impossible, or strange it may be.

As to the real number of Jews who died in the war: as pointed out, the Nazis themselves at the Wannsee Conference estimated that there were 4,536,500 Jews under their direct control. They would have no reason to lie to themselves over a topic dear to their hearts, and this figure ties in with all other estimates as well.

Yet there have been to date 4,384,138 individual claims for compensation by "victims" against the German government.

Simple mathematics reveals then that the difference between the number of claims and the total number of Jews represents those who died during the war (and were thus unable to make a claim, unlike the survivors).

This figure is 152,362.

Even if this figure is an underestimate, and the number is doubled or even tripled, it would still be a fraction of the claimed "Six Million" figure.

To put this figure into perspective, for example, more than one million Germans died during the mass expulsions from Poland and eastern Europe during the three years following the end of the war—a number far larger than the total number of Jews who died in the war under similar expulsion conditions.

Section 123: Why Was the Holocaust Story Invented?

The most important question remains however, why?

Why would the enemies of Nazi Germany go through all these efforts and contortions to create the lie known as "the Holocaust?" The reasons are fourfold:

Firstly, as mentioned above, the story germinated in the Soviet Union's desire to create war propaganda against its mortal foe, Nazi Germany, in retaliation for the latter's exposure of Communist atrocities.

Secondly, the tales of persecution of Jews have served to create a highly profitable business for large numbers of Jews, something which the honest Jewish professor Norman Finkelstein described as the "Holocaust Industry" in his book of the same name (*The Holocaust Industry: Reflections on the Exploitation of Jewish Suffering,* Verso Books, 2003).

Thirdly, the "Holocaust" served (and still serves) well in justifying the Zionist seizure of Palestine.

Any criticism of the overt human rights violations and atrocities committed by the state of Israel against the Palestinians is dismissed as "anti-Semitism."

This accusation, so closely linked to the story of "the Holocaust" is guaranteed to shut up any dissenting opinion, especially when backed by a powerful Zionist lobby with representatives in the mass media and many Western governments.

Finally, "the Holocaust" has served as a tool for those who seek to suppress any discussion of race, immigration, or ethnic issues.

This last factor has led to, for example, any group which advocates the preservation of its national identity or homogeneity, being dismissed as "Nazi" and therefore "one step away from the gas chambers."

It is vital for a number of reasons that this grotesque lie be overturned.

Firstly, it is a matter of freedom of speech and opinion, secondly it is a matter of grave historical injustice to the German people, and thirdly, it is a criminal swindle of international proportions, for whom the perpetrators must be called to account.

It is the author's earnest hope that this work be instrumental in bringing about the re-establishment of truth, honesty and justice in the world.

Appendix 1: Alois Brunner and the "I Would Do It All Again" Lie

The December 2014 announcement by the Simon Wiesenthal Center that one of their most sought-after "war criminals," Alois Brunner—the so-called "right hand man to Adolf Eichmann—died four years ago, has brought forth the usual outpouring of Holocaust stories about how he was responsible for "deporting tens of thousands of Jews to death camps during the second world war."

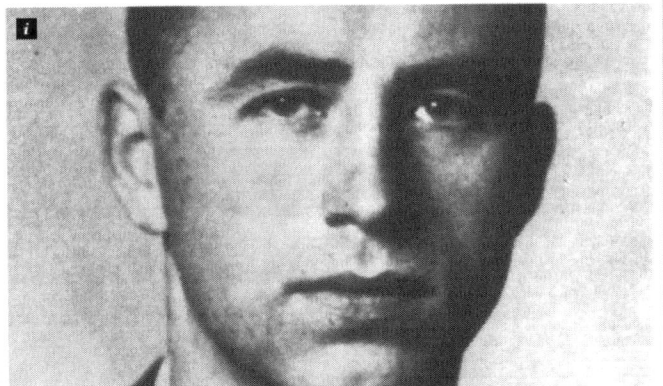

These stories have included the usual rehashing of a supposed interview he gave with the *Chicago Sun Times* in which Brunner was claimed to have said:

"All of [the Jews] deserved to die because they were the Devil's agents and human garbage. I have no regrets and would do it again." ("Nazi Butcher in Syria Haven", Nov. 1, 1987).

This incredible quote has been reused time and time again, and has once again made its appearance with the latest reports of Brunner's death.

Most media outlets—following the Holocaust Storyteller line—just repeat the quote without questioning its origin—even though Brunner denied ever saying such a thing.

So who actually conducted the interview? The article was written by a *Chicago Sun-Times* journalist named Chuck Ashman. He claimed he had conducted a telephone interview with Brunner in Damascus, "in front of a witness."

So who exactly was this "Chuck Ashman?"

According to an article in the *Chicago Reader* magazine, titled "Ashman: Adventures of an Uninteresting Person," all of Ashman's stories were well known in the Chicago newspaper world to be "hyperbolic" and "selective in its facts."

However, this is not the worst of it: Ashman was also a convicted fraudster who had spent time in a lunatic asylum.

According to the *Chicago Reader,* Ashman was a "habitual embellisher of reality, among whose many spurious claims were a law degree from the University of Tennessee and postgraduate study at Oxford University, schools that told the Press-Enterprise they had no record of him.

Most tellingly, the paper [the Press Enterprise] examined his past. At the age of 21, when an aide to Senator George

Smathers, he'd been named the Miami Beach Jaycees' outstanding young man of the year. But in 1964, seven years later, he was convicted of three counts of passing fraudulent checks. He avoided prison by pleading insanity and undergoing two years' confinement in a Florida state mental hospital."

After writing a whole series of outrageous stories about then Austrian president Kurt Waldheim—which were attacked by Clemens Coreth, the Austrian consul general in Chicago, in a letter to the Chicago Sun-Times in which he accused Ashman of "misrepresentation" and "malicious" insinuations—"The Sun-Times dropped him like a hot potato after finding out a few things about Ashman's highly erratic personal and professional history," as the Chicago Reader revealed.

This "quote" therefore comes from a "journalist" who was not only a convicted fraudster, and a certified lunatic, but who was also fired by the Chicago Sun-Times for making up news stories.

In fact the only correctly related interview ever conducted with Brunner—who left his native Austria after the war and eventually settled in Syria—was conducted in July 1987 by Austrian journalist Gerd Honsik, and published in his book Freispruch für Hitler (Burgenländischer Kulturverband, Wien, 1988).

Honsik's book was a series of interviews with some thirty-six witnesses, including six former concentration camp inmates and several historians on the topic of the war and the alleged mass-extermination story.

Honsik actually travelled to Damascus where he interviewed Brunner in person, even taking a picture of the former SS Hauptsturmführer, and reprinting it in his book.

In the interview, Brunner not only denied ever saying the infamous quote attributed to him, saying specifically that

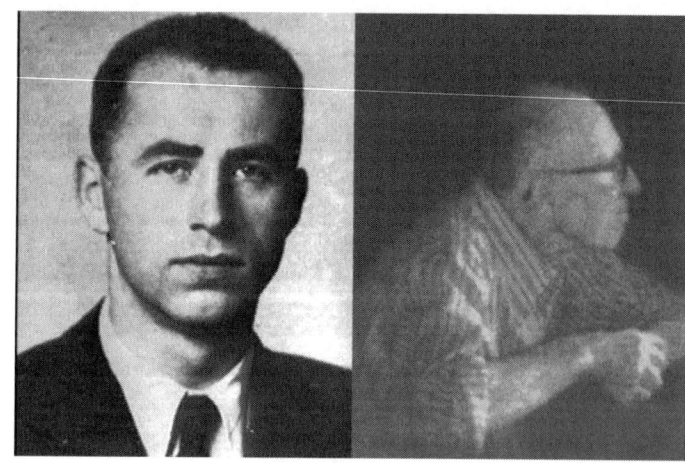

Brunner as a young man, left, and interviewed by Honsik in 1987, right. Picture from Honsik's book.

he had only said that he would "do it again" in reference to his attempts to resettle Jews outside Europe.

When Honsik specifically asked Brunner about gas chambers, the former senior SS man replied that he had "first heard about them in newspapers after the war" and had never even heard of such a thing during his period of service.

Instead, he continued, he had been actively involved in the project to create a Jewish homeland in Madagascar, and had never even heard of any mass extermination program.

It is an indication of the mass hysteria and media propaganda around the Holocaust that the word of a certified lunatic fraudster is taken to be true without question—even though Brunner denied ever making it.

* The Austrian journalist Honsik suffered the fate of many honest people in Europe. His book was outlawed, and he was sentenced to five years imprisonment for his "crime."

Appendix 2: Deceit, Lies and Swindles: The Psychology behind "Holocaust Survivor Testimonies"

A December 2014 article which appeared in the UK's *Daily Mail* newspaper, quoting a 101-year-old Jewish "Holocaust Survivor" as having survived being gassed because the Nazis "ran out of gas" is the perfect example of the psychology of mass deceit and lies which has come to typify this sort of "testimony."

In addition, the unquestioning acceptance of the easily-disproved lies of the "eye-witness" by the *Daily Mail* shows once again how the mass media is directly complicit in promoting the Six Million Story.

The *Daily Mail* story in question, titled "Woman who SURVIVED Auschwitz because Nazis ran out of gas turns 101," published on December 10, 2014, quotes one Klara Markus, who claims to have survived no less than three camps.

According to the *Daily Mail*, Markus "escaped [the] Auschwitz gas chambers because Nazis ran out of gas."

This incredible *Daily Mail* story is worth quoting in full in order to provide a proper analysis:

Mrs Markus, who had been imprisoned in Dachau and Ravensbruck before being sent to Auschwitz, survived the Nazi German camp in occupied Poland because the Nazis ran out of gas.

Mrs Markus was born Klara Schongut, on New Years Eve 1913, in Carei, Satu Mare County.

In August 1942, she was deported to a Jewish ghetto in Budapest, Hungary where she started work in an umbrella factory.

'My mother and older sisters were taken directly to Auschwitz. I never saw them again,' Klara Markus told a Romanian newspaper in 2010.

The mother-of-two remained in Budapest for another two years, before the Nazis ordered the remaining Jews in the city to march toward the concentration camps.

After a month-long march, Mrs Markus arrived at Dachau on October 20, 1944, and one week later she was sent to the notorious women's camp in Ravensbruck, before being transported to Auschwitz. Shortly before the evacuation and subsequent liberation of Auschwitz in January 1945, Mrs Markus, then 30 years old and weighing around 70lbs (32kg), was sent to the gas chambers.

She said: 'I was chosen towards the end of the day with a large group of other women and we were made ready for the gas chamber.

'But when they put us inside and went to turn the gas on, they found they had run out.

'One of the guards joked that it was our lucky day because they had already killed so many they didn't have any gas left for us.'

'God was watching over me that day.'

Mrs Markus says her narrow escape made her realise that she had nothing to lose and she managed to escape Auschwitz.

This is an astonishing story—but of course, a colossal lie from beginning to end.

According to the "official" Holocaust Storyteller version of events, Markus's "testimony" is blatantly untrue.

Even accepting the claim that it was possible to march thousands of people from Budapest to Dachau—a 403 mile or 650 kilometer route in wartime, during winter, without thousands of guards (!), Markus's story contains two astonishing lies:

Lie 1: Even the official Holocaust Storytellers Deny that Auschwitz had "gas chambers" in January 1945.

The most obvious lie is that Markus was sent to the "gas chamber" at Auschwitz in January 1945. According to the official Holocaust Storyteller version—as contained in, for example, the United States Holocaust Museum timeline of events at Auschwitz, the "gas chambers" were put out of commission in November 1944—in other words, before Markus even supposedly arrived at the camp.

Bear in mind that this "Holocaust survivor" claimed to have marched for a month to reach Dachau, where she claimed to have arrived on October 20, 1944. After a week, she claimed to have been transported to Ravensbruck camp. This camp was located north of Berlin, another 410 miles / 661 kilometers further north. This would have meant that she would have arrived in Ravensbruck during the first week of November at the earliest—just as the "gas chambers" at Auschwitz were being closed down, according to the official Holocaust Storytellers.

To claim that she was sent to the "gas chambers" in January 1945 is therefore impossible even by the "official" record.

Lie 2: The Nazis "ran out gas."

According to the official Holocaust Storyteller line, the Nazis did not pipe gas to the "gas chambers" but instead used Zyklon-B, an insecticide, to kill thousands of Jews in underground chambers at Auschwitz. Leaving aside the technical impossibility of killing thousands of people simultaneously in an underground chamber, * the Nazis would never have started an execution with thousands of people without making sure all the logistics were in place.

Markus's claim that the Nazis "ran out of gas" is as ludicrous as the claim that she was sent to a gas chamber in January 1945.

Finally, the reality is that Soviet troops reached Auschwitz on January 27, making Markus's claim to have "escaped" from the camp as unlikely as her claim to have escaped being "gassed." *(For example, the involuntary—and perfectly normal—defecation by executed persons as their bowel muscles relax, replicated by "thousands" of "victims" being killed simultaneously in a crowded, supposedly airtight, underground chamber, would quickly block up the room and make it unusable after even one such "mass gassing.")

This obviously fraudulent "survivor testimony" raises two important issues:

1. Why would someone invent a story which could be so easily disproved, even by consulting the "official" Holocaust Storytellers' version of events? And

2. Why would the *Daily Mail*—and other mass media outlets—carry this story without doing even the most basic of research to check if it was true or not? They would most certainly question and research any other such fantastic claim. The answer to the first question cuts to the very heart of so much "holocaust survivor" testimony which has been proven to be false. The vast majority of "survivors" are merely repeating the stories they have been told after the war.

Holocaust "Memoirs": A Long List of Lies and Fraud

Markus's "testimony" is but one of a long line of invented "memoirs", of which only a few can be reviewed here:

- Herman Rosenblat's *Angel at the Fence: The True Story of a Love That Survived* was a Holocaust memoir in which the author invented the story that, while he was imprisoned in the Buchenwald concentration camp, a young girl from the outside would pass him food through the fence daily and years later they accidentally met and married.

Rosenblat appeared twice on *The Oprah Winfrey Show*. Prior to the book's announced publication, Winfrey called the story "the single greatest love story, in 22 years of doing this show, we've ever told on the air." The book was scheduled for publication in February 2009 by Berkley Books, a division of Penguin Group USA, but was canceled after it was exposed as a lie from beginning to end.

Rosenblat and wife in happier days before their swindle was exposed.

- Binjamin Wilkomirski's *Fragments* (1995), was an acclaimed account of his supposed internment in Auschwitz and Majdanek.

The *New York Times* called the book "stunning," the *Los Angeles Times* described it as a "classic first-hand account of the Holocaust"; it received the 1996 National Jewish Book Award for Autobiography and Memoir.

In Britain, Wilkomirski's book received the *Jewish Quarterly* Literary Prize, and in France it was awarded the *Prix Memoire de la Shoah*.

In 1998, Wilkomirski was exposed as a liar by a Swiss journalist, who revealed the author had been nowhere near the camps; that he was in fact called Bruno Grosjean, and had been raised in an orphanage.

Appendix 3: The Ongoing "Survivor" Financial Swindles

Set against the backdrop of lies about the camps, it comes as little surprise to learn that from the very beginning, Jews have been swindling millions out of Germany—figuratively and literally.

The Ongoing Financial Swindle 1: The Philip Auerbach Case

Immediately after the war's end, a Jew by the name of Philip Auerbach, who claimed to have "survived" Auschwitz, was appointed head of the "Bavarian State Restitution Office" which was set up by the Allies, and tasked with overseeing "compensation payments" to his fellow Jews.

In January 1951, Auerbach became a member of the *Zentralrat der Juden in Deutschland* (Central Council of Jews in Germany)—but the very next month, he was arrested and charged with stealing 3 million Deutsch Marks (DM) from the "restitution fund."

He was found guilty, and in August 1952 was sentenced to 30 months' imprisonment. He committed suicide in jail.

Three of Auerbach's associates in the restitution office were also sentenced to prison in the same court case.

Left: Philip Auerbach, from the Central Council of Jews in Germany, arrested in 1951 for "reparations" swindling. Right: Werner Nachmann, president of the Central Council of Jews in Germany until 1988. Stole millions from "reparations" funding.

One of them, Rabbi Aaron Orenstein, was sentenced to a year's imprisonment and fined 10,000 DM. The second, Dr. Klaus Koenig-Ohnsorg, was sentenced to a year in prison and 200 DM fine. The third, Dr. Berthold Kernisch, received a four-month jail term and was fined 500 DM.

The Ongoing Financial Swindle 2: The Werner Nachmann Case

Werner Nachmann (1925–1988) was president of the *Zentralrat der Juden in Deutschland* (Central Council of Jews in Germany) from 1969 to 1988. He served on the organizing committee of the 1972 Summer Olympics in Munich, and in 1986 he received the Theodor Heuss prize for his services to the Jewish-German reconciliation and the peaceful coexistence of Jews and Christians in the Federal Republic of Germany.

After his death in 1988, it was discovered that from 1981 to 1987 he had defrauded about 33 million DM ($17 million in U.S. dollars at the time) from a German government fund intended for "victims." As reported in the *New York Times* of December 1988, half of the directors of the Central Council of Jews in Germany were forced to resign in the wake of the swindle.

The missing money was never found.

Conference on Jewish Material Claims Against Germany employee Semen Domnitser weeps after being exposed as a "reparations" fraudster.

The Ongoing Financial Swindle 3: The Semen Domnitser Case

In November 2010, the FBI in New York arrested 31 Jews in that city in connection with a $42.5 million organized fraud against a compensation fund for Holocaust victims. The U.S. Attorney's Office charged the 31, who included six current and former staff members of the *Conference on Jewish Material Claims Against Germany* conference, with making false financial claims using false documents.

In May 2013, the ringleader of the swindler gang, Semen Domnitser, was found guilty on all counts by a U.S. District Court jury in Manhattan. The verdict ended a four week trial in which two others, Oksana Romalis and Luba Kramrish, were also found guilty. The remaining 28 Jews who had participated in the fraud scheme had all pleaded guilty earlier. Cases such as these only scratch the surface of the ongoing "survivor" fraud industry.

Appendix 4: The Oskar Groening "I Saw the Gas Chambers" Story

The trial of Oskar Groening, the former SS so-called "Auschwitz bookkeeper" from April to July 2015 attracted much attention and allowed the mass media—and the BBC in particular—to recycle yet another old hoary lie on the topic: namely that Groening had said in a documentary that he had "seen the gas chambers."

The BBC's coverage of Groening's court date, as contained in their article of February 2, 2015, titled "Trial date set for 'Auschwitz bookkeeper' Groening" is clearly designed to be an attempt to beat back the growing Holocaust revisionist tide. The BBC article, in a subheading called "I saw the gas chambers," tells its readers that:

> "Groening, who began work at Auschwitz aged 21, does not deny witnessing the mass killing at Auschwitz. In 2005 he told the BBC: "I saw the gas chambers. I saw the crematoria. I saw the open fires. I was on the ramp when the selections [for the gas chambers] took place. I would like you to believe these atrocities happened—because I was there."

The documentary to which this article refers is the six-episode "Auschwitz: The Nazis and 'The Final Solution'" produced by the BBC and distributed all over the world.

As usual with these sorts of Holocaust stories, the truth is very far from reality. Groening was a lower-ranking SS man at Auschwitz—but in the BBC documentary, **he actually never used the words "gas chambers."**

This is a complete fiction, a made-up insertion. This overt lie was first pointed out by an alert viewer of the program from Portugal, one A. S. Marques, in a letter to historian David Irving, which was published on the latter's website. Marques' masterful treatment of the "Groening confession" lie cannot be bettered, so here it is, verbatim, as originally published:

> A. S. Marques of Portugal has spotted, Saturday, April 16, 2005, how BBC producer Laurence Rees faked what a German "eye-witness of gas chambers" actually said.
>
> What Gröning actually said
>
> I HAVE just read the article "The fight against Holocaust denial" by Raffi Berg, quoted by your site from BBC News. In that article, we read the following:
>
> "The fear that deniers could gain the upper hand led an SS camp guard, Oskar Gröning, to break a lifetime of silence earlier this year in a BBC documentary, Auschwitz: The Nazis and the Final Solution. 'I saw the gas chambers. I saw the crematoria. I saw the open fires. I was on the ramp when the selections [for the gas chambers] took

place,' said Mr Gröning, now in his 80s. 'I would like you to believe these atrocities happened—because I was there.'"

> Mr. Berg's quote is intriguing. I happen to have not only watched, but also tape-recorded, the BBC documentary he mentions, when it was broadcast last March 8 [2005] on the Portuguese channel RTP-2, in its original English version subtitled in Portuguese, and I was struck by the contradiction between the subtitles and the actual words one can hear in the film.
>
> They differ in one important detail from what one can distinctly hear, both in the German words spoken by Gröning and their superposed English translation. The Portuguese subtitles, like Mr. Berg's quote, follow what I gather to be the BBC-distributed text

that one can find here (Groening speaking):http://www.pbs.org/auschwitz/about/transcripts_6.html

"I see it as my task, now at my age, to face up to these things that I experienced and to oppose the Holocaust deniers who claim that Auschwitz never happened. And that's why I am here today. Because I want to tell those deniers: *I have seen the gas chambers*, I have seen the crematoria, I have seen the burning pits—and I want you to believe me that these atrocities happened. I was there."

Now here are the actual words one gets in the English superposed commentary, which is a faithful translation of the German words one is also able to hear beneath the English:

"I see it as my task, now at my age, to face up to these things that I experienced and to oppose the Holocaust deniers who claim that Auschwitz never happened. And that's why I am here today. Because I want to tell those deniers: I have seen the crematoria, I have seen the burning pits—and I want you to believe me that these atrocities happened. I was there."

Spot the difference.

A. S. Marques, Lisbon, Portugal.

The Trial Dissolves into a Farce

The trial soon dissolved into a farce after Groening accused "eyewitnesses" of exaggerating, and an analysis of his own account of a "gassing at Auschwitz" showed that his claims were fabricated, completely inconsistent with all established "evidence" and included a patently bogus claim that dead male corpses achieved erections while they were being cremated.

The following also emerged from Groening's testimony:
1. Groening said the Red Cross visited Auschwitz and were shown around Camp 1 despite the Holocaust storytellers claiming that there was a "gas chamber' at the entrance gates to that camp (the one still shown to tourists today);
2. That there was a brothel for prisoner use in Auschwitz Camp 1.
3. That Groening freely admitted that what knew about Auschwitz was limited to what **"other people had told him."** This included his claim that the camp could "dispose' of 5000 people every 24 hours, which he specifically said other people had told him.
4. Groening said he never saw or experienced any of the "5000 per day death process" himself, despite spending about two years at the camp.
5. That he contracted typhus from the prisoners and nearly died from the disease.
6. That he was reading from a script prepared for him, and could not remember questions asked of him only a few minutes before.

7. This prepared script was particularly relevant when it came to his account of witnessing a "gassing' at the camp, and the fact that his account was completely different to the "gassing in crematoria bunkers' told by the Holocaust storytellers.
8. Groening had, contrary to the English-speaking media's reporting, said so little of significance that one of the plaintiffs in the case, alleged "survivor' Eva Kor told the German media that "He did not really say much. I'm a little disappointed.'

The English-language coverage of the Groening trial was subjected to strict censorship in the controlled media in Britain and America, where the editors and journalists have both cherry-picked what they wanted to report and have even fabricated statements and claimed that Groening has made them in court.

Ironically, the court proceedings were much more accurately reported by the media in Germany, as exemplified, for example, by the coverage provided by the *Bild* newspaper.

Two articles in *Bild* in particular covered Groening's actual testimony in some detail, and, apart from a few sarcastic editorial insertions, have provided a completely different perspective on Groening's "confession' than claimed by the UK and US media.

The first *Bild* article, titled "Das Auschwitz-Geständnis des SS-Manns Oskar Gröning" (*The Auschwitz confession of SS man Oskar Groening*), dated 22-04-15, contains Groening's exact testimony regarding the "gassing' he claims to have witnessed. The original German is first and an English translation follows:

Im Dezember 1942 musste er bei der Suche nach Häftlingen helfen, die aus dem Vernichtungslager

108   *The Six Million*

flüchten konnten: „Irgendwie sind bei einem Transport einige Juden entwischt." Er wurde Zeuge einer Vergasungsaktion in einem Bauernhaus im Wald. „Das war das einzige Mal, wo ich eine Vergasung komplett beobachtet habe."

In December 1942, he had to help in the search for prisoners who escaped from the extermination camp: "Somehow, some Jews during transportation escaped." He witnessed a gassing in a farmhouse in the forest. "That was the only time I have seen a complete gassing operation."

„Einer schüttete Gas in die Klappe, dann wurden die Schreie immer lauter, aber bald wieder leiser." Erneut habe er um Versetzung gebeten – abgelehnt. „Über den Knüppel zu springen, dann komme ich noch nach Stalingrad, das war nicht immer so einfach."

"One guard poured gas into the opening, then the screams became louder, but soon quiet again." Again he asked for a transfer" declined. "To clear this hurdle, I would have to go to Stalingrad, which was not always such an easy matter."

Groening's Claims Completely Different to All Other "Eye-Witnesses" Accounts

Groening's account differs radically from all the "eye-witnesses" and official accounts, which have claimed that the gassings were carried out in underground bunkers attached to the crematoria in Auschwitz Camp 2.

Instead, as detailed above, Groening said the gassing he witnessed took place in a "farmer's house in the forest" and in the middle of the night.

Firstly, although it is clear that his "gassing in a farmhouse in the middle of the nights in the forest" bears no relation to any other account, claim or eye-witness, the controlled media all over the world blindly accepted this claim as the truth, and propagated it without comment.

Holocaust Storytellers will doubtless try and claim that this "farmhouse in the forest" was one the so-called "provisional gas chambers,' also known in Holocaust legend as the "red" and "blue" houses, or "bunker 1" and "bunker 2."

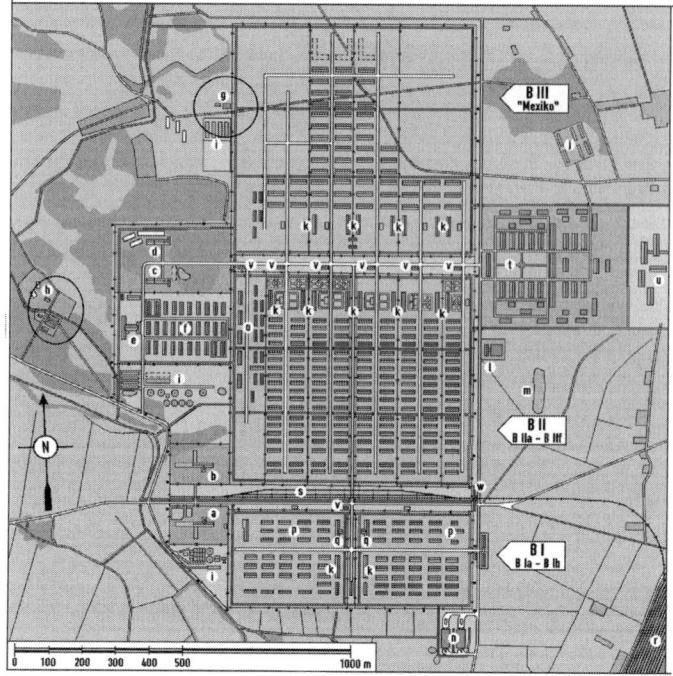

As can be seen from the "official' map of the Auschwitz camp, which claims to show all the "gassing locations," the "bunker 1" and "bunker 2" ("g" and "h" on the map above, circled) are located at the northern boundary at the western end of the Birkenau camp, and right up against the camp perimeter. Groening's claim that the farmhouse gassing was ***hidden in the forest*** is therefore clearly inconsistent even with the official Auschwitz Holocaust story.

Furthermore—and this is the most telling part—Groening's testimony in the Luneberg court room appears to be little more than a written summary of his 2005 interview with *Der Spiegel* magazine, titled "Der Buchhalter von Auschwitz,' (*The Accountant of Auschwitz*, 09.05.2005).

According to the coverage of the trial reported by the *Abendblatt* newspaper, titled "KZ-Buchhalter Gröning: "Die SS galt als zackige Truppe" (*Concentration Camp Accountant Groening: 'The SS was considered a smart troop'* 21.04.15), it was here that it became obvious that Groening was just reading from a script prepared for him. As the *Abendblatt* said:

"Hier steht umgebracht", sagt er fast irritiert mit einem kurzen Blick in das vor ihm liegende Manuskript.

"Here it says killed," he said, almost irritated with a brief look at the manuscript before him.

In fact, it seems that most of the script from which he has been reading in court, has been extracted almost verbatim from that *Spiegel* interview. There is however one important exception to this verbatim retelling, and that is the part which deals with the "gassing in the forest' allegation.

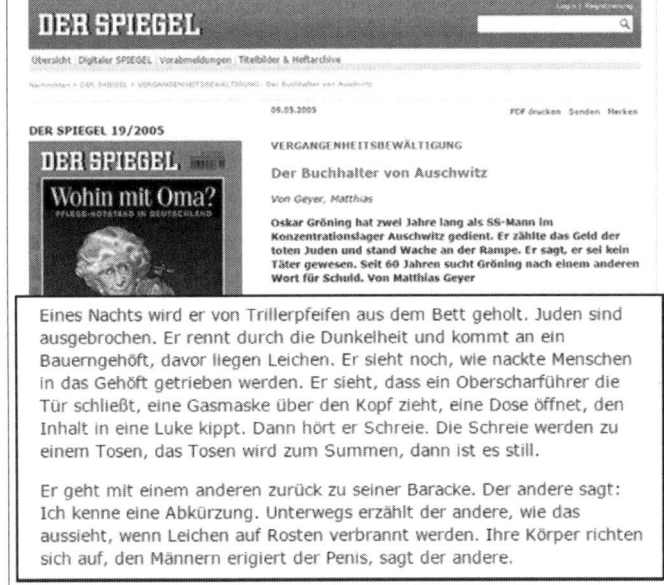

The Outrageous Claims in the Groening "Confession"

In the *Spiegel* interview, he described the "gassing' he witnessed as follows (German original in *Der Spiegel* first, then English translation):

Eines Nachts wird er von Trillerpfeifen aus dem Bett geholt. Juden sind ausgebrochen. Er rennt durch die Dunkelheit und kommt an ein Bauerngehöft, davor liegen Leichen. Er sieht noch, wie nackte Menschen in das Gehöft getrieben werden. Er sieht, dass ein Oberscharführer die Tür schließt, eine Gasmaske über den Kopf zieht, eine Dose öffnet, den Inhalt in eine Luke kippt. Dann hört er Schreie. Die Schreie werden zu einem Tosen, das Tosen wird zum Summen, dann ist es still. Er geht mit einem anderen zurück zu seiner Baracke. Der andere sagt: Ich kenne eine Abkürzung. Unterwegs erzählt der andere, wie das aussieht, wenn Leichen auf Rosten verbrannt werden. Ihre Körper richten sich auf, den Männern erigiert der Penis, sagt der andere.

"One night, he is hauled out of bed by a whistle alarm. Jews have escaped. He runs through the darkness and come to a farm, in front of which lie dead bodies. He also sees naked people driven into the homestead. He sees a SS Squad Leader close the door, pull a gas mask over his head, open a can and dump the contents into a hatch. Then he hears screams. The cries become a roar, the roar becomes a buzz, and all becomes quiet.

"He returns to his barracks with another man, who tells him he knows a shortcut. On the way, he meets another man, who tells him what it looks like when the corpses are burned on grates. Their bodies are lined up, and the men's penises are erect, he says.'

This account is clearly fantasy, particularly the part about the male corpses having erections as they are burned.

Apart from being physiologically impossible, such a claim smacks of the very worst of the hysterical lies and outrageous claims of the Holocaust storytellers.

Finally, it is highly significant that Groening's Luneberg testimony on the "gassing procedure' was deliberately vague compared with the detailed account in the *Spiegel* interview.

The "erect penises while being burned on grates" claim is the most obvious reason why this part has been edited out of Groening's new script at Luneberg.

But another reason is clearly the "fact" that, according to the Holocaust Storytellers, the "gassed Jews" at Auschwitz were cremated in industrial-scale crematoria inside Auschwitz Camp 2, and not on "grates" in the forest.

Significantly, Groening spent at least two years at the camp, but somehow he never heard of the supposed "big gas chambers and crematoria" inside the camp, and instead claims only to have seen this mysterious "house" in the forest.

Inconsistencies in Groening's Account Summarized

1. Groening's claim of a gassing facility "in a farmhouse in the forest" being operated in the middle of the night is completely unsubstantiated by any other evidence, even that put forward by the official Holocaust Storytellers;
2. Groening's claim in the 2005 *Der Spiegel* interview that the burning male corpses had erections while they were being cremated reveals confirms that the entire story is an outrageous fantasy; and
3. Groening's claim in the 2005 *Der Spiegel* interview that the cremations took place on "grates in the forest at night" is in complete contradiction to the Holocaust Storytellers' claim that the "gassing victims" were cremated in the crematoria which could "dispose of" 5000 people every day.
4. Groening only came forward with these bizarre claims 40 years after the end of the war—until then, he had never said a word about this mysterious, and until then, completely unknown gassing facility "in a farmhouse in the forest."

Why then would Groening make this bizarre—and completely unsubstantiated—claim of a new, never-before-heard-of "gassing' facility in a "farmhouse in the forest?"

The only possible answer must be that he has simply imagined it after reading wild claims in this regard, and then has transposed himself into the story over time.

That this appears to be the case is apparent from the fact that he only went public with this claim for the first time in 1985—some forty years after the end of the war! All the time prior to that date, he had never said a word about this "gassing in a farmhouse in the forest" to anyone, despite being a witness in several prior court cases.

That Groening could even claim that dead male corpses could have erections as they were being burned, as part of his "evidence" about a gassing, brings into serious doubt the truthfulness of his other claims.

The *Bild* article of 22-04-15 provides further insights into Groening's testimony:

> Am Mittwoch bestritt Gröning jedoch, an der Selektion eintreffender Juden regelmäßig beteiligt gewesen zu sein. An der Rampe in Auschwitz sei er nur dreimal im Einsatz gewesen. Nach seiner Beförderung zum SS-Unterscharführer im Jahr 1944 habe die Bewachung des Gepäcks an der Rampe nicht mehr zu seinen regulären Aufgaben gehört, sagte Gröning auf Nachfrage der Richter. Er habe nur wenige Male Kollegen vertreten und gewusst, was an der Rampe abgelaufen sei.

> **On Wednesday Groening however denied to have been regularly involved in the selection of incoming Jews. He had only served three times at the ramp at Auschwitz. After his promotion to Unterscharführer in 1944 to guard the baggage, he had never been the ramp as part of his regular duties, Groening told the judge. He only been told from a small number of colleagues what had transpired at the ramp.**

[Note the admission that he only knew of what happened from what he had been told by others].

> Für die ankommenden Menschen sei das mit Gewehren bewaffnete Wachkommando zuständig gewesen. „Die Kapazität der Gaskammern oder auch der Krematorien war reichlich begrenzt", sagte Gröning. „Man rühmte sich, dass man in 24 Stunden 5000 Tote entsorgen könnte."

> **For the incoming people, an armed guard detachment was sufficient. "The capacity of the gas chambers and the crematoria was really limited,' Groening said. "They boasted that they could kill 5,000 in 24 hours."**

[Note the "they boasted' claim" Groening never actually witnessed this, contrary to the impression created by the English-language media.] Groening's testimony continued, as reported by the *Bild*:

> An seinem ersten Abend auf seiner Stube habe er gefragt, was denn in Auschwitz gemacht werde. „‚Wie, das wisst ihr nicht?' Und dann wurde gesagt, dass die Personen, die nicht arbeiten konnten, – der Jargon war dort – entsorgt wurden."

> **On his first night in his living quarters, he asked what was done in Auschwitz. "What, do you mean you do not know?" And then it was said that the people who could not work, the jargon was, "disposed of."**

[Once again, note the admission that he only knew of what happened from what he had been told by others].

The *Bild* article continued:

> Gröning kam in die Devisenabteilung: „Ich hab diese Tätigkeit bekommen, weil ich Bankkaufmann gelernt hatte. Ich blieb dort bis Oktober 1944, bis ich aufgrund meines letzten Versetzungsgesuches an die Front gekommen bin. Ich war mit der Erfassung und Verwertung von Geldsachen befasst."

> **Groening was put into the foreign exchange department: "I was given this job because was trained as a banker. I stayed there until October 1944 until I was sent to the front because of my transfer request. My job was the collection and recovery of money."**

Groening then went into his description of the killing of a baby by a SS Guard on the ramp at Auschwitz. This story also features prominently in his 2005 *Der Spiegel* interview, almost verbatim.

While there is no evidence one way or another to prove or disprove Groening's claims with regard to this incident, the fact that he could simultaneously invent stories about bodies with erect penises being burned on "grates" casts a question mark over his outrageous story of baby-bashing as well.

The next part of the *Bild* article contains some editorial insertions, here highlighted by italics.

The *Bild's* comments inadvertently show three things:
- that the inmates of Auschwitz 1 were for the most part real criminals and not just political prisoners or Jews;
- that when he is not reading from his prepared manuscript, Groening rambles on; and
- that the prisoners in Auschwitz were given access to prostitutes (in a supposed "extermination center" !)

The *Bild* article continues (remember, *Bild* commentary text in italics):

> Dann spricht Gröning über einen Besuch des Roten Kreuzes. „Das Lager 1 bestand nur aus Berufsverbrechern, die ihre Strafe abgesessen hatten, Asozialen und Leuten der Wachturmgesellschaft." Damit meint er verschleppte Zeugen Jehovas. „Einmal hatte sich das Rote Kreuz zur Besichtigung angemeldet, denen wurde natürlich nur das Lager 1 gezeigt."

> *Then Groening spoke of a visit by the Red Cross [to Auschwitz].* "Camp 1 [Auschwitz I] consisted of professional criminals who had served their sentence, social misfits and people of the Watchtower Society." *By this he means Jehovah's Witnesses who had been deported.* "Once the Red Cross had registered for the tour, then they were of course only shown Camp 1."

Vor dem Besichtigungstermin seien „zehn Damen aus einem Bordell" ins Lager 1 geschickt worden; warum, erklärt Gröning nicht. Warum er das alles überhaupt erzählt, bleibt unklar, er neigt zum Abschweifen.

Before the [Red Cross] tour stated, "ten women from a brothel" were sent to Camp 1; *Groening did not explain why [this was so]. Why he was saying this at all remains unclear, as he started digressing.*

Vor dem Besichtigungstermin seien „zehn Damen aus einem Bordell" ins Lager 1 geschickt worden; warum, erklärt Gröning nicht. Warum er das alles überhaupt erzählt, bleibt unklar, er neigt zum Abschweifen.

The "ladies of the brothel" were for those [prisoners] *who still were strong enough* [to use them]. *That it amounted to forced prostitution, Groening appears not to have known before today.*
The *Bild* continues:

Ende 1943 erkrankte Gröning an Fleckthyphus, kam in Quarantäne in Kattowitz, sein Vater wurde einbestellt, weil man mit seinem Tod rechnete. „Und eines Tages stand mein Vater an meinem Bett. Das sind Szenen, die man nicht vergessen kann." Nach dem Genesungsurlaub geht es zurück nach Auschwitz.

As at the end of 1943, Groening contracted typhus and was put into quarantine in Katowice. His father was summoned because it was expected that Groening would die [from the disease]. "And one day my father stood by my bed. These are the sort of scenes that you cannot forget." After convalescing, he went back to Auschwitz.

[It is of significance that, according to Groening's own testimony, he contracted typhus from being at the camp. As it is now well-known, the use of Zyklon-B was precisely to exterminate typhus-bearing lice, and this was the reason for the delousing chambers at the camp, which have now been misrepresented as homicidal gas chambers" although, if Groening is to be believed, he had never heard of such a thing. The fact that a German guard could catch typhus was an indication of how serious the problem was, and also provides a rational explanation why the Germans would use the Zyklon-B insecticide at all the camps, not just Auschwitz].

Erst im Herbst 1944 wurde er an die Front versetzt – nach der sogenannten Ungarn-Aktion im Jahr 1944, die allein für die juristische Anklage im aktuellen Prozess zählt. Damals wurden innerhalb weniger Wochen mehr als 300 000 Juden aus dem Land in das Vernichtungslager gebracht. Die meisten von ihnen wurden sofort in Gaskammern ermordet. Der Richter möchte wissen, was an der „Ungarn-Aktion" anders war.

„Der Aufwand war größer", sagt Gröning.

It was not until the autumn of 1944 he was sent to the front—after the so-called Hungarian Action in 1944, one alone for legal prosecution in the current process. At that time, more than 300,000 Jews were taken out of the country to the extermination camp within a few weeks. Most of them were immediately murdered in gas chambers. The judge wants to know what was different about the "Hungarian Action."

"The effort was greater," said Groening.

[This is only relevant because Groening has been specifically charged with participation in the claimed "extermination' of 300,000 (!) Hungarian Jews. This figure dates from the time when it was claimed that over 4 million people had been exterminated at Auschwitz, whereas today the "official' estimate has been reduced to one million" but somehow the original "6 million' figure has never been reduced accordingly.]

Groening's testimony was met with disappointment by one of the plaintiffs in the case, alleged survivor Eva Kor. As the *Bild* reported:

„Er hat nicht wirklich viel gesagt. Ich bin ein wenig enttäuscht", sagt Eva Kor, Auschwitz-Überlebende und ebenfalls Nebenklägerin.

"He did not really say much. I'm a little disappointed," said Eva Kor, Auschwitz survivor and co-plaintiff.

On the third day of the trial, Groening expanded on some of his earlier testimony, reported once again by the *Bild* newspaper in an article titled "SS-Mann: Dienst an de Rampe war „nervig" ("SS man: Duty on the ramp was 'annoying'").

Groening Accuses "Eye-Witnesses" of Exaggerating

It was during this testimony that Groening accused the "eye-witnesses' giving testimony in the court room of having exaggerated their descriptions:

> Heute, am dritten Verhandlungstag, befragten die Anwälte der Nebenkläger Oskar Gröning. Sie wollten ihm entlocken, welche Rolle er bei den Vernichtungen gespielt hat. Er selbst hält viele Schilderungen aus Auschwitz für „übertrieben". Außerdem wurden die ersten Zeugen gehört: Max Tibor Eisen (86) aus Toronto (Kanada), der die Hölle von Auschwitz als 15-Jähriger überlebte und William Bill Glied (85).

> Today, on the third day of the trial, the lawyers interviewed the co-plaintiffs against Oskar Groening. They wanted to elicit from him the role he has played in the extrermination [process]. **He said [in turn] that many descriptions of Auschwitz [as claimed by the witnesses] were "exaggerated."**

> Als ein Anwalt der Nebenklage Gröning aus der Anklage vorliest, dass „die Gruppen der Ankömmlinge immer von Aufsehern umzingelt waren und eine Flucht ausgeschlossen war" sowie beim kleinsten Widerstand geschossen wurde, sagt Gröning: „Die meisten Dinge kann ich bestätigen, manche habe ich nie erlebt. Trotzdem halte ich die Schilderungen für übertrieben."

> Groening's advocate read out in court from the charge sheet, [quoting] that the "the groups of arrivals were always surrounded by guards and escape was impossible" and would have been shot at the slightest sign of resistance.

> [In response] Groening said "Most of these things I can confirm, but others I have never experienced. **Nevertheless, I think these descriptions have been exaggerated."**

Groening's refusal to listen to any more testimony on Thursday April 23, 2015, for example, after being forced to hear a "survivor' rehash the "I pulled gold teeth from dead corpses' fake horror story, provided yet another uncomfortable moment.

The Meaning of "Entlassung"

Then came the part where, according to many media reports, Groening was supposed to have said that he "could not imagine Jews leaving Auschwitz alive."

A close reading of the actual testimony, detailed in the *Bild* report, reveals that he in fact did not say this, and instead actually only said that he could "not imagine Jews being released."

The German word "entlassung" was deliberately mistranslated by the English-language mass media to mean "murdered" instead of its actual meaning, to be "released" or "laid off" (as in being laid off work).

Furthermore, the fact that Groening was reading off a prepared script became obvious once again when the judge asked him a question not related to the prepared manuscript, as the *Bild* reported:

> Frage: „Haben Sie sich damals vorstellen können, dass die Juden jemals lebend aus dem Lager rauskommen und Nachkommen haben könnten?"
>
> Gröning zögert sehr lange, bespricht sich mit seinen Anwälten. Dann: „Jetzt habe ich leider Ihre Frage vergessen."

> **Question: "Could you imagine at the time that the Jews ever could get out alive from the camp and could have descendants?"**
>
> **Groening hesitated for a long time, and then conferred with his lawyers. Then [he said]: "Now I have unfortunately forgotten your question."**

> Wieder bespricht er sich mit seinen Anwälten. Schließlich sagt er: „Ich konnte mir nur vorstellen, in Auschwitz 1 sind Entlassungen getätigt worden."
>
> Frage: „Auch Entlassungen von Juden?"
> Antwort: „Nein."
> Nachfrage: „Konnten Sie sich das vorstellen?"
> Gröning: „Nein, ich konnte mir das nicht vorstellen."

> **Again he conferred with his lawyers. Finally, he said: "I could only imagine in Auschwitz 1 that releases were made."**
> **Question: "Even Entlassungen of the Jews?"**
> **Answer: "No."**
> **Another question: "Could you imagine that?"**
> **Groening: "No, I could not imagine that."**

In other words, Groening actually said that he could NOT imagine Jews being released in Auschwitz: and not that he could not imagine Jews being killed there —which is precisely the opposite of how most English-language media outlets presented the exchange.

The Groening "Confession": Invented Hearsay

From the above it can be seen that Groening's ridiculous claims about "erect penises" on "dead men being cremated on grates" after being gassed in a "farmhouse hidden in the woods in the middle of the night" are clearly invented.

The "gassing in the forest" is clearly a fiction developed in his Groening's own mind, brought on by who knows what psychological impulse. Once caught up in the story, Groening was left with little alternative to follow the "don't-deny-it-happened-but-I-was-not-involved" type confession, the sort of which is detailed in Chapter 8 of this book ("The Psychology of Confessions"). It was a dangerous game which ultimately saw him sentenced to four years in prison —on the basis of a claim which was clearly untrue.

Appendix 5: Auschwitz—Reality versus the Claims

Before and After: The Fake "Chimney" at Auschwitz I

In chapter 10 of this book, "Auschwitz-Birkenau," sections 46 and 47 (*Auschwitz "Gas Chamber" Shown to Tourists Is Officially Admitted to be Fake*; and *Auschwitz Museum Finally Admits that "Gas Chamber" Was Built After the War*), it is discussed how the "chimney" of the "gas chamber" shown to tourists at Auschwitz I was "reconstructed" after the war--and totally faked.

The "chimney" is not even attached to the building which contains the alleged "gas chamber" and crematorium, which, of course, makes it physically impossible for the "chimney" ever to have been used for "crematoria."

Alongside are two images of what is now claimed to be the gas chamber at Auschwitz I.

The first image, above, was taken in 1945, after the German surrender, and shows no "chimney."

The second image was taken in 2013, and from that it can be seen that the "chimney" was added after 1945.

Above: "Crema 1" at Auschwitz, photographed in 1945. Below: The same building as it can be seen today at Auschwitz. The "chimney" has been added after 1945.

The Auschwitz Camp Orchestra

The story about the "Auschwitz camp orchestra" have entered nearly legendary status. Most often, the public is told, the evil Nazis (either themselves, or they forced Jews to do so) played classical music while they were mass-murdering Jews in the "gas chambers" or some other such activity.

So what was the reality of the Auschwitz Orchestra? The truth is revealed in original photographs, on display at the camp museum to this day. Below on the left is the real Auschwitz camp orchestra, assembled for an open

air concert in Auschwitz I. Note the crowds of prisoners standing round (not being "marched" or "carrying the dead" but quite relaxed, listening to some music., Note other prisoners on the left, standing at ease. . .It is, of course, also untrue that the camp orchestra was "forced" to assemble in one particular area only. Below, a picture taken in 1941, a Sunday afternoon (and not a "work" day, so, no "rows of prisoners "marching past") in which the details can be seen even more clearly:

114 *The Six Million*

Above, a picture of the camp choir, recruited from the workers at the IG Farben factory at Auschwitz--all well-fed prisoners, putting on a concert for the camp inmates.

Above: A stage performance at Auschwitz, dated by the German Federal Archive Service as "1941/1944.

The Treatment of Prisoners in Auschwitz

The image of Auschwitz, as promoted by the Holocaust Storytellers and their allies in the mass media, is that Auschwitz was a slave-extermination camp, dedicated only to murdering as many people as possible.

The image which the media and Holocaust Storytellers like to put forward is best summarized by this "survivor" drawing--this time by one David Olère, who claimed to have been at Auschwitz. Note the slave labor conditions, the smoking chimneys . . . . this is how they want Auschwitz to be presented...

The reality of life in Auschwitz was--needless to say--very different to these endless "survivor" lies.

Instead of being dedicated to the "mass murder" of any- and everyone, the Auschwitz Camp had a large number of facilities dedicated to saving the lives of prisoners-- including hospitals, dental clinics, recreational facilities, libraries, and so on.

Here follows some images from Auschwitz which the Holocaust Storytellers do not show.

Below: Block 10 at Auschwitz: the prisoner's hospital block. Ironically, this hospital is directly in front of what is now claimed to be a "gas chamber."

Below: Inside the Auschwitz prisoner's hospital: Nurses, doctors, prisoners, beds . . . completely inconsistent with an "extermination camp."

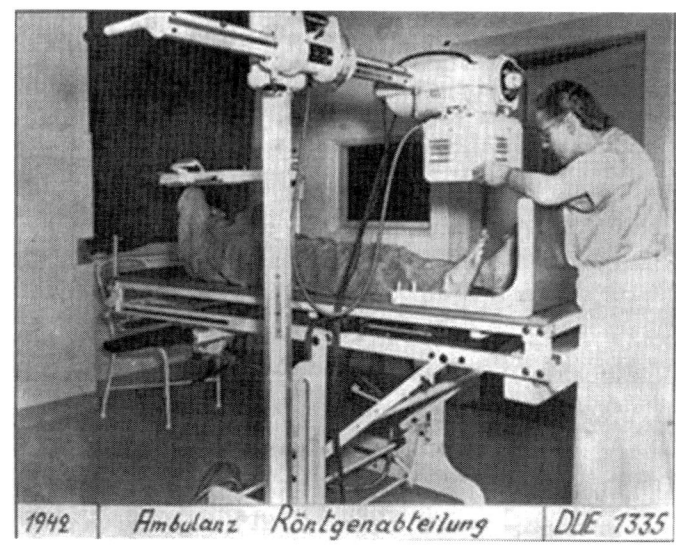

Below: A prisoner being X-Rayed at the Auschwitz hospital: once again, why do all this in a supposed "extermination camp" ?

Below, taken from the Yad Vashem (Israel's own "Holocaust memorial organization), a photograph showing prisoners at Auschwitz being treated in the ultra-modern dental clinic at the camp. Note the striped clothes of the prisoners:

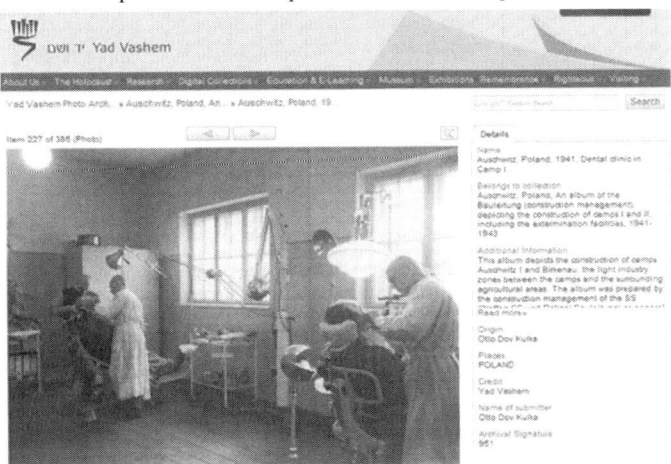

Below: It was a regular occurrence for children to be born in the camp. The Nazis even set up a nursery for the children. Picture from 1942.

Below, the dining hall at Auschwitz III, where the "big" gas chambers were supposed to be. Photograph from 1942.

Auschwitz also had its own greenhouse complex to provide food for the prisoners:

Sporting activities were also encouraged: below, a fencing tournament *for prisoners* at Auschwitz (note the sign in the background). Photograph from 1944.

There were prisoners from all over the world at Auschwitz, not just Jews. The camp had originally been built to accommodate Polish Prisoners of War, and later had many Russian POWS arrive as well. Below, the British POW soccer team at Auschwitz pose for their group photograph.

Index

A

Aktion Reinhard, program and camps 53, 54, 55, 61
American Jewish War Veterans, boycott of Germany 1933 6
Arad, Yitzhak 60
Arlosoroff, Chaim 4
Auerbach, Philip 28, 29, 63, 85, 105
Auschwitz camp 38ff
Auschwitz "gas chambers" change location 50
Auschwitz Museum admits that "gas chamber" is fake 40
Auschwitz Museum reduces death toll by 2.5 million 13
Auschwitz Swimming Pool 52
Austria 2, 9, 28, 82

B

Babi Yar "massacre" 25, 26, 27, 65
Babi Yar "massacre" disproved by aerial photography 25
Bach-Zelewski, SS General Erich von dem 27, 30
Bad Arolsen "International Tracing Service"--no record of "exterminations" 19
Bauer, Yehuda, dismisses Vrba as not credible 14
Belzec camp 57ff
Belzec Trial 58
Berenbaum, Michael 14
Bergen-Belsen camp 87ff
Black Book of Polish Jewry 64, 98
Bormann, Charlotte 94
Brunner, Alois 101, 102
Buber, Margarete 94

C

Central Council of Jews in Germany 105
Chelmno camp 55ff
Chelmno Trials 57
Communism 1, 99
Conan, Eric 42
Congressional Record 12

D

Dachau camp 81ff
Dachau fumigation cubicles 85
Dachau "gas chamber" 82
Daily Telegraph 13, 14
Daily Mail 103
Deir Yassin 8, 9
Delousing Chambers Used in All Camps 45

Demjanjuk, John, and trials 31, 32, 33, 34, 68, 88
Der Angriff 3, 4
Der Spiegel 15, 50
Diary of Anne Frank 90
Donat, Alexander 63
Domnitser, Semen 105
Düre, Arno, German officer hanged by Soviets for Katyn massacre 22

E

Eichmann, Adolf 11, 12, 14, 30, 31, 35, 54, 96, 97, 98
Ein Nazi Fahrt Nach Palastina—"A Nazi Travels to Palestine." 3
Einsatzgruppen, real role vs allegations 23
Einsatzgruppen Trials 22
Encyclopeadia Judaica 1
Encyclopedia of the Holocaust 29, 64
Ereignismeldungen (EM), "Event Reports" 24

F

Fake "guard towers" at Auschwitz 49
Feldhendler, Leon 60
Ferencz, Benjamin, Jewish prosecutor at Einsatzgruppen Trials 23, 24, 25, 28
"Final Solution"--actual meaning 17
Frankfurter, David 6, 7, 34
Franz, Kurt 64
Fuchs, Erich 60

G

"Gassing" by diesel engines 54
"Gas vans" 56
German architectural building plans for Crematorium II at Auschwitz 40
German "confessions" about Katyn 22
Gerstein, Kurt, and statement 15, 16, 60, 61
Gilbert, Martin 96
Gilead, Isaac 62
Goebbels, Joseph 3, 4, 7
Göring, Hermann 1, 7, 30
Gray, Martin 92
Groening, Oskar 105—107
Grynszpan, Herschel 7
Gustloff, Wilhelm 6, 7

H

Haavara Transfer Agreement 4, 5, 9
Hácha, Emil 19
Haimi, Yoram 62
Halifin transfer company, Poland 5

Hart, Kitty 92
Hentig, Werner Otto von 9
Hilberg, Raul, reduces death toll by 2.8 million 12
Himmler, Heinrich 7, 18, 19, 30, 60, 61, 87
Himmler's 1943 Posen Speech 18
Himmler's Personal Correspondence, 2013 19
Hitler, Adolf 1, 2, 5, 7, 16—19, 23, 24, 35, 56, 61, 67, 92, 97, 99
Hitler's remarks on "extermination" rumors 18
Hitler's "threat to Jews speech," Reichstag, 1939 17
Höfle Telegram 54
Höss, Rudolf 12, 13, 14, 38, 39, 52, 53
Höttl, Wilhelm 11, 12

I

IG-Farben factory at Auschwitz 51
Igrun 9
International Military Tribunal (IMT) 12, 16, 20, 27, 96, 97

J

Jerusalem Post 14, 58
Jewish Agency 4, 5
Jewish Chronicle 5
Jewish Cultural League 3
"Jewish soap" 16
Jewish terrorists in Palestine 8
Jewish Virtual Library 2
Jews Call for German Boycott, New York City, 1933 6
Jüdische Rundschau, supports Nuremberg Laws 2

K

Kaltenbrunner, Ernst 11
Kanada I delousing chamber 45, 46, 47, 48, 49
Kareski, Georg 3
Katyn massacre, blamed on Nazis 21
Kola, Professor Andrzej 59, 61, 62
Korherr, Dr. Richard, denies that "special treatment" meant extermination, 1977 15
Korherr Report 14, 15
Krakowsky, Dr. Shmuel, Yad Vashem 13
Kristallnacht 6, 7

L

Lanzmann, Claude 35, 36, 37
Law of Return, Israel 2
Lebensborn 19
Lehi Zionists offers to fight for Germany against Britain 9

Leleko, Paval 68
Lengyel, Olga 91
Leuchter, Fred, and *Leuchter Report* 49, 50, 75, 78
L'Express 42
Liebknecht, Karl 1
Life magazine 31, 88, 90, 91
Lipstadt, Deborah. denies "soap from Jews" story 16
Los Angeles Times 16, 17
Lubenchik, Naftali 9
Lüftl, Walter 54, 55
Luxemburg, Rosa 1, 17

M

Magna Carta, Jews in 1
Majdanek camp 70ff
Markus, Klara, 103
Marwitz, Vice Admiral Ralf von der 9
Marx, Karl 1
McCarthy, Senator Joe 12
Meaning of "ausrotten" 18
Metz, Zelda 60
Meyer, Fritjof 29, 50, 51
Mildenstein, Leopold von 3, 4
Montgomery, General Bernard 20
Müller, Filip 14, 80, 81, 93, 94, 97, 98
Mußfeldt, Erich 79, 80, 81

N

Nachmann, Werner 105
Nazi anti-Semitism 1
Nazi boycott of Jewish businesses, 1933 6
New York Times 7, 14, 35, 58, 97
Number of Jews under German Control 9
Number of post-war "Holocaust" claims against German government 10
Nuremberg Laws 2, 3
Nuremberg War Crimes Trials 19
Nyiszli, Miklos 93

O

Ohlendorf, Otto 27, 28, 29, 35
Operation "Harvest Festival" Hoax 79
Origin of "six million" number 11

P

Palestine 1—5, 8, 9, 100
Palestine Office, Berlin 1
Pawlicka-Nowak, Dr. Lucja 57
Pechersky, Alexander 60
Plaques at Auschwitz changed to reflect reduced death tolls 13
Pohl, Oswald 29, 30, 61
Pressac, Jean-Claude 14, 75, 77, 78, 97, 98

R

Rassinier, Professor Paul 95
Rath, Ernst vom 7
Rauff, Walter 56, 57
Ravensbruck 103
Reconstructed nature of Auschwitz 1's "gas chamber" 38
"Reconstruction" work at the Majdanek crematorium 71
Reich Central Office for Jewish Emigration 1
Reich Economics Ministry 5
Reich Main Security Office (RSHA) 11
Reinhard, Fritz 53
Reitlinger, Gerald 14, 52
Ribbentrop, Joachim von 7
Rosenblat, Herman 104
Rudolf, Germar, and *Rudolf Report* 13, 14, 38, 50, 52, 53, 91, 98
Rüter, Christiaan F. 34

S

Sachsenhausen camp 85ff
Sachsenhausen "gas chamber" 86
Schute, Ivar 67
Second Anglo-Boer 8
Sereny, Gitty 61, 70, 92
Shanghai 2
"Shower" gas chamber legend, origin of 45
Sicherheitsdienst (SD) 23
Siedlce, near Treblinka 64, 65
Silberschein, Dr. Abraham 58
Sklarek scandal 1
Sobibór 2014 "gas chamber" excavations 62
Sobibór camp 59ff
Sobibór Trials 61
Social Democratic Party 1
Soviet Union's invasion of Poland, 1939 20
Stahlecker, Franz, Einsatzgruppen leader killed in combat 23
Stangl, Franz 61, 70, 92
Steiner, Jean François 92
Stern Gang 9
Stolz, Sylvia 35
Sturdy Colls, Caroline 66
Suchomel, Franz 35, 36, 37

T

Thereisenstadt 8
Torture used to extract confessions in Soviet show trials 22
Treblinka camp 63
Treblinka Star of David "gas chamber tiles" hoax 67

Trotsky, Leon (Bronstein) 1
Tuchler, Kurt 3
Typhus 7, 8, 14, 41, 48, 49, 73, 79, 85, 87, 90, 95, 99

U

US Holocaust Memorial Museum 14, 29

V

Van Zyl, Lizzie 8
Vrba, Rudolf 14, 91

W

Wannsee Conference 1, 2, 9, 10, 17, 26, 31, 53, 54, 99
Warsaw Uprising 30
Washington Post 14, 23, 24
Weimar Constitution, legal basis for camps 7
Weizmann, Chaim 5
Wewelsburg, Himmler's 1941 speech at, 30
Wiesenthal, Simon 88, 90, 97, 98, 99
Wilkomirski, Binjamin 104
Wisliceny, Dieter 11, 12
World Jewry's Declaration of War against Germany, 1933 5
World Zionist Organization 4

Y

Yad Vashem reduces death toll at Auschwitz by 2.5 million 13
Yad Vashem, "Victim List" compiled on hearsay 11

Z

Zionist Federation of Germany, supports Nuremberg Laws 2
Zionist-Nazi cooperation 2, 4
Zionist State Organization 3
Zundel, Ernst 35
Zyklon-B 16, 43, 45—50, 54, 60, 72, 74, 75, 77—79, 83—88, 90, 92

Made in the USA
Middletown, DE
14 November 2015